A HISTORY OF EDUCATION

A HISTORY OF EDUCATION

IN MODERN TIMES

BY

FRANK PIERREPONT GRAVES, Ph.D.

PROFESSOR OF THE HISTORY OF EDUCATION IN THE UNIVERSITY OF PENNSYLVANIA. FORMERLY PROFESSOR OF THE HISTORY OF EDUCATION IN THE UNIVERSITY OF MISSOURI AND IN OHIO STATE UNIVERSITY

University Press of the Pacific
Honolulu, Hawaii

A History of Education in Modern Times

by
Frank Pierrepont Graves

ISBN: 1-4102-1498-2

Reprinted from the 1920 edition

University Press of the Pacific
Honolulu, Hawaii
http://www.universitypressofthepacific.com

In order to make original editions of historical works available to scholars at an economical price, this facsimile of the original edition of 1920 is reproduced from the best available copy and has been digitally enhanced to improve legibility, but the text remains unaltered to retain historical authenticity.

TO

JAMES ROWLAND ANGELL

TEACHER AND FRIEND

PREFACE

The present work is a continuation of *A History of Education before the Middle Ages* and *A History of Education during the Middle Ages and the Transition to Modern Times*. In a measure it covers the same period as the *Great Educators of Three Centuries;* but, as indicated in the preface to that book, the purpose and method of approach of the two works are quite different. The biographical material has here been reduced to a minimum; more attention is given to general educational movements than to individual reformers; and an attempt has been made to select and interpret the facts of the successive chapters in such a way as to form a connected narrative, and to furnish a suitable historical and social perspective. To obtain such a setting, it has seemed well to interweave a certain amount of political history. Owing, however, to the extent and ramifications of modern historical movements, such ancillary matter has proved less tractable and illuminating, and has been given less prominence than in the preceding volumes. And while I have continued to view the educational process from the standpoint of the development of individualism, the greater complexity of the subject-matter and a due respect for the facts have saved me from taking this interpretation too seriously. Save for the brief initial and concluding chapters, there is little express reference to it.

More striking characteristics of the book will probably be found in the emphasis laid upon educational institutions and practices, rather than upon theoretical development; and in the larger place given to American education. The account of each educational movement has included at least an attempt to trace its influence upon the content, method, and organization of education in this country, while three chapters have been devoted exclusively to the rise of our educational system. For this somewhat special point of view, I trust that no apology is needed, as the book is intended primarily for use in the United States, and will be of service to our teachers largely as it succeeds in focusing the educational progress of this country. It will be quite possible, however, for those readers in England and other countries, who have been so hospitable in their reception of my former works, to neglect or curtail these parts of the book, and still have a body of material sufficient to represent satisfactorily the history of education during the past two centuries.

While this book has been written to complete a series of three volumes and render them available for use as a continuous text in courses upon the history of education, it can be used quite independently of the previous publications. By itself it may serve as a reading circle adoption, a text-book, or a work of reference. In institutions where only a term or a semester can be afforded the history of education, or where the teacher holds that there is little material of significance to American education prior to the eighteenth century, it is hoped that it may fill a long-felt want. But whatever the particular purpose it may be made to serve, the liberal citation of sources and the selected lists of supplementary reading should prove of considerable value.

In preparing this volume for press, I have received help from several quarters. For rendering more accurate my descriptions of educational administration in Europe (Chapter IX) and of the modern scientific movement (Chapter X), I am greatly indebted to Professor F. E. Farrington of Columbia University and to Professor G. R. Twiss of the Ohio State University respectively. I owe a more extensive debt to Professor J. H. Coursault of the University of Missouri, Professor A. J. Jones of the University of Maine, and Professor W. H. Kilpatrick of Columbia University, who have read through practically my entire manuscript, and suggested a wide variety of changes. Likewise my wife, Helen Wadsworth Graves, has been ever at hand to advise and assist me.

F. P. G.

PHILADELPHIA,
November, 1913.

CONTENTS

CHAPTER VI

CHAPTER VII

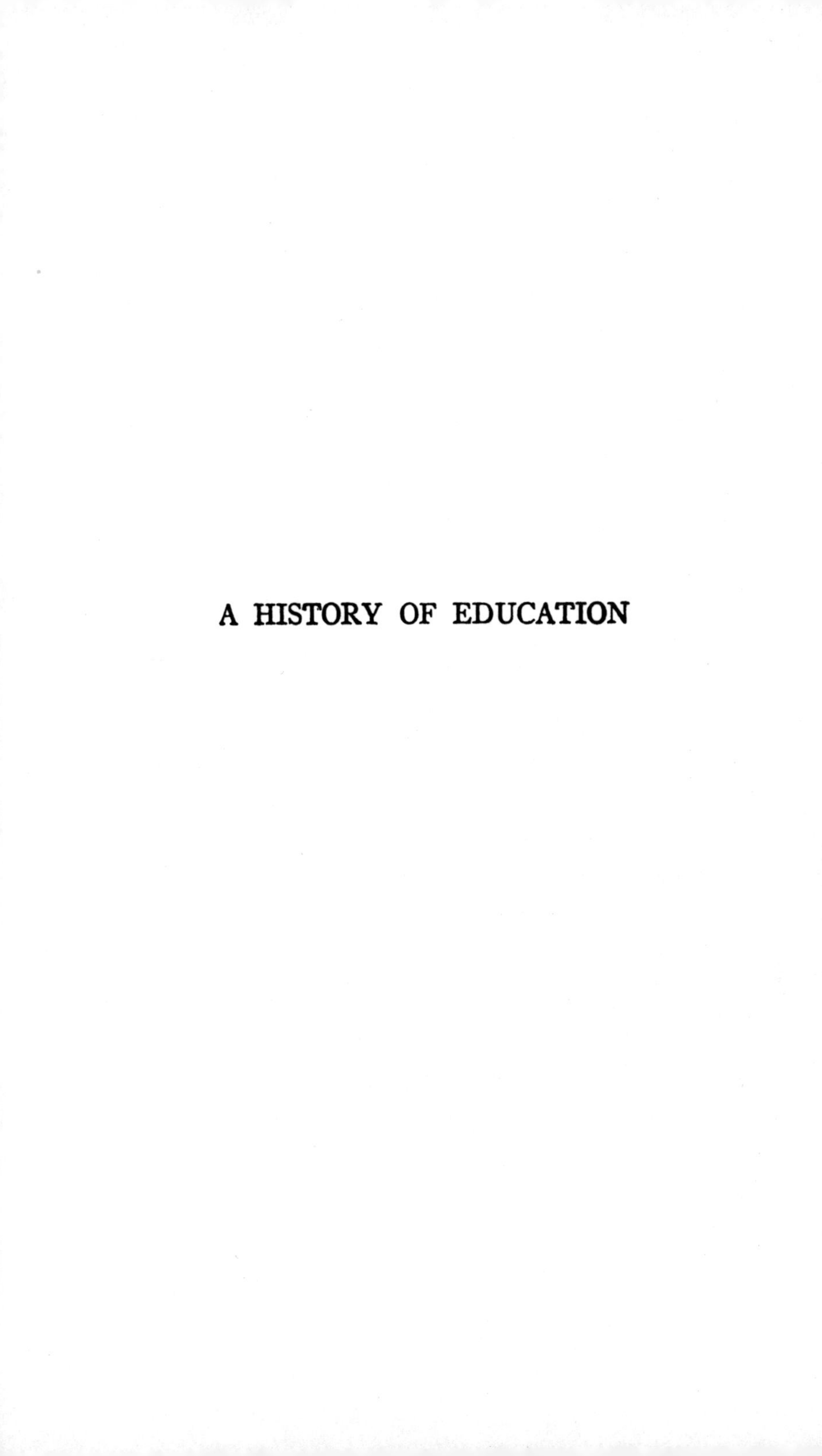

A HISTORY OF EDUCATION

A HISTORY OF EDUCATION IN MODERN TIMES

CHAPTER I

THE MISSION OF THE EIGHTEENTH CENTURY

The Eighteenth Century as a Period of Individualism.—In a work by that most brilliant of 'literary' historians, Thomas Carlyle, occurs the following characterization:—

> "This epoch of the eighteenth century was properly the End. The End of a Social System which for above a thousand years had been building itself together, and, after that, had begun, for some centuries (as human things all do), to moulder down. . . . At length, in the course of it, there comes a time when the mouldering changes into a rushing; active hands drive in their wedges, set to their crowbars. Instead of here and there a stone falling out, whole masses tumble down, torches too are applied, and the rotten easily takes fire." [1]

In the eighteenth century are found the climax of the rebellion against the arbitrary authority of church and state, and the period of extreme individualism.

And to one inclined to philosophize about the events of history, the eighteenth century is indeed filled with interest and significance. In this imaginary demarcation of time appear to be summed up all the institutions and developments of the seventeen preceding centuries of Christianity, and here may be found the climax of that rebellion against authority and the enslavement of

[1] Carlyle, *Diderot*, in the *Foreign Quarterly Review*, 1833.

the individual which had periodically been manifesting itself from the close of the Middle Ages. Prior to this century men had for the most part found their law in the realm of traditions and institutional activity. The two chief sources of authority and control were those powerful bodies, the church and the state. To these Europe was accustomed to look for guidance, and, as long as the reins were loosely held, there was but little complaint. It was generally the deprivation of rights and the curtailment of privileges that stirred up restless souls to wonder whence these institutions procured their authority and by what right they exercised their arbitrary rule. One revival after another—the Renaissance, the Reformation, realism, Puritanism, Pietism—had burst forth with great enthusiasm and promises of emancipation, only to fade gradually away or harden into a new formalism and authoritative standard. Yet with each effort something was really accomplished for freedom and progress, and the way was paved for the seemingly abrupt break from tradition that appears to mark the period roughly included in the eighteenth century.[1] At this point it is evident that despotism and ecclesiasticism were at length becoming thoroughly intolerable, and a series of effective revolts was made from the traditional, irrational, and formal in church and state. The individual tended to assert his right to be an end in himself, and at times all institutional barriers were swept aside. This destruction went to an extreme in the French Revolution, and for a time individualism ran wild.

The Development of Socialization.—But society could not pause here long. The freed individual had to be

[1] See Graves, *History of Education during the Transition*, Chapter XX.

given some direction, and some way had to be sought by which these rights he had secured might function. Without guidance or socialization of any sort, pure individualism must have resulted in anarchy. The more the individualistic movement succeeds, then, the more necessary it is to ascertain what the individual has to do and how he is to do it. The main tendencies of the eighteenth century would logically have resulted in disintegration, had not the nineteenth century made a conscious effort to justify the eighteenth, and bring out the positions that were only implied in the negations of the latter. It is not alone the individual as such that has interested the nineteenth century, but more and more the individual in relation to the social whole to which he belongs, as it is only in this way that his conduct can be evaluated. Thus, while the mission of the eighteenth century may be interpreted as tending largely toward free movement and getting the individual under way, the mission of the nineteenth and twentieth has been gradually to regulate this movement,—to know the law and help the individual to adjust himself to it. If the one period seem an abrupt revolution from the preceding centuries and 'the End of a Social System,' the other may be considered a natural evolution from its predecessor and the rude beginning of æons of possibilities for the individual and society. Thus the main movements of the eighteenth century may be said to have but cleared the deck for action in modern times.

But the nineteenth and twentieth centuries have tended to regulate this movement and produce an era of socialization.

The Two Epochs in the Eighteenth Century.—But this revolt of the eighteenth century from absolutism in politics, religion, and thought falls naturally into two parts. During the first half of the century the move-

In the first half of the eighteenth century the revolt was against eccle-

siastical repression; in the second, against political. The former movement is typified by the rationalism of Voltaire; the latter by the naturalism of Rousseau.

ment was directed against repression in theology and intellect, and during the second half against repression in politics and the rights of man. The former tendency appears in the onslaught upon the church made by the rationalism and skepticism of such men as Locke, Voltaire, and the encyclopedists,[1] while the latter becomes evident chiefly in the emotionalism and 'naturalism' of Rousseau. Although these aspects of the movement somewhat overlapped each other and had certain features in common, they should be clearly distinguished. The one prepared the way for the other by seeking to destroy existing abuses, especially of the Church, by the application of reason, but it soon degenerated into skepticism and an intellectual despotism. It undertook an absolute break from the old system of society and thought, but it gave no ear to the claims of the masses. It sought merely to replace the traditionalism and despotism of the clergy and monarch with the dogmatism and tyranny of an intellectual few and with irreligion and rationalistic materialism. In distinction to this rule of 'reason,' 'naturalism' declared that the intellect could not always be trusted as the proper monitor, but that conduct could better be guided by the emotions as the true expression of nature. It opposed the control of intellectual aristocracy and demanded rights for the common man. But to grasp the significance of this later phase of the eighteenth century revolt, with its far-reaching effect upon education and society in general, we must turn to another chapter and study more in detail the positions of Rousseau, its chief exponent and popularizer.

[1] *Op. cit.*, Chapter XIX.

CHAPTER II

NATURALISM IN EDUCATION

The Training and Times of Rousseau.—The exposition and advocacy of 'naturalism' by Rousseau find a ready explanation in his antecedents and career. The theories of no man are more clearly a product of his heredity, experience, and times, and they should be viewed in this setting. *Jean Jacques Rousseau* (1712–1778) was born in the simple Protestant city of Geneva, but his father, a watchmaker, was descended from a Parisian family. The latter inherited much of the romanticism, mercurial temperament, and love of pleasure of his forbears, and was most irresponsible in his attitude toward his son. The mother of Rousseau, too, although the daughter of a clergyman, was of a morbid and sentimental disposition. She died at the birth of Jean Jacques, and the child was brought up by an indulgent aunt, who made little attempt to instil in him any real moral principles. Naturally Rousseau early showed a tendency toward emotionalism and a want of self-control. His early years from eight to ten were spent in the village of Bossey, just outside Geneva, where he had been sent with a cousin of about the same age to be educated. Here his love of nature, which had already been cultivated by the beauties of Genevan environment, was greatly heightened. He found a wonderful enjoyment in the rural life, until a severe

Rousseau's parentage and early surroundings largely account for his want of control, love of nature, sympathy for the poor, and unsystematic education.

punishment for a boyish offense turned all to dross. After this the boy returned to Geneva and spent a couple of years in idleness and sentimentality. Then, during trade apprenticeships, lasting four years, he was further corrupted by low companions. Eventually he ran away from the city, and spent several years in vagrancy, menial service, and dissoluteness. During this time the beauties of nature were more than ever impressed upon the youth by the wonderful scenery of the Savoy country through which he passed. His education meanwhile was somewhat improved by incidental instruction from a relative of one of the families he served and through Madame de Warens, a person of easy morals and considerable beauty. Through occasional wanderings he also learned to sympathize with the condition of the poor and oppressed. At length he gravitated to Paris, where he was forced to earn a livelihood for himself and a coarse and stupid servant girl, with whom he lived for the rest of his life. He thus began to develop some sense of responsibility.

These personal characteristics were in keeping with certain general sentiments of the times.

While Rousseau's days of vagabondage were now over, they had left an ineffaceable stamp upon him. His sensitiveness, impulsiveness, love of nature, and sympathy for the poor, together with his inaccurate and unsystematic education, were ever afterward in evidence. Further, it should be noted that these characteristics of Rousseau blended well with a body of inchoate sentiments and vague longings of this period that were striving for expression. These were the days of Louis XV and royal absolutism, when the administration of all affairs in the kingdom was controlled nominally by the monarch, but really by the small clique of idle and extravagant courtiers about him. It was necessary for those who had any desire for advancement to seek to attach themselves to the court and adopt its elaborate rules and customs. In consequence, a most artificial system of etiquette and conduct had grown up everywhere in the upper class of society. Under this veneer and extreme conventionality the degraded peasants were ground down by taxation, deprived of their rights, and obliged to minister to the pleasure of a vicious leisure class. But against this oppression and decadence there had gradually arisen an undefined spirit of protest and a tendency to hark back to simpler conditions. There had come into the air a feeling that the despotism and artificiality of the times were due to the departure of civilized man from an original beneficent state of nature, and that above all legislation and institutions was a natural law in complete harmony with the divine will. Hence it happened that Rousseau, emotional, uncontrolled, and half-trained, was destined to bring to consciousness and give voice to the revolutionary and naturalistic ideas and tendencies of the century. He was overwhelmed by the number of existing abuses and bad institutions, and easily came to hold that all social regulation was wrong, and, having turned his back upon social traditions, he found his guide in nature.

To these tendencies he gave voice in his prize essays upon *The Progress of the Arts* and *The Origin of Inequality*, and

Rousseau's Earlier Works.—It was some time before Rousseau crystallized this spirit of the age and resultant of his own experience in any writing. But in 1750, by a curious accident, he undertook a literary work, which at once lifted him into fame. The preceding year the Academy of Dijon [1] had proposed as a theme for a

[1] A few of the larger cities of France had, in imitation of Paris, founded

prize essay: *Has the progress of the sciences and arts contributed to corrupt or to purify morals?* This inquiry seems to have suddenly brought to a focus all the chaotic thought that had been surging within him, and with much fervor and conviction, though rather illogically, he declared that the existing oppression and corruption of society were due to the advancement of civilization. Rousseau's essay was successful in the competition and created a tremendous stir. Three years later he competed for another prize offered by the same academy on the subject: *The Origin of Inequality among Men.* In this discourse Rousseau again holds that the physical and intellectual inequalities of nature which existed in primitive society were scarcely noticeable, but that, with the growth of civilization, most oppressive distinctions arose, especially through the institution of private property.

This point of view in a somewhat modified form he continued to embody in writings at the village of Montmorency, whither he soon withdrew from the hypocritical and cold-blooded atmosphere of Paris. Here in 1759 he produced his remarkable romance, *The New Heloise*, and three years later he published his influential essay on political ethics, known as the *Social Contract*, and that most revolutionary treatise on education, the *Emile*. *The New Heloise* departs somewhat from the complete return to nature sought in the two prize discourses. It commends a restoration of as much of the primitive simplicity of living as the crystallized traditions and

in *The New Heloise, Social Contract,* and *Emile.*

'academies' for the discussion of scientific and philosophic questions. Of these institutions one of the earliest and most prominent was that of Dijon.

institutions of society will permit. In the *Social Contract*, Rousseau also finds the ideal state, not in that of nature, but in a society managed by the people, where simplicity and natural wants control, and aristocracy and artificiality do not exist.

The *Emile* aims to replace the formal education of the day with a natural training.

Purpose of the *Emile*.—But the work that has made the name of Rousseau famous and most concerns us here is his *Emile*. This treatise and the two prize discourses their author declared to be "three inseparable works, which together form a single whole." He might well have included also the *New Heloise* and the *Social Contract*, especially as the *Emile* assumes more nearly the modified position of the later works, and undertakes to show how education might minimize the drawbacks of civilization and bring man as near to nature as possible. As the *Social Contract* and his discourses were written to counteract the oppressive social and political conditions, the *Emile* aims to replace the conventional and formal education of the day with a training that should be natural and spontaneous. We learn that under the current *ancien régime* little boys had their hair powdered, wore a sword, "the chapeau under the arm, a frill, and a coat with gilded cuffs," that a girl was dressed in equally ridiculous imitation of a fashionable woman, and that education was largely one of deportment and the dancing master, for "this is to be the great thing for them when they become men and women, and for this reason it is the thing of chief importance for them as children." [1] On the intellectual side, education was

[1] Taine, *The Ancient Régime*, p. 137. Read S. C. Parker's clear and interesting presentation of this 'dancing-master education' in his *History of Modern Elementary Education*, Chap. VII.

largely traditional and consisted chiefly of a training in Latin grammar, words, and *memoriter* work. Rousseau scathingly criticised these practices and pleaded for reform. In the *Emile* he applies his 'negative' and naturalistic principles to the education of an imaginary pupil of that name "from the moment of his birth up to the time when, having become a mature man, he will no longer need any other guide than himself." He begins the work with a restatement of his basal principle that "everything is good as it comes from the hands of the Author of Nature; but everything degenerates in the hands of man." After elaborating this, he shows that we are educated by "three kinds of teachers—nature, man, and things, and since the coöperation of the three educations is necessary for their perfection, it is to the one over which we have no control (*i. e.* nature) that we must direct the other two." Education must, therefore, conform to nature.

In the first period, Emile's education consists of physical activities;

The Five Books of the *Emile*.—Now the natural objects, through which Emile is to be educated, remain the same, but Emile himself changes from time to time. In so far, therefore, as he is to be the guide of how he is to be educated in a natural environment, his impulses must be examined at different times in his life. Hence the work is divided into five parts, four of which deal with Emile's education in the stages of infancy, childhood, boyhood, and youth respectively, and the fifth with the training of the girl who is to become his wife. The characteristics of the different periods in the life of Emile are marked by the different things he desires. In the first book, which takes him from birth to five years of age, his main desire is for physical activities, and he should, therefore, be placed under simple, free, and healthful conditions which will enable him to make the most of these. He must be removed to the country, where he will be close to nature, and farthest from the contaminating influences of civilization. His growth and training must be as spontaneous as possible. He must have nothing to do with either medicine or doctors, "unless his life is in evident danger; for then they can do nothing worse than kill him." His natural movements must not be restrained by caps, bands, or swaddling clothes, and he should be nursed by his own mother. He should likewise be used to baths of all sorts of temperature. In fact, the child should not be forced into any fixed ways whatsoever, since with Rousseau, habit is necessarily something contrary to impulse and so unnatural and a thing to be shunned. "The only habit," says he, "which the child should be allowed to form is to contract no habit whatsoever." His playthings should not be "gold or silver bells, coral, elaborate crystals, toys of all kinds and prices," but such simple products of nature as "branches with their fruits and flowers, or a poppy-head in which the seeds are heard to rattle." Language that is simple, plain, and hence natural, should be used with him, and he should not be hurried beyond nature in learning to talk. He should be restricted to a few words that express real thoughts for him.

in the second, of sense training, although incidentally he is given some idea of conduct and property;

The education of Emile during infancy is thus to be 'negative' and purely physical. The aim is simply to keep his instincts and impulses, which Rousseau holds to be good by nature, free from vice, and to afford him the natural activity he craves. Next, in the period of childhood, between the years of five and twelve, which is treated in the second book, Emile desires most to touch, to see, and in other ways to sense things. This, therefore, is the time for training his senses. "As all that enters the human understanding comes there through the senses, the first reason of man is a sensuous reason. Our first teachers of philosophy are our feet, our hands, and our eyes. . . . In order to learn to think, we must then exercise our limbs, our senses, and our organs, which are the instruments of our intelligence." To obtain this training, Emile is to wear short, loose, and scanty clothing, go bareheaded, and have the body inured to cold and heat, and be generally subjected to a 'hardening process' similar to that recommended by Locke.[1] He is to learn to swim, and practice long and high jumps, leaping walls, and scaling rocks. But, what is more important, his eyes and ears are also to be exercised through natural problems in weighing, measuring, and estimating masses, heights, and distances. Drawing and constructive geometry are to be taught him, to render him more capable of observing accurately. His ear is to be rendered sensitive to harmony by learning to sing. This body and sense training should be the nearest approach to an intellectual training at this period. Rousseau condemns the usual unnatural practice of requiring pupils to learn so much before they have reached the proper years. In keeping with his 'negative' education, he asks rhetorically: "Shall I venture to state at this point the most important, the most useful, rule of all education? It is not to gain time, but to lose it." During his childhood

[1] See Graves, *History of Education during the Transition*, p. 308; *Great Educators*, p. 62.

Emile is not to study geography, history, or languages, upon which pedagogues ordinarily depend to exhibit the attainments of their pupils, although these understand nothing of what they have memorized. "At the age of twelve, Emile will hardly know what a book is. But I shall be told it is very necessary that he know how to read. This I grant. It is necessary that he know how to read when reading is useful to him. Until then, it serves only to annoy him."

Incidentally, however, in order to make Emile tolerable in society, for he cannot entirely escape it, he must be given the idea of property and some idea of conduct. But this is simply because of practical necessity, and no moral education is to be given as such, for, "until he reaches the age of reason, he can form no idea of moral beings or social relations." He is to learn through 'natural consequences' until he arrives at the age for understanding moral precepts. If he breaks the furniture or the windows, let him suffer the inconveniences that arise from his act. Do not preach to him or punish him for lying, but afterward affect not to believe him even when he has spoken the truth. If he carelessly digs up the sprouting melons of the gardener, in order to plant beans for himself, let the gardener in turn uproot the beans, and thus cause him to learn the sacredness of property. As far as this moral training is given, then, it is to be indirect and incidental.

in the third, of instruction in the natural sciences through curiosity and interest in investigation;

However, between twelve and fifteen, after the demands of the boy's physical activities and of his senses have somewhat abated, there comes "an interval when his faculties and powers are greater than his desires," when he displays an insistent curiosity concerning natural phenomena and a constant appetite for rational knowledge. This period, which is dealt with in his third book, Rousseau declares to be intended by nature itself as "the time of labor, instruction, and study." But it is obvious even to our unpractical author that not much can be learned within three years, and he accordingly decides to limit instruction to "merely that which is useful." And even of useful studies the boy should not be expected to learn those "truths which require, for being comprehended, an understanding already formed, or which dispose an inexperienced mind to think falsely on other subjects." After eliminating all useless, incomprehensible, and misleading studies, Rousseau finds that natural sciences alone remain as mental pabulum for the boy. Later in this third book, in order that Emile may informally learn the interdependence of men and may himself become economically independent, Rousseau adds industrial experience and the acquisition of the trade of cabinet-making to his training. But at this point Rousseau next considers the natural and so most effective method for acquiring these subjects. "Ask questions that are within his comprehension, and leave him to resolve them. Let him know nothing because you have told it to him, but because he has comprehended it himself; he is not to learn science, but to discover it. If you ever substitute in his mind authority for reason, he will no longer reason."

Rousseau holds that this may best be accomplished by appealing to the curiosity and interest in investigation, which are so prominent in the boy at this time. He illustrates with lesson plans this solution of the problem of imparting knowledge. He contrasts the current methods of teaching astronomy and geography by means of globes, maps, and other misleading representations, with the more natural plan of stimulating inquiry through observing the sun when rising and setting during the different seasons, and through problems concerning the topography of the neighborhood. Emile is taught to appreciate the value of these subjects by being lost in the forest, and, in his efforts to find a way out, discovering a use for them. He learns the elements of electricity through meeting with a juggler, who attracts an artificial duck by means of a concealed magnet. He similarly discovers through experience the effect of cold and heat upon solids and liquids, and so comes to understand the thermometer and other instruments. Hence Rousseau feels that all knowledge of real value may be acquired most clearly and naturally without the use of rivalry or textbooks. "I hate books," he says; "they merely teach us to talk of what we do not know." But he finds an exception to this irrational method in one book, "where all the natural needs of man are exhibited in a manner obvious to the mind of a child, and where the means of providing for these needs are successively developed with the same facility." This book, Defoe's *Robinson Crusoe,*[1] he felt, should be carefully studied by Emile.

The fourth book takes Emile from the age of fifteen to twenty. At this period the sex interests appear and

[1] Hence Campe of the 'Philanthropinum,' which attempted to put Rousseau's doctrines into practice, wrote in imitation *Robinson Crusoe Junior*, and numerous similar works were produced. Of these the only well-known survivor is *Swiss Family Robinson*, written by Johann David Wyss in 1813.

and in the fourth, of moral training through contact with the unfortunate and the criminal elements of society.

should be properly guided and trained, especially as they are the basis of social and moral relationships. "As soon as Emile has need of a companion, he is no longer an isolated being." His first passion calls him into relations with his species, and he must now learn to live with others. "We have formed his body, his senses, and his intelligence; it remains to give him a heart." He is to become moral, affectionate, and religious. Here again Rousseau insists that the training is not to be accomplished by the formal method of precepts, but in a natural way by bringing the youth into contact with his fellowmen and appealing to his emotions. Emile is to visit infirmaries, hospitals, and prisons, and witness concrete examples of wretchedness in all stages, although not so frequently as to become hardened. That this training may not render him cynical or hypercritical, it should be corrected by the study of history, where one sees men simply as a spectator without feeling or passion. Further, in order to deliver Emile from vanity, so common during adolescence, he is to be exposed to flatterers, spendthrifts, and sharpers, and allowed to suffer the consequences. He may at this time also be guided in his conduct by the use of fables, for "by censuring the wrongdoer under an unknown mask, we instruct without offending him."

The fifth book describes the inconsistently repressive training of Sophie, whom Emile is to marry, now that he has arrived at manhood.

Emile at length becomes a man, and a life companion must be found for him. A search should be made for a suitable lady, but "in order to find her, we must know her." Accordingly, the last book of the *Emile* deals with the model Sophie and the education of woman. It is the weakest part of Rousseau's work. He entirely misinterprets the nature of women, and does not allow them any individuality of their own, but considers them as simply supplementary to the nature of men. Accordingly, he completely abandons the individualistic training to be given the man. He insists:—

> "The whole education of women ought to be relative to men. To please them, to be useful to them, to make themselves loved and honored by them, to educate them when young, to care for them when grown, to counsel them, to console them, to make life agreeable and sweet to them—these are the duties of women at all times, and what should be taught them from infancy."

Like men, women should be given adequate bodily training, but rather for the sake of physical charms and of producing vigorous offspring than for their own development. Their instinctive love of pleasing through dress should be made of service by teaching them sewing, embroidery, lacework, and designing. Further, "girls ought to be obedient and industrious, and they ought early to be brought under restraint. Made to obey a being so imperfect as man, often so full of vices, and always so full of faults, they ought early to learn to suffer even injustice, and endure the wrongs of a husband without complaint." Girls should be taught singing, dancing, and other accomplishments that will make them attractive without interfering with their submissiveness. They should be instructed dogmatically in religion at an early age. "Every daughter should have the religion of her mother, and every wife that of her husband." In ethical matters they should be largely guided by public opinion. A woman may not learn philosophy, art, or science, but she should study men. "She must learn to penetrate their feelings through their conversation, their actions, their looks, and their gestures, and know how to give them the feelings which are pleasing to her, without even seeming to think of them."

To make a fair estimate of the *Emile*, one must forget the offensive personality of the author, and the inconsistencies and contradictions of the work itself.

Merits and Defects of the *Emile*.—Such was Rousseau's notion of a natural individualistic education for a man and the passive and repressive training suitable for a woman, and of the happiness and prosperity that were bound to ensue. To make a fair estimate of the *Emile* and its influence is not easy. It is necessary to put aside all of one's prejudices against the weak and offensive personality of the author and to view the contradictions of his life and work in the proper perspective. It must also be admitted at the start that the *Emile* is often illogical, erratic, and inconsistent. Rousseau constantly sways from optimism to pessimism, from spontaneity to authority, from liberalism to intolerance. While he holds that society is thoroughly corrupt, he has great confidence in the goodness of all individuals of which it is composed. In the face of history and psychology, he opposes nature to culture, and creates a dualism between emotion and reason. Although the instincts and reactions of Emile are apparently given free play, they are really under the constant guidance of his tutor. Emile is to have his individuality developed to its utmost, but Sophie's is to be trained out of her. However, in spite of such glaring inconsistencies, the *Emile* has at all times been accounted a work of great richness and power. The brilliant thought, the underlying wisdom of many of its suggestions, the sentimental appeal, and the clear, enthusiastic, and ardent presentation have completely overbalanced its contradictions and logical deficiencies. Its errors and illusions are fully outweighed by great truths, lofty sentiments, and definite contributions to educational theory and practice.

The anti-social education of the *Emile* is absurd, but tradition had to be broken, and an extreme doctrine was necessary.

The Break with Social Traditions.—The most marked feature of the Rousselian education and the one most subject to criticism has been its extreme revolt against civilization and all social control. A state of nature is held to be the ideal condition, and all social relations are regarded as degenerate. The child is to be brought up in isolation by the laws of brute necessity and to have no social or political education until he is fifteen, when an impossible set of expedients for bringing him into touch with his fellows is devised. The absurdity of this anti-social education has always been keenly felt. Children cannot be reared in a social vacuum, nor can they be trained merely as world citizens to the complete exclusion of specific governmental authority. And although society may become stereotyped and corrupt, it furnishes the means of carrying the accumulated race experience and attainments. One should remember, however, that the times and the cause had need of just so extreme a doctrine. The reformer is often forced to assume the position of a fanatic, in order to secure attention for his propaganda. Had Rousseau's cry been uttered a generation later, when society had become less artificial and more responsive to popular rights, it might have contained less exaggeration. But at the time such individualism alone could enable him to break the bondage to the past. By means of paradoxes and exaggerations he was able to emphasize the crying need of a natural development of man, and to tear down the effete traditions in educational organization, content, and methods.

By this destruction of traditionalism Rousseau brought education into closer relations with human welfare and opened the way to numerous social movements in modern education.

The Social Movements in Modern Education.—Hence, although Rousseau's mission was largely to destroy traditionalism, and most of the specific features of his naturalism have in time been modified or rejected, many important advances in modern education would seem to go back to him. His criticism caused men to rush to the defence of existing systems, and when they failed in their attempts to reinstate them, they undertook the construction of something better. In the first place, his attitude toward the artificial, superficial, and inhuman society of the times led him to oppose its arbitrary authority and guidance of education. He advocated the virtues of the primitive men and a simpler basis of social organization, and held that all members of society should be trained industrially so as to contribute to their own support and to be sympathetic and benevolent toward their fellows. Through him education has been more closely related to human welfare. The industrial work of Pestalozzi and Fellenberg, the moral aim of education held by Herbart, the social participation in the practice of Froebel, and the present-day emphasis upon vocational education, moral instruction, and training of defectives and of other extreme variations, alike find some of their roots in the *Emile*. In fact, the fallacy involved in Rousseau's isolated education is too palpable to mislead any one, and those who have best caught his spirit and endeavored to develop his practice have all most insistently stressed social activities in the training of children and striven to make education lead to a closer and more sympathetic coöperation in society. Hence in Rousseau's negative and apparently anti-social training are clearly implied many of the social movements in modern education.

The Scientific Movement in Modern Education.—Moreover, since Rousseau repudiated all social traditions and accepted nature as his only guide, he was absolutely opposed to all book learning and exaggerated the value of personal observation and influence. He consequently neglected the past, and wished to rob the pupil of all the experience of his fellows and of those who had gone before. But he stressed the use of natural objects in the curriculum and developed the details of nature study and observational work to an extent never previously undertaken. Partly as a result of this influence, schools and colleges have come to include in their course the study of physical forces, natural environment, plants, and animals. Therein Rousseau not only anticipates somewhat the nature study and geography of Pestalozzi, Basedow, Salzmann, and Ritter, but, in a way, foreshadows the arguments of Spencer, Huxley, and the modern scientific movement in education.

By his rejection of books and the experience of the past, in favor of nature study and observational work, Rousseau helped develop the use of sciences in the curriculum.

The Psychological Movements in Modern Education.—A matter of even greater importance is Rousseau's belief that education should be in accordance with the natural interests of the child. Although his knowledge of children was defective,[1] and his recommendations were marred by unnatural breaks and filled with sentimentality, he saw the need of studying the child as the only basis for education. In the *Preface to the Emile* he declares:—

Although Rousseau's knowledge of children was defective, he started the study of their development, and while his theory of 'delayed maturing' divided the pupil's development into too definite

"We do not know childhood. Acting on the false ideas we

[1] His *Confessions* tell us how he declined to rear his own children, but consigned all five to the public foundling asylum.

stages, it outlined the characteristics at different periods.

have of it, the farther we go the farther we wander from the right path. The wisest among us are engrossed in what the adult needs to know and fail to consider what children are able to apprehend. We are always looking for the man in the child, without thinking of what he is before he becomes a man. This is the study to which I have devoted myself, to the end that, even though my whole method may be chimerical and false, the reader may still profit by my observations. I may have a very poor conception of what ought to be done, but I think I have the correct view of the subject on which we are to work. Begin, then, by studying your pupils more thoroughly, for assuredly you know nothing about them. Now if you read this book of mine with this purpose in view, I do not believe it will be without profit to you."

As a result of such appeals, the child has become the center of discussion in modern training, and we may thank Rousseau for introducing a new principle into education. And, despite his limitations and prejudices, this unnatural and neglectful parent stated many details of child development with much force and clearness and gave an impetus to later reformers, who were able to correct his observations and make them more practicable in education. In this connection should especially be considered Rousseau's theory of 'delayed maturing,' which is later restated by Froebel. He makes a sharp division of the pupil's development into definite stages that seem but little connected with one another, and prescribes a distinct education for each period. This is often cited as a ruinous breach in the evolution of the individual, and the *reductio ad absurdum* of such an atomic training would seem to be reached in his hope of rendering Emile warm-hearted and pious, after keeping him in the meshes of self-interest and doubt until he is fifteen. But such a criticism loses sight of the remarkable contribution to educational theory and practice made thereby. Rousseau has shown that there are characteristic differences at different stages in the child's life, but each "has a perfection or maturity of its own," and that only as the proper activities are provided for each stage will it reach that maturity or perfection. It can be seen how these principles fulfill his contention that the child must be studied, and mark Rousseau as a progenitor of the child study movement.

And through this sympathetic understanding of child development, rather than from any scientific principles, he started marked improvements in child study and in methods of teaching, and gave a great impulse to the modern psychological tendencies in education.

In keeping with this, Rousseau also held that education should be conducted according to the way in which the mind of the child works under the stimulation of the interests that are characteristic of the various periods. This is the fundamental consideration with him in determining the course of study and methods of teaching. He may, therefore, be credited to a great degree with the increasing tendency to cease from forcing upon children a fixed method of thinking, feeling, and acting, and for the gradual disappearance of the old ideas that a task is of educational value according as it is distasteful, and that real education consists in overcoming meaningless difficulties. Curiosity and interest are rather to be used as motives for study, and Rousseau therein points the way for the Herbartians. It is likewise due to him primarily that we have recognized the need of physical activities and sense training in the earlier development of the child as a foundation for its later growth and learning. To these recommendations may be traced much of the object teaching of Pestalozzianism and the motor expression of Froebelianism. Thus Rousseau made a large contribution to educational method by showing the value of motivation, of creating problems, and of utilizing the senses and activities of the child, and may be regarded as the father of the psychological movements in modern education. He could not, however, have based his study of children and his advanced methods upon any real scientific knowledge, for in his day the 'faculty' psychology absolutely prevailed. Instead of working out his methods from scientific principles, he obtained them, as did Pestalozzi afterwards, through his sympathetic understanding of the child and his ability to place himself in the child's situation and see the world through the eyes of the child. It is not until the time of Herbart that a scientific formulation of method and a scientific system of psychology first appear.

Hence Rousseau has had a remarkable influence upon most modern movements in educational organization, method, and content in Europe and America, beginning with the 'Philanthropinum' of Basedow.

The Spread of Rousseau's Doctrines.—Thus the influence of Rousseau upon education in all its aspects has been most weighty and far-reaching. It is shown by the library of books since written to contradict, correct, or disseminate his doctrines. During the quarter of a century following the publication of the *Emile*, probably more than twice as many books upon education were published as in the preceding three-quarters of a century. This epoch-making work created and forced a rich harvest of educational thinking for a century after its appearance, and it has affected our ideas upon education from that day to this. As indicated, then, most modern movements in educational organization, method, and content, find their roots in Rousseau, and he is seen to be the intellectual progenitor of Pestalozzi, Herbart, Froebel, Spencer, and many other modern reformers. But his principles did not take immediate hold on the schools themselves, although their influence is manifest there as the nineteenth century advanced. In France they were apparent in the complaints and recommendations concerning schools in many of the *cahiers* [1] that were issued just prior to the revolution, and afterward clearly formed a basis for much of the legislation concerning the universal, free, and secular organization of educational institutions. In England, since there was no national system of schools, little direct impression was made upon educational practice. But in America this revolutionary thought would seem to have had much to do with causing the unrest that gradually resulted in upsetting the aristocratic and formal training of the young and in secularizing and universalizing the public school system. The first definite attempt, however, to put into actual practice the naturalistic education of Rousseau occurred in Germany through the writings of Basedow and the foundation of the 'Philanthropinum,' and is of sufficient importance to demand separate discussion.

The erratic Basedow was, through the *Emile*, inspired to reform the unnatural education of the day.

Development of Basedow's Educational Reforms.— *Johann Bernhard Basedow* (1723–1790) was by nature the very sort of person to be captivated by Rousseau's doctrines. He was talented, but erratic, unorthodox, tactless, and irregular in life. He had been prepared at the University of Leipzig for the Lutheran ministry, but proved too heretical, and giving up this vocation, became a tutor in Holstein to a Herr von Quaalen's children. With these aristocratic pupils he first developed methods of teaching through conversation and play connected

[1] These were lists of grievances and desired reforms prepared by the various towns and villages throughout France at the request of the king (Louis XVI), in accordance with an old custom.

with surrounding objects. A few years after this, in 1763, Basedow fell under the spell of Rousseau's *Emile*, which was most congenial to his methods of thinking and teaching, and turned all his energy toward educational reform. As in the case of Rousseau with education in France, he realized that the German education of the day was sadly in need of just such an antidote as 'naturalism' was calculated to furnish. The school-rooms were dismal and the work was unpleasant, physical training was neglected, and the discipline was severe. Children were regarded as adults in miniature, and were so treated both in their dress and their education. The current schooling consisted largely of instruction in artificial deportment. The study of classics composed the entire intellectual curriculum, and the methods were purely grammatical. As a result, suggestions made by Basedow for educational improvement attained as great popularity as his advanced theological propositions had received abuse.

Through his *Address on Schools* he raised a sufficient subsidy to publish his *Elementarwerk,* and *Methodenbuch,* which contain principles from Comenius and other sources, as well as from Rousseau.

In 1768 by his *Address on Schools and Studies, and their Influence on the Public Weal*, he called generally upon princes, governments, ecclesiastics, and others in power, to assist him financially in certain definite educational reforms. In addition to suggesting that the schools be made nonsectarian and that public instruction be placed under a National Council of Education, he proposed that, in contrast to the formal and unattractive training of the day, education should be rendered practical in content and playful in method. To assist this reform, he planned to bring out a work on elementary education, which he described in outline. Great interest in his proposals was shown throughout

Europe by sovereigns, nobles, prominent men, and rich and poor alike that were interested in a nonsectarian and more effective education. A subsidy to the sum of ten thousand dollars was speedily raised. Six years later, Basedow completed his promised text-book, *Elementarwerk*, and the companion work for teachers and parents known as *Methodenbuch*. The *Elementarwerk* was accompanied by a volume containing one hundred plates, which illustrated the subject matter of the text, but were too large to be bound in with it. In his manuals Basedow does not seem to see the problem exactly as Rousseau did, but accepts some of the old traditions. For instance he retains Latin in his suggested training. Nevertheless, he did get many naturalistic ideas from Rousseau, and through them saw that further study was necessary to answer more fully the problems with which these things were connected.

The *Elementarwerk* clearly combines ideas taken from many sources, including many of the principles of Comenius as well as of Rousseau. It has, in fact, been often referred to as 'the *Orbis Pictus*[1] of the eighteenth century,' and gives a knowledge of things and words in the form of a dialogue. The *Methodenbuch*, while not following Rousseau completely, contains many ideas concerning natural training that are suggestive of him. In this study of the nature of children, the book makes some advance upon the Rousselian doctrine by finding that they are especially interested in motion and noise, although Basedow would have shocked Rousseau by being so much under the control of tradition as to sug-

[1] For the *Orbis Sensualium Pictus* and its method, see Graves, *History of Education during the Transition*, p. 274; *Great Educators*, p. 31.

He and his followers also produced children's books in imitation of *Robinson Crusoe*, recommended by Rousseau.

gest using these interests in the teaching of Latin. Later, Basedow, together with Campe, Salzmann, and others of his followers, also produced a series of popular story books especially adapted to the character, interests, and needs of children. These works are all largely filled with didactics, moralizing, religiosity, and scraps of scientific information. The best known of them is *Robinson der Jüngere* (*Robinson Crusoe Junior*), which was published by Campe in 1779. It seems to have been suggested by Rousseau's recommendation of *Robinson Crusoe* as a text-book, and in turn a generation later it became the model for *Der Schweizerische Robinson* (*The Swiss Family Robinson*) of Wyss, which has been so popular with children in America and elsewhere.

Through Prince Leopold, Basedow founded the 'Philanthropinum' at Dessau, to embody his naturalistic ideas.

Course and Methods of the Philanthropinum.— Eight years before this, however, Prince Leopold of Dessau had been induced to allow Basedow to found there a model school called the 'Philanthropinum,' which should embody that reformer's ideas. Leopold granted him a salary of eleven hundred thalers,[1] and three years later gave him an equipment of buildings, grounds, and endowment. At first Basedow had but three assistants, but later the number was considerably increased. The staff then included several very able men,—such as Wölke, who had taught at Leipzig; Campe, formerly chaplain at Potsdam; Salzmann, who had been a professor at Erfurt; and Matthison, the poet. The underlying principle of the Philanthropinum was "everything according to nature." The natural instincts and interests of the children were only to be

[1] A *thaler* was equivalent to about three shillings, or seventy-three cents.

directed and not altogether suppressed. They were to be trained as children and not as adults, and the methods of learning were to be adapted to their stage of mentality. That all of the customary unnaturalness, discomfort, and want of freedom might be eliminated, the boys were plainly dressed in sailor jackets and loose trousers, their collars were turned down and were open at the neck, and their hair was cut short and was free from powder, pomade, and hair-bags.

Universal education was advocated, but social distinctions were recognized. Every one was given industrial and physical training, and a wide objective course was planned.

While universal education was believed in, and rich and poor alike were to be trained, the traditional idea still obtained that the natural education of the one class was for social activity and leadership, and of the other for teaching. Consequently, the wealthy boys were to spend six hours in school and two in manual labor, while those from families of small means labored six hours and studied two. Every one, however, was taught handicrafts,—carpentry, turning, planing, and threshing, as suggested in the third book of the *Emile*, and there were also physical exercises and games for all. On the intellectual side, while Latin was not neglected, considerable attention was paid to the vernacular and French. According to the *Elementarwerk*, Basedow planned especially to create a wide objective and practical course very similar to that suggested by Comenius. It was to give some account of man, including bits of anthropology, anatomy, and physiology; of brute creation, especially the uses of domestic animals and their relation to industry; of trees and plants with their growth, culture, and products; of minerals and chemicals; of mathematical and physical instruments; and of trades, history, and commerce. He afterward admitted that he had overestimated the amount of content that was possible for a child, and greatly abridged the material.[1]

Languages were taught by conversation, games, and drawing; arithmetic by mental methods; geometry by drawing; and geography by beginning with the home.

The most striking characteristic of the school, however, was its recognition of child interests and the consequent improved methods. Languages were taught by speaking and then by reading, and grammar was not brought in until late in the course. Facility in Latin was acquired through conversation, games, pictures, drawing, acting plays, and reading on practical and interesting subjects. Similar linguistic methods had been recommended by Montaigne, Ratich, and Locke, and largely worked out by Comenius, but were never before made as practical as by Basedow and his assistants. His instruction in arithmetic, geometry, geography, physics, nature study, and history was fully as progressive as that in languages, and, while continuing Rousseau's suggestions, seems to anticipate much of the 'object teaching' of Pestalozzi. Arithmetic was taught by mental methods, geometry by drawing figures accurately and neatly, and geography by beginning with one's home, and extending out into the neighborhood, the town, the country, and the continent. In a similarly direct way the pupils were instructed in matters of actual life. For example, they cast lots in the classroom to see who should have the privilege of describing the tools and processes of a trade depicted in an engraving.

Great expectations were had for the school, and it proved a stimulus for younger children.

Influence of the Philanthropinum.—The attendance at the Philanthropinum was very small in the beginning, since the institution was regarded as an experiment, but eventually the number of pupils rose

[1] The actual program of each day is given in full in Barnard, *German Teachers and Educators*, pp. 519f.

to more than fifty. Most visitors were greatly pleased with the school, especially on account of the interested and alert appearance of the pupils. Kant had such high expectations of its results as to declare in 1777 that it meant "not a slow reform, but a quick revolution," and felt that "by the plan of organization it must of itself throw off all the faults which belong to its beginning." He afterward admitted that he had been too optimistic, but he still felt that the experiment had been well worth while, and had paved the way for better things. Although it may not have served well for older pupils, it was certainly excellent in its stimulus to children under ten or twelve, who too often are naturally averse to books, and can be captured only by such appeals to the physical activities, the senses, and other primary interests.

The Philanthropinum was soon closed, but similar institutions sprang up throughout Germany, including the famous school of Salzmann at Schnepfenthal and those of Rochow at Rechahn and elsewhere.

Basedow, however, proved temperamentally unfit to direct the institution. He soon left, and began to teach privately in Dessau and write educational works along the lines he had started. *Joachim Heinrich Campe* (1746–1818), who first superseded him, withdrew within a year to found a similar school at Hamburg. Institutions of the same type sprang up elsewhere, and some of them had a large influence upon education. The most striking and enduring of these schools was that established in 1784 by *Christian Gotthilf Salzmann* (1744–1811) at Schnepfenthal under the patronage of the royal family of Saxe-Gotha. The natural surroundings—mountains, valleys, lakes—were most favorable for the purpose of the institution, and much attention was given to nature study, 'lessons on things,' organized excursions, gardening, agricultural work, and care of domestic animals. Manual training, gymnastics, sports, informal moral and religious culture, and other features that anticipated later developments in education also formed part of the course. During the decade before the establishment of Salzmann's school, institutions embodying many of Basedow's ideas were opened at Rechahn and his other Brandenburg estates by *Baron Eberhard von Rochow* (1734–1805). His schools were simply intended to improve the peasantry in their methods of farming and living, but, when this step toward universal education proved extraordinarily successful, Rochow advocated the adoption of a complete national system of schools on a nonsectarian basis.

And while the philanthropinic movement became a fad, and came into the hands of mountebanks, it introduced many new ideas concerning methods and industrial training.

In 1793 the Philanthropinum at Dessau was closed permanently. Its teachers were scattered through Europe, and gave a great impulse to the new education. An unfortunate result of this popularity was that the Philanthropinum became a fad, and schools with this name were opened everywhere in Germany by educational mountebanks. These teachers prostituted the system to their own ends, degraded the profession into a mere trade, and became the subject of much satire and ridicule. Nevertheless, the philanthropinic movement seems not to have been without good results, especially when we consider the educational conditions and the pedagogy of the times. It introduced many new ideas concerning methods and industrial training into all parts of France and Switzerland, as well as Germany, and these were carefully worked out by such reformers as Pestalozzi, Froebel, and Herbart. In this way there were embodied in education the first positive results of the destructive 'naturalism' of Rousseau, and there appeared further progress in the social, scientific, and psychological movements of modern education. The significance of the naturalistic movement will be patent when we come to the work of the later reformers, but we must now turn for a time to a different phase of educational development.

SUPPLEMENTARY READING

I. Sources

BASEDOW, J. B. *Elementarwerk* and *Methodenbuch.*

CAMPE, J. H. *Robinson der Jüngere* and *Theorophon.*

ROUSSEAU, J. J. *Confessions*, *Letters*, and *Reveries; Discourse on the Sciences and Arts* and *Discourse on Inequality; The New Heloise*, *Social Contract*, and *Emile.*

SALZMANN, C. G. *Conrad Kiefer.*

II. Authorities

BARNARD, H. *American Journal of Education.* Vol. V, pp. 459–520; XX, 349–350; and XXVII, 497–508.

BARNARD, H. *German Teachers and Educators.* Pp. 459–520.

BOYD, W. *The Educational Theory of Jean Jacques Rousseau.*

BROUGHAM, H. *Rousseau* (*Lives of Men of Letters*).

BROWNING, O. *An Introduction to the History of Educational Theories.* Chap. IX.

BRUNETIÈRE, F. *Manual of the History of French Literature.* (Translated by Derechif.) Pp. 333–414.

CAIRD, C. *Literature and Philosophy.* Vol. I, pp. 105–146.

COMPAYRÉ, G. *History of Pedagogy.* (Translated by Payne.) Chap. XIII.

COMPAYRÉ, G. *Jean Jacques Rousseau and Education from Nature.* (Translated by Jago.)

DAVIDSON, T. *Rousseau and Education according to Nature.*

FRANCKE, K. *Social Forces in German Literature.* Chaps. VII–VIII.

GARBOVICIANU, P. *Die Didaktik Basedows in Vergleiche zur Didaktik des Comenius.*

GIRALDIN, ST. M. *J. J. Rousseau, sa vie et ses ouvrages.*

GÖRING, H. *Ausgewählte Schriften mit Basedows Biographie.*

GRAVES, F. P. *Great Educators of Three Centuries.* Chaps. VII and VIII.

HUDSON, W. H. *Rousseau and Naturalism in Life and Thought.*

LANG, O. H. *Rousseau and his Emile.*

LANG, O. H. *Basedow: His Educational Work and Principles.*

LINCOLN, C. H. *Rousseau and the French Revolution* (*Annals of the American Academy of Political and Social Science*, X, pp. 54–72).

MACDONALD, F. *Studies in the France of Voltaire and Rousseau.* Chaps. II and VII.

MONROE, P. *Textbook in the History of Education.* Chap. X.

MORIN, S. H. *Life and Character of Rousseau* (*Littell's Living Age*, XXXVIII, pp. 259–264).

MORLEY, J. *Rousseau.*

MUNROE, J. P. *The Educational Ideal.* Chap. VII.

PARKER, S. C. *The History of Modern Elementary Education.* Chaps. VIII–X.

PAYNE, J. *Lectures on the History of Education.* Pp. 91–96

PINLOCHE, J. A. *Basedow et le Philanthropinisme.*

QUICK, R. H. *Educational Reformers.* Chaps. XIV and XV.

SCHLOSSER, F. C. *History of the Eighteenth Century.* Vols. I and II.

TEXTE, J. *Jean Jacques Rousseau and the Cosmopolitan Spirit in Literature.* (Translated by Matthews.) Bk. I.

WEIR, S. *The Key to Rousseau's Emile* (*Educational Review*, V, pp. 278–290).

CHAPTER III

PHILANTHROPY IN EDUCATION

In the eighteenth century there were reconstructive as well as destructive forces in society and education.

English Social and Educational Conditions in the Eighteenth Century.—The eighteenth century cannot be regarded altogether as a period of revolution and destruction. While such a characterization describes some of the prevailing tendencies, there were also social and educational forces that looked to evolution and reform rather than to a complete disintegration of society and a return to animal or to primitive living. There was still some attempt to build upon the past, and, while modifying traditions and conditions, to alleviate and improve, and not entirely ignore or reject society as it existed. Moreover, even in Rousseau, the arch-destroyer of traditions, we found many evidences of a reconstruction along higher lines, and beginnings of the development of social, psychological, and scientific movements in modern education. And such a positive movement was decidedly obvious in Basedow, Salzmann, and other philanthropinists. But reforms were even more apparent in England. In the land of the Briton, progress is proverbially gradual, and sweeping victories and Waterloo defeats in affairs of society and education are alike unwonted. The French tendency to cut short the social and educational process and to substitute revolution for evolution is out of accord with the spirit across the English Channel. Hence in England educational movements took place in the eighteenth century largely as a continuation of those characterizing the seventeenth, and were the outgrowth of philanthropy on the part of the upper classes rather than the result of a general uprising of the unfortunate masses.

Philanthropy and educational reform were greatly needed, especially in England, to relieve the poverty and lack of elementary schools for the lower classes.

And yet conditions could scarcely have been worse even in France. The terrible poverty of England in the early part of the eighteenth century can now be imagined with difficulty. The great industrial and mining development had not yet begun. Wages were low, employment was irregular, and the laboring classes, who numbered fully one-sixth of the total population, were clad in rags, lived in hovels, and often went hungry. The opportunities for elementary education had become greatly reduced. The few elementary schools that remained after the acts of dissolution under Henry VIII and Edward VI had largely lost their endowments through embezzlement or had been perverted into secondary schools, and had suffered through a type of patronage whereby the master secured a vested interest in his emoluments, regardless of his ability or attention to duty. Education was further injured by the political and religious upheaval of the times. During the arbitrary reign of the first two Stuarts, and the civic changes and theological controversies of the Commonwealth and Restoration, schools were alternately abused and neglected. Both sides in turn had the schoolmasters of opposing opinions ejected and forbidden to teach. Hence it gradually came to be almost impossible for the lower classes to educate their children at all, and they generally failed themselves to appreciate the value of an education.

The Foundation of 'Charity Schools' by Endowment and Subscription.—However, some people of wealth must have realized the seriousness of the problem and their own responsibility in the premises, and before the close of the seventeenth century had put forth vigorous efforts at a solution. During the early part of the century there sprang up a succession of 'charity schools,' in which children of the poor were not only taught, but boarded and sometimes provided with clothes, and the boys were prepared for apprenticeship and the girls for domestic service. The movement for the establishment of these schools for the lower classes by endowment or subscriptions reached its height during the comparative peace and toleration that followed the 'bloodless revolution' of 1688. The first few endowments were even made a generation before this change of government, and for about sixty years they steadily continued. Through such bequests the opportunities for elementary education were much increased, and it was estimated in the middle of the nineteenth century that anywhere from one-third to one-half of all the schools then in existence were the product of endowment in this period. According to an investigation of the Charity Commissioners at that time, some eight or nine hundred elementary schools had come down from these days, and, if the diversion of numerous endowments is taken into account, there must have been at least one thousand schools founded during the period.

Charity schools were started even in the seventeenth century, and by the middle of the eighteenth a large number had been opened through bequests or subscriptions.

Of these 'charity schools,' however, a great many were not founded through endowment. In fact, the term has always included and has more generally been applied to the institutions established and maintained by private

Numerous subscription schools were also established before this in Wales by Thomas Gouge.

subscriptions. These arose in England for the most part after the movement toward endowed schools was well under way, but similar institutions had also been established in Wales in the latter half of the seventeenth century, especially through the efforts of Thomas Gouge. Gouge was among the English clergy ejected from their charges by the Act of Uniformity in 1662. By means of contributions from wealthy Londoners, he set up schools in eighty-six of the chief towns and parishes, and was soon having about twelve hundred poor children taught to read and write English and cast accounts. In 1674, to receive and manage the necessary funds for his work, he organized a corporation composed of churchmen and nonconformists, and at his death seven years later there were by this means over three hundred free schools maintained in Wales.

But most charity schools were established through the S. P. C. K., founded by Dr. Bray.

The Charity Schools of the Society for the Promotion of Christian Knowledge.—In England itself the great majority of 'charity schools' were established through the 'Society for the Promotion of Christian Knowledge' (often abbreviated to S. P. C. K.). In order to counteract the low ebb in religion, morals, and education that still prevailed toward the close of the century, this society was founded in 1698 by *Rev. Thomas Bray, D.D.* (1656–1730) and four other clergymen and philanthropists. Its chief project and that which is especially pertinent here, was "to set up catechetical schools for the education of poor children." As a rule, these S. P. C. K. charity schools were established, supported, and managed by local people, but the society guaranteed their maintenance, assisting them from its own treasury whenever a temporary stringency in local funds occurred. Before long the local subscriptions were often supplemented by endowments and by systematic church collections, for which sermons were preached at stated periods. The S. P. C. K. also inspected the schools, advised and encouraged the local managers, and furnished bibles, prayer books, and catechisms at the cheapest rates possible. It made stringent regulations of eligibility for its schoolmasters. Every one of them had not only to stand all the usual tests of religious, moral, and pedagogical efficiency, but to be a member of the Church of England, at least twenty-five years of age, and to be approved by the minister of his parish. Each master was required to teach the children the catechism of the church twice a week and "more largely inform them of their duty by the help of the *Whole Duty of Man*." He was also to "take particular Care of the Manners and Behaviour of the Poor Children," and purge them of lying, swearing, Sabbath breaking, and other vices. This religious training was given them in addition to the regular work in reading, writing, and "the Grounds of Arithmetick, to fit them for Service or Apprentices." Parents were also required, under penalty of their children's being dismissed from the school, to see that the children did not absent themselves, save for sickness, and that they came to school cleanly and neat. Besides being educated, the pupils were clothed, boarded, and at times even lodged.

These schools undertook to train their pupils in religion, morals, and neatness, as well as in reading, writing, and sufficient arithmetic for apprenticeship.

As a result of the efforts of the S. P. C. K., the charity schools in London and throughout England and Wales increased by leaps and bounds. During the first three years at least a dozen of these institutions sprang up in

S. P. C. K. schools continued to increase until, before the middle of the eighteenth century, the number in England and Wales reached nearly two thousand, with about fifty thousand pupils.

London, and by the close of the first decade there were within a radius of ten miles of London eighty-eight schools, with an attendance of 2,181 boys and 1,221 girls. The subscriptions had grown to nearly £4,200, and the special collections to almost half as much again, while the gifts from the beginning had amounted to £9,517. Nearly one thousand boys and over four hundred girls had been sent out as apprentices. Moreover, there were two hundred and fifty schools elsewhere in England and twenty-five in Wales. After another decade the charity schools increased to over twelve hundred and had an attendance of nearly twenty-seven thousand pupils, while before the middle of the eighteenth century the total number of charity schools in England and Wales reached nearly two thousand, with about fifty thousand boys and girls in attendance. This increase in facilities for the education of the poor was not kindly received by many in the upper classes, who would often have agreed with Mandeville in his *Essay on Charity Schools* that "there is no Need for any Learning at all for the meanest Ranks of Mankind: Their Business is to Labour, not to Think: Their Duty is to do what they are commanded, to fill up the most servile Posts, and to perform the lowest Offices and Drudgeries of Life for the Conveniency of their Superiors, and common Nature gives them Knowledge enough for this Purpose." On the other hand, the charity schools had the warm support of the numerous advocates of religious and social reform. Many of these philanthropists, indeed, were over-sanguine in their estimate of what these schools were destined to accomplish. Joseph Addison even went so far as to say: "I have always looked on this institution of

Charity Schools, which of late years has so universally prevailed through the whole nation, as the glory of the age we live in. . . . It seems to promise us an honest and virtuous posterity. There will be few in the next generation who will not at least be able to write and read, and have not an early tincture of religion." But while the benefactions for these institutions continued to increase for nearly half a century, until in many cases they virtually became endowments, by the middle of the eighteenth century popular interest had waned. The subscriptions began to fall off, the system of inspection became less effective, teachers again came to be regarded as having a vested interest, and the schools ceased to expand. Nevertheless, the Society for the Promotion of Christian Knowledge had succeeded in impressing the Church of England with a sense of responsibility for the establishment of a national school system upon a religious basis. The S. P. C. K. schools were largely continued throughout the eighteenth century, and were in most instances absorbed after 1811 by the 'National Society for Promoting the Education of the Poor in the Principles of the Established Church.'[1] Some of the best of these foundations have even existed until the present day upon an independent basis.

While later the work became less effective, the S. P. C. K. had impressed England with a responsibility for the establishment of national schools.

Other British Charity Schools.—These institutions of the S. P. C. K. may be taken as typical of British charity schools in general. While under the control of the Church of England, they were at first assisted by wealthy nonconformists and often attended by the children of poor dissenters. But as a result of increasing sectarian hostility the nonconformists soon set up schools

The 'Gravel Lane School' and about sixty other charity schools were founded by nonconformists before the close of the eighteenth century.

[1] See pp. 55ff.

of their own. The first of these foundations was the 'Gravel Lane School,' founded in Southwark, London, in 1687, "for the instruction of children in reading, writing, and arithmetick, and the girls in sewing and knitting, and furnishing them with books for their instruction in these arts, and with Testaments, Catechisms, and Bibles." This school was maintained by voluntary subscriptions, annual collections, and legacies, and the number of pupils soon rose from forty at the beginning to over two hundred. Half a dozen other such nonconformist institutions seem to have been established in London during the early part of the eighteenth century. By the middle of the century there were in the metropolis at least five charity schools belonging to the Presbyterians, three to the Independents, two to the French Protestants, and one to the Quakers, and before the close of the century there must have been sixty charity schools founded in various parts of England and Wales by different nonconforming denominations.

and 'circulating schools' were also founded in Wales.

Later there was also founded in Wales an interesting type of philanthropic institution known as 'circulating schools.' These institutions simply aimed to teach pupils to read the Bible in Welsh, and when this had been accomplished in one neighborhood, the school was transferred to another. Their organization was begun in 1737 by the Reverend Griffith Jones, but in their support they were largely assisted by the S. P. C. K. Under the management of Jones over one hundred and fifty thousand children and adults were taught to read through some three thousand of these schools, and under his successor, who continued the organization until 1779, there was an even larger number of schools and pupils.

The Society for the Propagation of the Gospel in Foreign Parts, and Its Charity Schools in America.— The charity school movement of the mother country also had a counterpart in the American colonies. A number of earlier charity schools were started in America by various organizations, but most of the institutions of this sort developed during the eighteenth century through an offshoot of the Society for the Promotion of Christian Knowledge. This association had from the first contemplated religious education in the colonies as well as in England. Dr. Bray undertook the commissaryship of Maryland for the Bishop of London with the understanding that he should be assisted in providing libraries and schools in America. Before starting for the colony himself, he sent over many missionaries, and furnished libraries and money to be used in education. While schools never came to be organized in America by the society, it was evidently intended that they should be encouraged in time, but before any definite action could be taken, the other work in the colonies had grown to such proportions that Bray deemed it wise to organize a separate society to manage education. Thus, three years after its own creation, the Society for the Promotion of Christian Knowledge gave birth to the 'Society for the Propagation of the Gospel in Foreign Parts' (commonly known as the 'S. P. G.'), and after 1701 the parent association was enabled to limit its efforts largely to the home field. Through liberal subscriptions and wise investments the S. P. G. eventually came to have a fund of its own amounting to over £400,000. Missionaries were sent to America in 1702, and soon spread through all the colonies, but no schools were founded for several years.

The S. P. G. was founded in 1701 for missionary and educational work in America.

The first S. P. G. school was opened in New York City in 1709 upon a similar plan to that of the S. P. C. K. schools in England.

The first school of the society was opened in New York City. William Huddleston, who had been conducting a school of his own there, was in 1709 placed upon the society's payroll, "upon condition that he should teach forty poor children gratis." It was intended that the new school should follow the plan of the charity schools in England, but while free tuition and free books were guaranteed from the beginning, it was not until many years later that the expense of clothing the children was provided. Under different masters and with varying fortunes, the school was supported by the society until 1783, when the United States had finally cut loose from the mother country and started upon a career of its own. Meanwhile Trinity Church had come more and more to take the initiative in the support of the school, and finally accumulated an endowment of £5000. The institution came to be known as 'Trinity Church School,' and ever since the withdrawal of the society from America, it has been continued under that name.

The same type of school was supported in all the colonies, except Virginia.

Schools of the same type were soon established by the S. P. G. missionaries throughout the colonies. For the colony of New York, we possess more or less complete accounts of schools established in Westchester County at Rye, West Chester, White Plains, Yonkers, and East Chester; in two or three centers on Staten Island; at Hempstead, Oyster Bay, North Castle, Huntington, Jamaica, Southampton, and Brookhaven, on Long Island; among the German Palatinates on the Hudson at New Windsor and Newburgh; and at Albany and Johnstown. In Pennsylvania there were well-known schools in Philadelphia, Lancaster, and Chester; while similar institutions were supported at Burlington,

Shrewsbury, and Second River in New Jersey. The S. P. G. schoolmasters seem to have been likewise active in all the other colonies, except Virginia.

All these schools, except for size and local peculiarities, closely resembled that in New York City. The attendance ranged from eighteen or twenty pupils to nearly four times that number. From one-quarter to one-half of them were taught gratuitously. Girls were generally admitted, and occasionally equalled or exceeded the boys in number. As a rule, children of other denominations were received on the same terms as those of Church of England members, and at times nearly one-half the attendance was composed of dissenters, but often those outside the Church were given secondary consideration, or the catechism was so stressed by the school that the dissenting children were withdrawn and rival schools set up. The character of the course of study in these charity schools is further indicated by the books furnished by the society. In packets of various sizes it sent over hornbooks, primers, spellers, writing-paper and inkhorns, catechisms, psalters, prayer books, testaments, and bibles. There is also some evidence that secondary instruction was carried on intermittently in the various centers by the missionaries or by the schoolmasters in conjunction with their elementary work. The character of the work done by the society's schools varied somewhat. Some masters were notoriously inefficient, but as a whole they ranked above the average of the times.

The instruction was generally elementary and religious.

Throughout its work in the American colonies the S. P. G. met with various forms of opposition. The dissenters, Quakers, and others were often openly hostile through fear of the foundation of an established national

The S. P. G. schools met with much opposition. Yet, while the society

was sectarian, it exerted a great influence toward universal education.

church similar to that of England, and both sides displayed considerable sectarianism and bigotry. After 1750 the opposition to the society increased in bitterness and became more general, owing to the feeling that its agents were supporting the king against the colonists. It was gradually forced to give up its schools, and by 1783 had entirely left the country. Yet its patronage of schools was most philanthropic and important for American education in the eighteenth century. While it insisted upon the interpretation of Christianity adopted by the Church of England, it stood first and foremost for the extension of religion and education to the virgin soil of America. It carried on its labors with devoted interest and showed great generosity in the maintenance of schools. Where it refused to establish a school or made any retrenchment, the action can generally be explained through an actual lack of funds or a want of coöperation on the part of the colonists. The hope was frequently expressed that the people of the colonies would soon be able to assist in the support of these charity schools, or to assume the entire charge themselves, but, except for the aid given in New York by Trinity Church, the time never came. Nevertheless, the support of schools in the colonies by the S. P. G. exerted some influence toward universal education, and among the colonists where the Church of England prevailed it afforded the nearest approach to a public school system. It can hardly be claimed that the society would have encouraged a genuine state support and control of schools, but it certainly furnished a generous example and paved the way for such an educational policy.

Charity Schools among the Pennsylvania Germans.— During the eighteenth century the efforts of the S. P. G. were supplemented by the formation of minor associations and the establishment of other charity schools in various colonies. The most noteworthy instance was the charity school movement among the German sects of Pennsylvania. The Germans had come to the colony in the early part of the century at the invitation of Penn. They had there found peace and content, and by the middle of the century they numbered not far from one-half of the entire population. But the educational facilities, on account of their poverty, the sparseness of population, and the dearth of efficient schoolmasters, soon proved inadequate, both in quantity and quality. An attempt to improve these conditions was made in 1751 by raising funds among the Calvinists in Holland and Scotland, and through an appeal to the S. P. G. in 1753 by Provost Smith of the new College at Philadelphia (afterward the University of Pennsylvania). In addition to the arguments of religion and education, Dr. Smith urged the political reason that "by a common Education of English and German Youth at the same Schools, acquaintances and connexions will be formed, and the English language and a conformity of manners will be acquired." In response to his petition, an additional fund of £20,000 was raised through contributions by the S. P. G., the royal family, and the proprietaries of the colony. This fund, "from the interests of which free schools were here to be established and sustained, was placed in the hands of certain trustees, constituting A Society for Propagating the Knowledge of God among the Germans." In accordance with a plan of Smith's,

Through contributions from the S. P. G. and other sources, a number of charity schools were started among the German settlers of Pennsylvania about the middle of the century, and there was appointed a general colonial board of six trustees. One or more of the trustees were to visit each of the schools annually and award one prize for the best oration in English by a boy of German parentage, and one for the best oral examination passed by any boy in civil and religious duties. The course of study included instruction in "both the English and German languages; likewise in Writing, keeping of common accounts, Singing of Psalms, and the true Principles of the holy Protestant Religion."

while the aid was withdrawn after a decade, the organization of these institutions paved the way for a system of public schools for the state.

It had been planned to establish twenty-five such schools, but owing to lack of funds, insufficiency of teachers, and quarrels as to location, there were probably always less than half that number. In the various schools and at different seasons of the year, the attendance ranged from twenty-five to sixty-six, and at most the number of pupils accommodated at any one time in all the charity schools must have been well under one thousand. The schools lasted only about a decade. From the beginning the minor sects—Dunkers, Mennonites, Schwenkfelders, Moravians, Siebentagers—eyed them with suspicion, and later the Lutherans and Calvinists were likewise persuaded that this English schooling threatened their language, nationality, and institutions. The resulting opposition ultimately led to their abandonment by the S. P. G. and the king. Yet the organization of these institutions left some good results. They stimulated the Germans to provide schools to maintain their own language and religion, they helped unify the people of Pennsylvania, and paved the way for the establishment of a system of public schools in 1834.[1]

[1] See pp. 102f.

Sunday schools for instruction in religion and the rudiments were established in Gloucester, England, in 1780 by Robert Raikes,

Robert Raikes and the 'Sunday School' Movement in Great Britain.—A variety of charity school, quite different from those already mentioned, sprang up in England toward the close of the century under the name of 'Sunday schools.' The reputed originator of these institutions was *Robert Raikes* (1735–1811) of Gloucester, England. This city was a manufacturing center, and child labor, with all the attendant ignorance, vice, and squalor, was everywhere in vogue. Several clergymen and philanthropists of the vicinity had sought with more or less success to improve conditions by gathering children and adults together on Sunday for instruction in religion and the rudiments, but until the time of Raikes no general system arose, and the Sunday schools scarcely spread to the neighboring parishes. The success of Raikes came largely through the publicity he was able to give the institutions in the columns of his *Gloucester Journal*, the proprietorship of which he had inherited from his father. He opened his first Sunday school in 'Sooty Alley' in 1780 under the direction of a Mrs. Meredith, whom he paid a shilling each Sunday to train the children. After six months he started a new school in Southgate street under Mrs. Mary Critchley, and further schools were soon established. The formal instruction in these Sunday schools was very rudimentary. It consisted at the best in teaching the pupils to read in the Bible, spell, write, and absorb the elements of religion. The religious training did not emphasize any particular creed, and was not obscured by sectarian bitterness. But even so mild an attempt at reform could not pass unchallenged by the conservatives. The upper classes held that "the lower orders of mankind are incapable of improvement," and feared that, unless the masses were kept in their place, there would be a social upheaval in England like that going on at the time in France. The poor, on their side, were suspicious of "people taking pains to bestow benefits without having some selfish object," and declared that "reading only serves to make poor folk proud and idle." Yet the new movement was not without warm and influential friends among the nobility and others interested in reform, and Wesley even incorporated Sunday schools as one of the features of his religious 'societies.'

In fact, despite opposition, the Sunday schools were a success from the start, and soon spread from the county of Gloucester to all corners of the United Kingdom. As early as 1784, schools of this type were opened in London, and the year following a general Sunday School Society was founded. In the course of a decade this organization distributed nearly one hundred thousand spellers, twenty-five thousand testaments, and over five thousand bibles, and trained approximately sixty-five thousand pupils in a thousand schools. The Sunday schools that appeared in Wales were probably independent in their origin, although they may have been stimulated by the Raikes movement. They were largely developed through a clergyman of Bala, named Charles, who started them in 1785 as the best substitute within his means for the former 'circulating schools' of Jones,[1] and instructed adults as well as children. Even in Scotland, where religious instruction in the family was excellently organized, there was a 'Sabbath Evening School' founded in 1797. Eight years before, Sunday schools were

and soon spread through England, Wales, Scotland, Ireland, and the Channel Islands.

[1] See p. 42.

formally organized in Down County, Ireland, and were thence extended to Dublin and other centers. The Channel Islands, Jersey and Guernsey, also opened similar institutions during the early part of the nineteenth century. Hence before the death of Raikes there were nearly half a million pupils in the Sunday schools of the British Isles, and by the middle of the century the attendance had grown to two and one-half millions. Meanwhile the teachers had gradually come to serve without pay and to instruct less efficiently, and the schools had largely given up all training save the religious. An investigation of the London Sunday schools in 1858 revealed the fact that the teaching was "certainly not secular, but as purely as possible religious." In no instance were pupils instructed in writing, "and reading was taught only incidentally and by means of Bible lessons." Nevertheless, the Sunday schools were continued as a nominal part of secular education until the public system was started in 1870, when they came to occupy the distinctly religious field of the present day.

Sunday schools of the Raikes type were likewise organized in various cities of the United States, and a little later associations were formed for promoting this kind of Sunday instruction.

The 'Sunday School' Movement in the United States.—The Raikes system of Sunday instruction was also soon introduced in America. Sunday schools had not been uncommon in the colonies even more than a century before this, but they had been exclusively for religious teaching. The first school on the new basis was organized in 1786 by Bishop Asbury at the house of Thomas Crenshaw in Hanover County, Virginia, in the hope of combating the ignorance, infidelity, and sectarianism that were rampant after the American revolution. Within a quarter of a century a number of other schools arose at Charleston, Pittsburg, Pawtucket

(R. I.), Boston, New York, Paterson (N. J.), Stockbridge (N. Y.), Albany, and elsewhere. In these communities schools were provided for the laboring classes, whose children were generally very ignorant and vicious, and, as in the British movement, the teachers were at first usually paid. The chief texts used were the speller and hymn-book. But the organization of the system in the United States soon became more extensive than these isolated cases of Sunday schools. In 1791 the first permanent association for promoting Sunday instruction, 'The First Day or Sunday School Society,' was organized at Philadelphia. It arose from the lack of free schools in the city and the need of improving material and intellectual conditions. It was formed by prominent men of several creeds, and was purely nonsectarian. By the close of the century it was training over two thousand children. During the first two decades of the nineteenth century a number of similar societies for secular instruction on Sunday were founded in New York, Boston, Philadelphia, and elsewhere. In 1823 these associations were all absorbed into a new and broader organization, called the 'American Sunday School Union.' For a time this society continued secular instruction. It published suitable reading-books, and furnished primers, spellers, testaments, and hymn-books to needy Sunday schools at a reasonable rate, but it has gradually come to confine itself to the publication of religious literature and the encouragement of religious instruction. In fact, after the first quarter of the nineteenth century the prevailing tendency in the Sunday schools of the United States was to substitute voluntary teachers and purely religious training for the system of

But the tendency soon arose of substituting voluntary teachers and purely religious training for the system of Raikes.

Raikes. The growth of free education everywhere in America has gradually rendered secular instruction on Sunday unnecessary.

Value of the Instruction in 'Sunday Schools.'—In fact, the value of secular instruction in both British and American Sunday schools was not large at its best. These institutions were not unimportant in their effect upon the extension of education, but their work was necessarily limited to a few hours once a week, and their secular training was always subordinate to the religious. And finally, when the teachers became voluntary, the instruction was rendered with more zeal than ability, and the secular element in the content gradually disappeared altogether. Both Raikes and all others interested in these institutions recognized their inadequacy as a means of securing universal education, and regarded them merely as auxiliary to a more complete system of instruction. But while a makeshift and by no means a final solution for national education, they performed a notable service for the times, and, like all philanthropic schools, helped point the way to a system of universal instruction at public expense.[1]

While the Sunday schools were a makeshift in both England and America, they helped point the way to universal public instruction.

Lancaster's School in Southwark.—It has been evident that while most varieties of philanthropic education came into existence in the eighteenth century, some of the schools continued into the nineteenth. This was even more the case with the schools of the 'monitorial' system, which became prominent entirely within the first half of the latter century. This system may be said to have started in 1798 with a school for the children

Joseph Lancaster started 'monitorial' schools for the poor of England in 1798,

[1] For their influence in starting primary schools in the city of Boston, see p. 69.

of the poor, opened in Southwark, London. The teacher was *Joseph Lancaster* (1778–1838), an English Quaker only twenty years of age. The youthful philanthropist had come to feel that "the want of system and order is almost uniform in every class of schools within the reach of the poor." To overcome the lack of organization and the resulting illiteracy, he undertook to educate as many of the bare-foot and unkempt children of the district as he could. His school-room was soon crowded with a hundred or more pupils, and, in order to teach them all, he used the older scholars as assistants. He taught the lesson first to these 'monitors,' and they in turn imparted it to the others, who were divided into equal groups. Each monitor cared for a single group. The work was very successful from the first, and Lancaster called further attention to it in 1803 by an account he published under the title of *Improvements in Education as it respects the Industrious Classes of the Community*. He also lectured on his methods throughout England and established 'monitorial' schools everywhere, and it was generally believed that an effective means had at length been found for educating everyone with little cost. Lancaster, however, proved most reckless, and his venture had by 1808 plunged him deeply in debt. Having rescued him from the debtors' prison, certain philanthropic men of means in that year founded 'The Royal Lancasterian Institution,' to continue the work on a practical basis. But within half a dozen years, Lancaster withdrew from the association and started a school of his own. A few years later he left England for foreign lands, where he again met with failure and poverty, and finally died in the city of New York, a disappointed man.

The 'British and Foreign' and the 'National' Societies.—Yet the organization for perpetuating his work, which after the withdrawal of Lancaster became known as 'The British and Foreign Society,' continued to flourish and perform a splendid service for education. So successful was it that the Church of England began to fear its liberalistic influence upon education. Following the nonconformist attitude of its Quaker founder, the education of the society included religion and reading the Bible, but permitted no catechism or denominational instruction of any sort. To most Anglican churchmen such religious teaching seemed loose and colorless, and in 1811 'The National Society for Promoting the Education of the Poor in the Principles of the Established Church' was founded by them. This long-named association was to use the 'monitorial' system, and to have a Doctor Bell as its manager. *Andrew Bell* (1753–1832) had been an army chaplain and the superintendent of an orphanage in India, and had the idea of monitorial instruction suggested to him by the Hindu education. A year before Lancaster opened his school, Bell had published his treatise known as *An Experiment in Education Made at the Male Asylum of Madras;* and while the Quaker philanthropist began his system independently, it is not unlikely that he received help later from Bell. Although they formed no part of Bell's original methods in Madras, the catechism and the prayer book were now taught dogmatically in the schools founded by the National Society, and as Bell proved an admirable director, the affairs of the organization prospered marvelously. In consequence, a healthy rivalry with the older association of the Lancasterians rapidly grew up.

and the British and Foreign Society was founded to perpetuate his work.

To combat the liberalistic influence of Lancasterianism upon education, Anglican churchmen founded the National Society, under the management of Andrew Bell.

The Systems of Lancaster and Bell.—'Monitorial' or 'mutual' instruction, however, was not original with either Lancaster or Bell. Besides being used by the Hindus,[1] it has formed part of the Jesuit system of education,[2] was practiced by Trotzendorf in his school,[3] and was confidently recommended by Comenius in his *Didactica Magna*.[4] Nevertheless, it was the work of Lancaster and Bell that greatly developed the method and brought it into prominence. The plans of the two men, while analogous, differed somewhat in spirit and details. Without considering the methods of religious instruction, the system of Lancaster was generally animated by broader motives. While he failed to teach certain subjects, it was simply because his resources were limited; but the National Society purposely curtailed the range of its instruction on the ground that "there is a risk of elevating those who are doomed to the drudgery of daily labour above their station, and rendering them unhappy and discontented with their lot." In the matter of details, both men worked out systematically the idea of instructing through monitors, and both used a desk covered with sand as a means of teaching writing; but in other respects Lancaster elaborated the method more than Bell. By having the speller or other text printed in large type and suspending it from the wall, he made one book serve for a whole class, or even for the entire school. Through the use of slates and dictation he had five hundred boys spell and write the

The system of Lancaster was broader than that of the National Society, and was more elaborate.

[1] See Graves, *History of Education before the Middle Ages*, pp. 87f.

[2] See Graves, *History of Education during the Transition*, p. 218.

[3] *Op. cit.*, pp. 188f.

[4] *Op. cit.*, pp. 274f.

same word at the same time. He arranged a new method in arithmetic whereby any child who could read might teach the subject with accuracy. Moreover, he instituted company organization, drill, regimental control, precision, and a prompt observance of the word of command. He also developed a system of badges, tickets, offices, and other rewards, and, in order to avoid flogging, a set of punishments by which the offender was made an object of ridicule rather than physical pain. There were likewise a number of unessential differences between the two systems.

The monitorial system, while it accomplished much when little attention was given to education, was formal and mechanical.

Value of the Monitorial System in England.—Neither Bell nor Lancaster deserves much praise as an educational reformer. Each was vain and pedagogically ignorant, and saw but one side of education. While both societies accomplished much good at a time when little attention was given to instruction and less to the problems of education, the monitorial systems overemphasized repetition in the teaching process and treated education purely from the standpoint of routine. The monitorial method was not real instruction, but a formal drill. It had no principles and little of the elasticity that was apparent in the more psychological methods of the reformers on the Continent. The mechanical basis of such a system is exposed by the arithmetical boast of Lancaster. He calculated: "Each boy can spell one hundred words in a morning. If one hundred scholars can do that two hundred mornings yearly, the following will be the total of their efforts at improvement." He then shows that there will be an annual achievement of two million words spelt. Similarly, in arithmetic he seems to hold that it is simply a question of the number of sums done in a given time, and not at all a matter of principles.

But it afforded a national education in England before it could be otherwise obtained.

Yet the Lancaster-Bell schools were productive of some achievements. Most of them afforded a fair education in the elementary school subjects and added some industrial and vocational training. They also did much to awaken the conscience of the English nation to the need of general education for the poor, and the system emphasized the school as an organized community for mutual aid. The British and Foreign and the National Societies afforded a substitute, though a poor one, for national education in the days before the government was willing to pay for general education or the denominations were able to furnish it, and they became the avenues through which such appropriations as the government did make were distributed. In 1833 the £20,000, constituting the first aid to elementary education, was equally divided between the two societies,[1] and this method of administration was continued as the annual grant was gradually increased, until universal public education was enacted. Likewise, in 1839, £10,000 for normal instruction was voted to the societies, and was used by the British and Foreign for its Borough Road Training College, and by the National for St. Mark's Training College. These were followed by several other training institutions established by each society through government aid. In 1870, when the 'board,' or public elementary, schools were at length founded,[2] the schools of the British and Foreign Society, with their nonsectarian instruction, fused naturally with them; but the institutions of the National Society, though

[1] See pp. 303f.

[2] See pp. 305f.

transferred to school boards in a few cases, have generally come to constitute by themselves a national system on a voluntary basis.

The Lancasterian system was introduced into many American cities,

Results of Lancasterianism in the United States.— In the United States, where complete freedom in religion obtained, the system of Dr. Bell and the National Society found little footing. The monitorial system in its Lancasterian form, however, was introduced into New York City in 1806. The 'Society for the Establishment of a Free School,' after investigating the best methods in other cities and countries, decided to try the system of Lancaster.[1] The method was likewise introduced into the charity schools of Philadelphia. The monitorial system then spread rapidly through New York, Pennsylvania, Massachusetts, Connecticut, and other states. It is almost impossible to trace the exact extent of this organization in the United States, but before long it seems to have affected nearly all cities of any size as far south as Augusta (Georgia), and west as far as Cincinnati. There are still traces of its influence everywhere throughout this region,—in Hartford, New Haven, Washington, Baltimore, and Albany, as well as in the cities already mentioned. In 1818 Lancaster himself was invited to America, and assisted in the monitorial schools of New York, Brooklyn, and Philadelphia. A dozen years later the system began to be introduced generally into the high schools and academies. Through the efforts of Dr. John Griscom, who had been greatly pleased with the monitorial high school of Dr. Pillans in Edinburgh, a similar institution was established in New York City in 1825, and the plan was soon adopted by a number

[1] See pp. 97f.

of high schools in New York and neighboring states. Likewise, the state system of academies in Maryland and in Indiana, which became high schools after the Civil War, was organized on this basis. For two decades the monitorial remained the prevailing method in secondary education. Training schools for teachers on the Lancasterian basis also became common.

and did a great service where free schools had been few

In fact, the monitorial system was destined to perform a great service for American education. At the time of its introduction, public and free schools were generally lacking, outside of New England. Even in that section the early Puritan provision for schools had largely become a dead letter, and the facilities that existed were meager, and available during but a small portion of the year. In all parts of the country illiteracy was almost universal among children of the poor. This want of school opportunities was rendered more serious by the rapid growth of American cities, which was evident even in the earliest part of the century, and by the consequent increase and concentration of ignorance, poverty, and crime. 'Free school societies,' like that in New York City, formed to study and relieve the situation, were driven to the conclusion that gratuitous education must be instituted, if the poorer classes were to be trained to habits of thrift and virtue. Because of its comparative inexpensiveness, these philanthropic associations came to regard the system of Lancaster as a very godsend for their purpose. And when, before long, the people awoke to the crying need of public education, legislators found the monitorial schools the cheapest way out of the difficulty, and the provision they made for these schools gradually opened the road to the ever increasing expenditures and taxation that had to be made before satisfactory schools could be established. Hence the introduction of Lancasterianism may well be considered to have provided a basis for the substantial public support of education now universal in the United States.

and the work ineffective,

Moreover, the Lancasterian schools were not only economical, but most effective, when the educational conditions of the times are taken into consideration. Even in the cities, the one-room and one-teacher school was the prevailing type, and grading was practically unknown. The whole organization and administration was shiftless and uneconomical, and a great improvement was brought about by the carefully planned and detailed methods of Lancaster. The schools were made over through his definite mechanics of instruction, centralized management, well-trained teachers, improved apparatus, discipline, hygiene, and other features. We can, then, well understand the enthusiasm for these new schools that is apparent in the utterances and writings of statesmen, educators, and other persons of the times that felt responsible for the training of the people. One of the earliest and best known estimates is that of De Witt Clinton, afterward (1817–23 and 1825–28) governor of New York, who in 1809 declared in his address at the dedication of the new building of the Free School Society:

"When I perceive that many boys in our school have been taught to read and write in two months, who did not before know the alphabet, and that even one has accomplished it in three weeks—when I view all the bearings and tendencies of this system—when I contemplate the habits of order which it forms, the spirit of emulation which it excites, the rapid improvement which it produces, the purity of morals which it inculcates—when I behold the extraordinary union of celerity in instruction and economy of expense—and when I perceive one great assembly of a thousand children, under the eye of a single teacher, marching with unexampled rapidity and with perfect discipline to the goal of knowledge, I confess that I recognize in Lancaster the benefactor of the human race. I consider his system as creating a new era in education, as a blessing sent down from heaven to redeem the poor and distressed of this world from the power and dominion of ignorance."[1]

but disappeared when educational sentiment improved.

But while the monitorial methods met a great educational emergency in the United States, they were clearly mechanical, inelastic, and without psychological foundation. Naturally their sway could not last long, and as public sentiment for education increased, and enlarged material resources enabled the people to make greater appropriations for education, the obvious defects of the monitorial system became more fully appreciated and brought about its abandonment. Before the middle of the century its work in America was ended, and it gave way to the more psychological conceptions of Pestalozzi and to those afterward formulated by Froebel and Herbart.

Oberlin opened infant schools in every village of his parish, and, besides teaching reading, writing, and arithmetic, afforded a religious and industrial training.

'Infant Schools' in France.—Another form of philanthropic education that came to be very influential during the nineteenth century and has eventually been merged in several national systems is that of the so-called 'infant schools.' These institutions may be said to have started with *Jean Frédéric Oberlin* (1740–1826), Lutheran pastor in Ban de la Roche, a wild district in the Vosges

[1] For Clinton's complete eulogy of the system adopted by the Free School Society, of which he was president, see Bourne, *History of the Public School Society of the City of New York*, pp. 18–20.

Mountains of Northeastern France. Among the institutions that the young minister opened in every village were 'infant schools' for very young children. In these schools he endeavored to inculcate morality and religion, as well as to teach the elements of reading, writing, and arithmetic. The Scriptures, natural history, and geography were taught through pictures, maps, and drawing; and excursions to search for flowers and other products of nature were taken. The older children also learned to knit and spin, and meanwhile the younger were allowed to play. These infant schools did much to dispel ignorance, immorality, and shiftlessness, and soon spread into various parts of France.

This plan was imitated at Paris in institutions that developed into the *ecoles maternelles* of the French national system of education.

Among the institutions inspired by this example, was the *salle d' hospitalitê* ('room of entertainment'), which was opened at Paris in 1801. It did not last long at the time, but a quarter of a century later it was revived through a study of the infant schools that had meanwhile grown up in England,[1] and it then rapidly expanded into a system. In 1833 these institutions were adopted as part of the French national system of education, and in 1847 a normal school was founded to prepare directresses and inspectors for them. In 1881 they became permanently known as *écoles maternelles* ('mother schools'), and the curriculum was given its present form.[2] These schools have striven to fulfill a function of their own, and not imitate the formal education given older children. Besides reading and writing, they have always included exercises in the mother tongue, drawing, knowledge of common things, the elements of geography and natural history, manual

[1] See pp. 65ff.

[2] See p. 297.

and physical exercises, and singing. In place of the elements of religion, with which the schools started, the secularized curriculum now furnishes the first principles of moral education.

Robert Owen opened independently at New Lanark, Scotland, an infant school, and furnished young children of the factory population with a moral and physical training, combined with play and nature study.

Robert Owen and his 'Infant School.'—Quite independently, though over a generation later than Oberlin's work, an 'infant school' was opened in 1816 at New Lanark, Scotland. The founder was *Robert Owen* (1771–1858), a philanthropic cotton-spinner, who endeavored to put certain theories of social reform into practice near his factory. Up to his time poor children from six to eight years of age had been sent to the factories, and were required to labor from six in the morning until seven in the evening. After these hours they attended night school, but they were generally too fatigued "to acquire much proficiency in education, and many of them became dwarfs in body and some of them deformed." Instead of employing children so early, Owen wished them "to acquire health and education until they were ten years old." At first he was able to have only the older children trained, but seven years later he bought out his conservative partners and put into practice his scheme for the education of very young children. For this an 'infant school' was started in the lower story of the so-called 'New Institution.' Children were received at the age of three, and were given a careful moral and physical training. They were taught for two or three years whatever was useful and within their understanding, and this instruction was combined with much singing, dancing, amusement, and out-of-door exercise. They were not 'annoyed with books,' but were taught about nature and common objects through maps, models, paintings, objects from nature, and familiar conversation, and their "curiosity was excited so as to ask questions respecting them."

For this almost Pestalozzian training Owen found it difficult to get the right teachers, but he at length secured "a poor simple-hearted weaver named *James Buchanan*, who at first could scarcely read, write, or spell," but who, by following the instructions of Owen literally, made a great success of the school. Owen published his methods in his *New View of Society*, and the work at New Lanark attracted a great deal of attention both in Europe and America. But the socialistic and free thought opinions held by Owen soon offended many of his supporters, and the management of the school was at length taken away from its founder. In 1823 he came to the United States and started a communistic society at New Harmony, Indiana, in which for a short time he continued his theories of education. In this plan he coöperated with William McClure and Joseph Neef,[1] who were interested in spreading the Pestalozzian doctrines and practices, and was assisted by his son, who had been educated with Fellenberg at Hofwyl.[2]

While Owen soon left the work and went to the United States,

'Infant Schools' in London and the Work of Wilderspin.—Before this, however, the infant school at New Lanark had been copied in 1818 at Brewer's Green, Westminster, by a group of peers and distinguished men. Buchanan, who had been transferred to London by Owen at their request, took charge of the school. While it was intended to have the Westminster school based upon the principles in use at New Lanark, Buchanan seems, when placed upon his own responsibility, to have been

Buchanan, whom he had engaged to teach the school, started a similar institution in London. This school became the inspiration for Wilderspin, the chief exponent of infant schools.

[1] See p. 150.

[2] See p. 153ff.

too lacking in intelligence and force to accomplish this. He was soon obliged to withdraw, and the school was closed within a decade, but it proved largely the source of inspiration for *Samuel Wilderspin* (1792–1866), who was destined to become the leading exponent of the 'infant schools' for Great Britain and America. Wilderspin started a school in Spitalfields, London, on the same basis as that at Westminster, but he soon put forward the claim: "Mr. Owen's institution was intended merely for an asylum; I alone had the merit of inventing what is now known in this country by the name of the Infant System." The school at Spitalfields, which was opened in 1820, was immensely successful. Through the large number of visitors it attracted, and half a dozen books that Wilderspin produced upon infant schools, some weight was lent to his claims.

Wilderspin's schools were mechanical, and while using the moral, physical, and play features of Owen, they stressed books and apparatus, depended upon the memory rather than the understanding, and gave a formal religious training.

The infant schools of Wilderspin were far more mechanical than those of Owen, but they had some similar principles underlying them. For example, the school was organized on the basis of a family, and much attention was given to developing kindly feelings, morality, and coöperation. Recreation and physical exercises on a playground were provided, as well as mental and moral training. For this, various apparatus, amusements, and games were used, especially those imitating occupations. A peculiar grouping of the children for receiving object lessons was invented by Wilderspin. This 'gallery,' as he called it, was effected through a succession of steps, the highest of which was occupied by the oldest child and the lowest by the youngest. For teaching the children to count, he also employed an instrument of his own, called the 'arithmeticon,' which consisted of a number of balls in a frame of wires. The defects of the system were most apparent. Wilderspin thought too highly of 'books, lessons, and apparatus,' and confounded instruction with education. He overloaded the child with verbal information, depending upon the memory rather than the understanding. Before the child was six, it was expected that he had been taught reading, the fundamental operations in arithmetic, the tables of money, weights, and measures, a knowledge of the qualities of common objects, the habits of different animals, the elements of astronomy, botany, and zoölogy, and the chief facts of the New Testament. Wilderspin did not himself understand object teaching, and confused words with things. His method was catechetical and mechanical, and, to assist the memory in carrying its heavy burden, the lessons were often made rhythmical or put into rhyme. Even the games were stereotyped, and the religious teaching was most formal. Despite the attempt to train the feelings, 'natural depravity' was inculcated as a prime tenet.

Through Wilderspin infant schools were spread throughout the United Kingdom.

Development and Spread of the 'Infant Schools.'— While not the real founder of infant schools, Wilderspin certainly gave them vogue. He lectured upon the subject throughout the United Kingdom, often demonstrating his methods with classes of children he had taken along, and organized infant schools everywhere. In 1824 an 'Infant School Society' was founded through subscriptions, with the Marquis of Lansdowne as president, and while it lasted only sixteen years, it was remarkably active during this period. It was reported the year following the society's organization that thirty-four new schools were opened and that fourteen more were nearly

Stow established in Scotland a modified type of his own;

ready, and this increase continued throughout the subsequent years of the society. In 1829 Wilderspin also visited Scotland at the invitation of *David Stow* (1793–1864) of Glasgow,[1] who had three years before established infant schools upon a modified plan of his own. He adopted the playground and 'gallery' of Wilderspin, but was much less mechanical and *memoriter* in his method, and broader in his purpose.

The Home and Colonial School Society of London undertook to combine the infant schools with Pestalozzianism;

An important organization for training infant school teachers, known as 'The Home and Colonial School Society,'[2] was established at London in 1836. The founder of the society was a retired civil officer, but the most influential members were *James Pierrepont Greaves* (1777–1842) and *Rev. Charles Mayo, D. D.* (1792–1846), who had studied with Pestalozzi at Yverdon. Through them it was decided to extend Pestalozzi's principles to the poor, and the society undertook to graft Pestalozzianism upon the infant school stock. Object teaching and the training of the senses were emphasized rather than verbal training and the use of the memory. A great improvement in observation took place in the infant schools, but even then there was still too much imitation of the formal instruction of older children, and memorizing of material not fully understood. Moreover, there remained a tendency to cultivate infant prodigies by an appeal to emulation and by public exhibitions, which puffed up the brilliant pupils and quite discouraged the mediocre. A

[1] A detailed account of this visit is found in Wilderspin's *Early Discipline*, Chaps. VI–X.

[2] This association was founded as 'The Home and Colonial Infant School Society,' but in 1845 the words 'and Juvenile' were inserted in the title, to show a widened purpose, and, when this proved too cumbrous, the name was reduced to the form given in the text above.

training college was opened, and after 1843 the course became greatly improved through Mayo's sister, Elizabeth, who arranged to give all her time to the institution.

The work of Wilderspin, Stow, and the Home and Colonial School Society was so influential that infant schools spread rapidly in Great Britain, and were adopted as a regular part of the public system, when it was established in 1870. Schools for children between three and seven were organized in a separate department under the guidance of a trained teacher. Improvements were gradually introduced into the methods of these infant schools. By 1874 a marked change was made through merging in them some of the methods and games of the kindergarten.

and, when the public system was established, infant schools were eventually adopted as a regular part.

Schools open to all younger children likewise sprang up generally in the United States. They first arose toward the end of the first quarter of the nineteenth century, but for many years were not regarded as an essential part of the public school system, and were managed separately. The establishment of these schools in American cities and their gradual fusion with the public system is of sufficient importance to demand separate consideration.

'Primary Schools' in Boston.—In Boston one of the most influential factors in bringing about the establishment of these schools for younger children was the introduction of Sunday schools.[1] Through these institutions were discovered the illiteracy of three-fourths of the poor children in attendance, and the need of their learning to read, if any attention were to be given to religion. As pupils were not admitted to the public

Similar institutions were established separately in the United States.

[1] See p. 53.

schools until they could read and write, and as many of the parents were unable to teach their children themselves and could not afford the slight expense of the 'dame' schools, a considerable number of children were altogether debarred from even an elementary education. Hence those citizens actively engaged in the work of religious and philanthropic associations became interested in the agitation for 'primary schools.' After two petitions and much discussion in town meeting, in 1818 the first modest appropriation, $5000, was made for 'primary schools,' 'to provide instruction for children between four and seven years of age.' While the 'Primary School Committee' was nominally a sub-committee of the city board of management, it was in effect a separate organization. By 1844 the weakness of the organization and methods in this dual school system had become apparent, although Horace Mann met with great opposition in his endeavors to improve the situation. The Primary School Committee remained a separate body for a decade longer, but all public schools were in 1854 consolidated and the existing committees merged in a single organization. These primary schools were divided into four grades, beginning with the study of the alphabet and closing with reading in the New Testament. Besides reading, writing, and spelling, sewing and knitting were taught the girls, since their poverty made these accomplishments useful. As a whole, a formal course of instruction and the 'monitorial' system [1] were employed until about 1840, when the primary schools became generally permeated with the subjects and methods started by Pestalozzi.[2]

'Primary schools' were started in Boston under a separate board in 1818, and were not united with the rest of the public system until 1854;

[1] See pp. 56f. [2] See pp. 139ff.

'Infant Schools' in New York and Other Cities.— Schools for younger pupils were first opened in New York almost a decade later than in Boston. In 1827 an 'Infant School Society' was organized there to furnish the means of instructing poor children between three and six years of age, and an 'infant school' was opened in the basement of the Canal Street Presbyterian Church. A 'junior department' was also established in the basement of 'School No. 8,' where hitherto, as in the case of the other institutions belonging to the 'Public School Society,' [1] the pupils of all grades had been taught on the 'monitorial' [2] basis in a single department. Early the following year a committee of the Public School Society visited these two infant schools. They were much pleased with the Pestalozzian principles they saw embodied there and pronounced them "a judicious combination of instruction and amusement, . . . calculated to form and elicit *ideas*, rather than mere literal knowledge, though this was by no means neglected." They recommended the continuance of the 'junior department' and the establishment of an 'infant school' in the basement of 'School No. 10,' and this was shortly done. Hence, while the infant schools came under the immediate control of the Public School Society, they were really the offspring of the Infant School Society, and after some discussion, it was decided to use the Pestalozzian system rather than the Lancasterian. Although both societies would have been glad to extend the number of infant schools, they were for a time prevented by financial and legal considerations. In 1830, however, these schools became known as the 'primary departments' of the schools in

an Infant School Society of New York City in 1827 opened schools, which three years later became the 'primary departments' of the Public School Society's institutions;

[1] See pp. 60 and 97f.

[2] See pp. 53ff.

which they were located, and thereafter formed a regular feature of all the Public School Society's institutions.[1] A committee was appointed in 1832 to examine the Society's schools and suggest improvements. Upon the recommendation of two of this committee, who had inspected education in Boston, primary schools were established in rented rooms in sufficient numbers to be within easy reach for the young children. The subject-matter and methods were likewise made less formal.

after 1827 Philadelphia and other centers of Pennsylvania organized infant and primary schools; and about the same time Hartford, Baltimore, and other American cities established them.

In the same year that the first infant school was opened in New York, three similar institutions were founded in Philadelphia and other centers in Pennsylvania through Robert Baux. By 1830 the number of infant schools in the state had risen to ten, with two to three thousand pupils. As the numbers would indicate, the schools were largely organized upon the Lancasterian plan. Two years later a model infant school was started in Philadelphia, and in 1834 six others were organized. By 1837 there were thirty primary schools in Philadelphia alone. Several other cities started infant schools early. Hartford began them in 1827, and Baltimore in 1829. These institutions were in most cases fostered by the leading men of the community, and the ultimate service performed for American education by this form of philanthropy was considerable. Among other improvements, the infant schools developed a better type of school-room, secured separate rooms for different classes, introduced better methods and equipment, encouraged

[1] Hence the arrangement of two principals, a woman in the primary and a man in the grammar department, still exists in many of the New York public schools.

a movement toward playgrounds, and brought women into the city schools of the United States.

Thus the various types of charity schools that arose during the eighteenth century and spread throughout the British Isles, America, and France, while much opposed and a makeshift, paved the way for national and public education.

The Importance of Philanthropic Education.—Many other types of charity school arose during the eighteenth century both in Great Britain and America, but the chief movements have been described, and sufficient has been said to indicate the important part in education played by philanthropy. The moral, religious, and economic condition of the lower classes had been sadly neglected, and by means of endowment, subscription, or organized societies, a series of attempts was made to relieve and elevate the masses through education. As a result, charity schools of many varieties and more or less permanent in character arose in all parts of the British Isles, the United States, and even France. In many instances the pupils were furnished with lodging, board, and clothes. The course in these institutions was, of course, mostly elementary. It generally included reading, spelling, writing, and arithmetic, while a moral and religious training was given through the bible, catechism, prayer book, and psalms, and sometimes through attendance at church under supervision of the master. Frequently industrial or vocational subjects were taught, or the pupils apprenticed to a trade or domestic service. The course was usually most formal both in matter and method, but occasionally in the later types drawing, geography, nature study, physical exercises, and games were added, and the more informal methods of Pestalozzi or Froebel were partially employed. Sometimes the training was especially intended for and adapted to children under the usual school age.

These efforts to improve social conditions by means of

philanthropic education encountered various sorts of opposition. Often the upper classes held that the masses should be kept in their place, and feared that any education at all would make them discontented and cause an uprising. The poor themselves, in turn, were often suspicious of any schooling that tended to elevate them, and were unwilling to stamp themselves as paupers. Moreover, the sectarian color that sometimes appeared in the religious training not infrequently repelled people of other creeds or kept the schools from receiving their children. However, this philanthropic education may, in general, be considered a fortunate movement, although its greatest service consisted in paving the way for better things. In contrast to the negative phase of 'naturalism,' it represented a positive factor in the educational activities of the century. Instead of attempting to destroy existing society utterly, it sought rather to reform it, and when the work of destruction gave opportunity for new ideals, it suggested and even furnished a reconstruction along higher lines. Hence philanthropy in education complemented and continued the work of Rousseau, and led to universal, national, and public training for citizenship. It was in many of its forms merged in such a system in several countries, and in succeeding chapters many references to the charity, S. P. C. K., S. P. G., Sunday, monitorial, and infant schools will naturally appear. But while philanthropic education occasionally utilized some of the recent tendencies in method and content, its contribution to the modern psychological and scientific movements was not large. But in providing schooling for the poor and making them more efficient intellectually, morally, and economically, it represents one of the most prominent of the social movements in modern education.

SUPPLEMENTARY READING

I. Sources

BELL, A. *An Experiment in Education.*

HOME AND COLONIAL SCHOOL SOCIETY. *Annual Reports.*

LANCASTER, J. *British System of Education* and *Improvements in Education.*

MANDEVILLE, B. de. *Essay on Charity and Charity Schools.*

OWEN, R. *Autobiography.*

OWEN, R. D. *An Outline of the System of Education at New Lanark.*

RAIKES, R. *The Gloucester Journal.*

WILDERSPIN, S. *Early Discipline, Education of the Young, Infant Education, On the Importance of Educating the Children of the Poor, The Infant System,* and *Reports.*

II. Authorities

ADAMS, F. *History of the Elementary School Contest in England.*

ALLEN, W. O. B. and MCCLURE, E. *Two Hundred Years: The History of the Society for Promoting Christian Knowledge, 1698–1898.*

BARNARD, H. *American Journal of Education.* Vol. IX, 229–293 and 449–486; X, 323–531; XV, 489–490; XVI, 403–416 and 620–622; and XVII, 177–192.

BARTLEY, G. C. T. *The Schools for the People.*

BOURNE, W. O. *History of the Public School Society of the City of New York.*

BROWN, J. R. *Essay on the Cultivation of the Infant Mind.*

BROWN, MARIANNA C. *Sunday School Movements in America.*

BUTLER, JOSEPHINE E. *The Life of Jean Frédéric Oberlin.*

EVANS, D. *The Sunday Schools of Wales.*

FRASER, W. *Memoirs of the Life of David Stow.*

GILL, J. *Systems of Education.* Pp. 162–202.

GRAVES, F. P. *Great Educators of Three Centuries.* Chaps. IX and XII.

GRÉARD, O. *Éducation et Instruction.*

GREGORY, A. *Robert Raikes, Journalist and Philanthropist.*

GREGORY, R. *Elementary Education.*

HARRIS, J. *Robert Raikes; the Man and his Work.*

HOLMAN, H. *English National Education.* Chap. II.

JONES, L. *Life of Robert Owen.*

KEMP, W. W. *The Support of Schools in Colonial New York by the Society for the Propagation of the Gospel in Foreign Parts.*

LEITCH, J. *Practical Educationalists and their Systems.* Pp. 121–165.

MEIKLEJOHN, J. M. D. *An Old Educational Reformer, Dr. Andrew Bell.*

MONTMORENCY, J. E. G. *State Intervention in English Education.* Chaps. III and V–VII.

MONTMORENCY, J. E. G. *The Progress of National Education in England.*

OLIVER, N. K. *Advantages and Defects of the Monitorial System of Instruction.*

PALMER, A. E. *The New York Public School.* Chaps. II–XVI.

PASCOE, C. F. *Two Hundred Years of the S. P. G.*

RANDALL, S. S. *History of the Common School System of the State of New York.* Pp. 28–32.

ROBERTS, R. D. *Education in the Nineteenth Century.* Chap. II.

SADLER, M. E. *Great Britain, Department of Education, Special Reports.* Vols. II and VIII.

SALMON, D. *Joseph Lancaster.*

SALMON, D. *The Education of the Poor in the Eighteenth Century.*

SALMON, D. and HINDSHAW, W. *Infant Schools, their History and Theory.*

SECRETAN, C. F. *Memoirs of the Life and Times of Robert Raikes.*

SOUTHEY, R. and C. C. *The Life of the Rev. Andrew Bell.*

SPALDING, T. A. *The Work of the London School Board.* Pp. 10–16.

STEINER, B. C. *History of Education in Maryland.* Pp. 57–62.

STOCKWELL, T. B. *History of Public Education in Rhode Island.* Pp. 254–294.

TRUMBULL, H. C. *Yale Lectures on the Sunday School.*

WATSON, W. H. *The History of the Sunday School Union* and *The First Fifty Years of the Sunday School.*

WEBER, S. E. *The Charity School Movement in Pennsylvania.*

WICKERSHAM, J. P. *A History of Education in Pennsylvania.* Chaps. IV, VII–VIII, and XIV.

WIGHTMAN, J. M. *Annals of the Boston Primary School Committee.*

CHAPTER IV

RISE OF THE COMMON SCHOOL IN AMERICA

Gradual Development of Public Education in the United States.—Philanthropy in education and the institution of charity schools constituted only a half-way house in the progress of modern educational organization. As a reform of the moral, religious, and economic conditions of the masses in the eighteenth century, philanthropic training served a great purpose, but its real mission would now seem to have been to pave the way to the common schools. Through the charity schools the conception of the importance and value of education to society was greatly enlarged, and the need of a generous financial support was gradually recognized. These institutions were a makeshift to relieve the burdens of the poor and were ofttimes sectarian and narrow in their attitude, but they became the foundation for a completely nonsectarian and universal training for citizenship at public expense. Out of them were largely evolved the conception of a state or national system of education for all and the idea of the common school.

Universal education under public control and support, which grew out of philanthropic education, has naturally reached its most consistent form in the United States.

Such a development of universal education under state control and support has reached its most consistent form in the United States. And this is not surprising. America has long stood, in theory at least, for equality of opportunity, and this conception of society is apparent in its views of education. The distinguishing characteristic of the American schools has throughout been the attempt of a free people to educate themselves, and, through their elected representatives, the people of the various states have now come, in harmony with the genius of American civilization, to initiate, regulate, and control their own systems of education. The universal, free, and secular schools of the United States are a natural accompaniment of its republican form of government. But, like the new democracy itself, this development of popular education was not reached at a bound. The American schools are the offspring of European institutions, and have their roots deep in the social soil of the lands from which the colonists came to America. At first they resembled the schools of the mother countries as closely as the frontier life in the new world would permit. In American education the seventeenth century was distinctly a period of transplantation of schools, with little or no conscious change, and it is only toward the middle of the next century, as new social and political conditions were evolving and the days of the Revolution were approaching, that there are evident a gradual modification of European ideals and the differentiation of American schools toward a type of their own. This period of transition from inherited ideals is not marked off until the eighteenth century and the first half of the nineteenth, and the purely American conception of education cannot be fully discerned before the middle of the latter century.

Conditions in Europe from Which American Education Developed.—We have hitherto had little occasion to speak of American education, except by way of anticipating certain great waves of influence and important institutions that have come into America from Europe. But in the rest of our study of educational history the practices of education in the new world will become increasingly distinctive and influential, and, to get at their origins, we must now turn back in our narrative to the early part of the seventeenth century and briefly consider the social and educational situation in Europe, especially England and Holland. This may seem like a serious breach both in logic and chronology, but only in the light of the conditions out of which they sprang can the developed ideals and practices of universal public education in the United States be really understood.

Education in the American colonies was colored by the religious interests of the Reformation period, during which the colonists left the old world.

The thirteen American colonies were started while the fierce agitations of the Reformation period were still at their height. The settlers, for the most part, were Protestants, and many of them had emigrated in order to establish institutions—political, ecclesiastical, educational—that would conform to their own ideals, and in all cases education in the new world was given a peculiar importance by the dominant religious interests and conflicts of the old. At this time in practically all the states of Europe, educational institutions were controlled and supported by the church and religious orders, with the assistance of private benevolence; but a few schools everywhere, and especially in Teutonic countries, were maintained by pre-Reformation craft gilds, and so had a close connection with municipalities. Thus the American schools at first naturally adopted the religious conception of education and ecclesiastical domination, but had some acquaintance with free schools and municipal management. In addition to these characteristics, the religious reformers, like Luther and Calvin, generally held to the idea that a system of schools should be supported, or at least established, by the state, and that all children should have an opportunity to secure an education sufficient to make them familiar with the Scriptures. If people were to be guided by the word of God, they must all be able to read it. But this view of education was not held by those for whom, as in the English Church, the Reformation was not primarily a religious and theological, but rather an ecclesiastical and political revolt. In Holland and Scotland, for example, where Calvinism prevailed, universal education was upheld by the mass of the people, but in France and England only a small minority, the Huguenots and Puritans respectively, adopted this attitude. Hence it happens that, wherever in America the influence of Puritanism, the Dutch Reformed religion, Scotch Presbyterianism, or other forms of Calvinism was felt, the nucleus of public education appeared, while in the colonies where the Anglican communion was dominant, the aristocratic idea of education prevailed and training of the masses was neglected. However, even among the Calvinists, who held that elementary education should be universal, and that the state as well as the church should hold itself responsible for its being furnished, the logical solution of the problem was not perceived for scores of years. In the Calvinistic colonies it was not at first believed that education should be the same in character for all or that the state should bear the expense through taxation. This distinctively American interpretation of public education did develop later, but in the beginning even the most advanced colonies to some extent

Wherever the influence of Calvinism or Lutheranism appeared, there was a tendency toward universal education, but where the Anglican communion was dominant, the aristocratic idea of education prevailed.

But even among the Calvinistic colonists the logical solution of public education did not appear at first.

placed the financial responsibility upon the parent or guardian.

There were three chief types of school organization in the colonies: (1) the *laissez faire*, in Virginia and the South; (2) the parochial, in New Netherlands and Pennsylvania; and (3) the governmental activity, in Massachusetts and Connecticut.

Early Education in the South.—With these general traditions and characteristics in mind, it may be of interest to trace the development of educational facilities, especially of the common schools, in America during the colonial period and the first half century of statehood. In this way it may be possible to understand the various obstacles that universal education had to meet, and its very gradual success in overcoming them. Briefly, it may be stated that there are three chief types of school organization in the colonies to be discussed. These are (1) the *laissez faire* method, current in Virginia and the South, (2) the parochial organization of New Netherlands and Pennsylvania, and (3) the governmental activity in Massachusetts and Connecticut. There are also various modifications, but attention will be mainly confined to these typical organizations. As each colonial type is discussed, an account will be given of its further development up to the educational awakening in the first half of the nineteenth century.

Virginia as the Type of Aristocratic Education.—We may then turn first to the aristocratic colonies and states of the South. Here the prevailing ideals were inherited directly from England and education became 'selective' in character. These English colonists brought with them the idea of a classical higher and secondary training for the upper classes in the semi-monastic type of university and the Latin grammar school, and but little in the way of elementary education, except the private 'dame' schools and the catechetical training by the clergy. There was, in addition, the family 'tutorial'

In Virginia we find the 'selective' education, inherited from England.

education, both secondary and elementary, for the children of the wealthy, and some provision of the old English industrial training through apprenticeship for orphans and children of the poor, but no such institution as a public elementary school was at first known. Virginia, the oldest of these provinces, may serve as a type. This colony constituted the first attempt of England at reproducing herself in the new world, and here are found an order of society, form of government, established church, and distinction between classes, similar to those of the mother country. The gentry or landowning class perpetuated the methods of educating their families that were customary in England, while the masses, including the landless, the indentured servants, and other dependents, were without any means of formal instruction.

Hence educational legislation was concerned with the organization of a college or of secondary schools, and with apprenticeship education for the poor.

Hence we find that the educational legislation in colonial Virginia concerns itself mainly with (1) the organization of a college or university, (2) individual schools of secondary grade, and (3) apprenticeship education for the poor. During the first quarter of a century most educational efforts were in behalf of the foundation of an institution of higher learning, and were aided by the king, the Anglican bishops, and the London Company. By 1619 over £2000 and a grant of ten thousand acres of land had been obtained for a university at Henrico, but this rather indefinite plan was brought to a violent end by the Indian massacre of 1622, and the funds were diverted to a school in the Bahamas. An even more fruitless endeavor to found a college was made in 1624 by Sir Edwin Palmer upon an island in the Susquehanna. During this period also there was at least one abortive attempt to establish a school by collections and gifts, and during the second quarter century of the colony there were chartered a number of secondary schools, endowed with bequests of land, money, cows, horses, slaves, or other property. These schools, however, were local, and resembled the endowed Latin schools of England, except that they may sometimes have been obliged by circumstances to include more or less elementary instruction. By 1660 a number of these colonial secondary schools had been chartered, and in that year there was a renewed attempt to establish by subscriptions a college and 'free' [1] school 'for the advance of learning, education of youth, supply of the ministry and promotion of piety.' But none of the efforts at founding schools could have been very successful, for, a decade later, when interrogated as to what kind of education existed in the colonies, Governor Berkeley made his famous reply:

> "The same course that is taken in England out of towns; every man according to his ability instructing his children. . . . I thank God there are no free schools, and I hope we shall not have them these hundred years; for learning has brought disobedience and heresy and sects into the world."

However, despite these biassed remarks of the testy governor, by 1692 the constant efforts to obtain an institution of learning were finally rewarded. Through the management of the Reverend James Blair, D. D., the bishop's commissary in Virginia, a charter for the College of William and Mary, a gift of £2000 and of

[1] Probably a school in which tuition was 'free' to some pupils by virtue of an endowment. The exact significance of the word, however, is in dispute. See Jackson, *School Support in Colonial Massachusetts* (New York, 1909), Chap. VI.

twenty thousand acres of land, and the right to certain colonial taxes were obtained from the king, and large donations were made by the planters and additional support provided by the assembly. In fact, the college was munificently endowed for the times, and it did a great work in training the greatest scholars, statesmen, judges, military officers, and other leaders during the struggle for independence. Moreover, 'free' schools now greatly increased in number and their courses were much improved, and sons of the more prominent families were often sent to England or the Continent to be educated. But education was throughout this early period regarded as a special privilege, and the masses were mostly employed in making tobacco, and other manual pursuits. For the sons of these people the only educational legislation was that provided between 1643 and 1748 in various acts concerning the industrial training of the poor, apprentices, wards, and orphans. In keeping with English precedents, these children were taught a trade by the masters to whom they were indentured, or trained in the flax-house established by public funds at James City.

Thus up to the Revolution little interest in elementary schools was shown by the responsible classes.

Thus, by the outbreak of the Revolution a fair provision of secondary and higher education had been voluntarily made in various localities, but as yet no real interest in common elementary schools had been shown by the responsible classes in Virginia. The nearest approach to such institutions is found in the plantation 'field school.' Organized by a group of neighbors, these schools were supported by tuition fees and were not dependent upon any authority other than the good sense of the parents and pupils. But by the close of the war a desire for genuine public education began to appear. The leader in the movement was the great statesman, Thomas Jefferson. As early as 1779, he first introduced into the legislature a scheme of universal education. His bill proposed to lay off all the counties into small districts five or six miles square, to be called 'hundreds.' Each hundred was to establish at its own expense an elementary school, to which every citizen should be entitled to send his children free for three years, and for as much longer as he would pay. The leading pupil in each school was to be annually selected by a school visitor and sent to one of the twenty 'grammar' (*i. e.* secondary) schools, which were to be erected in various parts of the state. After a trial of two years had been made of these boys, the leader in each grammar school was to be selected and given a complete secondary course of six years, and the rest dismissed. At the end of this six-year course, the lower half of the geniuses thus determined were to be retained as teachers in the grammar schools, while the upper half were to be supported from the public treasury for three years at the College of William and Mary, which was to be greatly expanded in control and scope.

But in 1779 Jefferson introduced a proposal for universal education,

This comprehensive plan for a system of common schools was, in the face of most discouraging opposition, constantly adhered to by Jefferson, although he did not live to see universal education an accomplished fact. He did, however, stimulate some movements toward this end. In 1796 the legislature passed an ineffective law whereby the justices of each county were *permitted* to initiate a school system by taxation, and in 1810 a 'literary fund' was established for public education. When, in 1816, this fund had been increased to a

and, although he did not live to see it fulfilled, he stimulated some movements toward this end, including the foundation of the University of Virginia and the support of 'poor schools.'

million dollars, those in charge of it recommended to the legislature the establishment of "a system of public education, including a university, to be called the University of Virginia, and such additional colleges, academies, and schools as should diffuse the benefits of education through the Commonwealth." This revision of Jefferson's suggestion did not immediately result in any legal steps toward universal education, except the appropriation in 1818 of $45,000 from the income of the literary fund to have the poor children of each county sent to a proper school, but it did bring about in 1820 the foundation of the University of Virginia and a generous grant for the erection of a set of buildings. In the same year the effectiveness of the 'permissive' law for common schools of 1796 and of the appropriation act of 1818 was somewhat strengthened by the division of the counties into districts, among which the appropriation for education of the poor was distributed and managed by special commissioners.

While this law marked one more step in advance, it was hampered by several of the features that in various states continually delayed the establishment of common schools at public expense. In the first place, it was based on the conception of public education as poor relief, rather than universal training for citizenship. It was often viewed with hostility or indifference by the wealthy, who felt that they were paying for that from which they received no benefit, and with pride and scorn by the poor, who refused to be considered objects of charity. Moreover, the sum distributed ($45,000) was totally inadequate for over one hundred thousand children, and every variety of school, private as well as public, was

While the system of 'poor schools' was much opposed and totally inadequate, it gradually improved and prepared the way for public education.

subsidized without distinction. The system lacked a strong central organization, and the commissioners, often appointed by the county judges from the classes most opposed to the arrangement, were notoriously inefficient. The teachers also were generally incompetent, as it was practically impossible to persuade college or academy graduates to undertake the instruction of the poor. Nevertheless, under this apology for a people's common school, the state went on for a score of years, and there was a steady growth in the literary fund, the appropriations, the length of the school term, and the number of pupils who were willing to take advantage of such opportunities as it afforded. State officials of wide vision, moreover, sought in every way to improve the teaching corps and the defective administration. While the great majority of the school children still attended the denominational, private, and 'field' schools, this system of subsidies was educating public opinion for something better. By the close of the first half century of statehood, while Virginia was not yet ready to establish a complete system of public education, we shall later [1] see that the ground had been prepared for the development of common schools that was spreading throughout the country.

Peculiarities in the Other Southern Commonwealths.—In general, the *laissez faire* foundation of schools and colleges during the colonial period, and the slow development of an approach to a system of public education during the first fifty years of independence, which was evident in Virginia, is found to be typical of the four other colonies of the South. Practically all of them seem to have begun with the aristocratic and semi-feudal society

[1] See pp. 165ff. and 267ff.

and education inherited from England, and to have been handicapped in their evolution of public schools by the wide separation of households, Indian wars, poverty, and the subsidizing of private schools. But the problems were in every case a little different, and in each there were variations in development that are worthy of special attention. Maryland, for example, while mainly following the same random foundation of schools as Virginia, also made a determined attempt to support schools in every county by a general colonial tax. In 1696, through encouragement and gifts from the governor, and general subscriptions from legislators and others, the assembly was enabled to pass an act to establish a county system of 'free' [1] schools, and authorize a corporation to manage them and receive bequests and donations. Eight years later the fund for these schools was increased by a duty upon various imports and exports, and between 1723 and 1776 several acts concerning the land endowment, support, and administration of these institutions were passed. Thus Maryland undertook a new movement in secondary education, and while the plan met with little success before the Revolution, it eventually resulted in a county academy system with a permanent annual subsidy. Unfortunately, these academies, being close corporations, somewhat delayed the establishment of common schools, but during the first half century of statehood, Maryland, like Virginia, began to move slowly toward universal education by subsidizing the education of the poor (1816) and by the passage of a 'permissive' law for common schools in the counties (1825).

Maryland, while mainly following the *laissez faire* organization of Virginia, made an attempt to establish a county system of schools.

There was also a gradual movement toward universal education through 'poor schools' and a 'permissive' law.

[1] See p. 84 and footnote.

South Carolina undertook to found parish schools (1712), and later county schools (1722), although neither attempt proved much of a success; and an effort to found 'free schools' (1811), was injured by social discrimination and an inequitable apportionment.

South Carolina likewise made an unsuccessful attempt (1722) at establishing a county system of secondary schools. But a decade before this it had also undertaken an original plan of its own by agreeing to pay to the schoolmaster approved by the vestry of any parish £10 per annum and to grant £12 towards a parish school building. The parish system, however, did not prove much more of a success than the county arrangement, and most of these schools, while well subsidized, were first organized after the Southern method of local endowment by some individual or of support by some philanthropic society. Early in the nineteenth century, however, the sentiment for universal education began to develop. While, prior to the Civil War, South Carolina never established a 'literary,' or permanent school fund, and failed to provide an administrative organization of schools, an annual appropriation for 'free schools' was started in 1811. A law was passed establishing a number of schools in each election district equal to that of its members in the legislature and providing $300 for each school. While this act was intended to produce universal education, its terminology, giving preference to poor orphans and children of indigent parents where the school facilities were limited, caused a social discrimination against the free schools to arise, and they came to be regarded largely as pauper institutions. Moreover, because legislative representation was based upon property, the distribution of the appropriation was very inequitable, and the inland parts of the state, which most needed assistance in providing schools, received the least. However, despite poor organization and management, the amount of the appropriation was gradually increased, and the sentiment for universal education continued to develop.

Georgia until the Revolution had its budget financed by Parliament, and, while in early statehood it provided for a school system under the title of the 'University of Georgia,' small land values and heterogeneity of population permitted only the foundation of Franklin College and county academies for the dominant classes.

Georgia also presents some peculiar educational features. Both as a proprietary (1732) and a royal (1752) province, it had its entire budget, including the items for education, financed by the English parliament, and not until the Revolution do its educational history and its evolution of common schools begin. Within the first half dozen years of statehood it had provided a generous land endowment for schools in every county, academies in three counties, and the University of Georgia, and had caused the 'university' to signify an organization of all the schools maintained or subsidized by the state.[1] But the value of the lands was exceedingly small, and even the comparatively democratic type of population in Georgia was not sufficiently homogeneous to establish a genuine system of public education so soon. Franklin College, representing the higher education of the 'university,' was soon on its feet, and by 1840 some two or three hundred chartered academies had arisen, and from 1825 to 1838 the state appropriated some $25,000 annually to secondary schools, mostly county academies. But a tuition fee was charged for this training, and, except for subsidized education of the poor, these institutions were largely limited to the dominant classes. Yet, while little was done toward providing elementary education before the general development of common schools (1835–1860), an administrative organization had been furnished, a permanent school fund had been started, and sentiment for public education had begun to grow.

[1] A similar meaning was later attached by Napoleon to his state organization of schools in France. See p. 294.

While repressed until the Revolution, North Carolina, through the accession of an influential 'middle class,' formulated a system of public schools (1816) and established a common school fund (1825).

North Carolina, as the result of a more influential 'middle class,' made much earlier progress toward common schools than any other Southern state. The colony had been originally settled in the seventeenth century under English proprietors, but after its sale to the crown in 1728, a large number of Irish and Scotch Presbyterians, German Protestants, and other immigrants, mostly from Pennsylvania, came in and formed a vigorous opposition to the aristocratic ecclesiastical and civic policy of the colonial government. While they were closely repressed before the Revolution, with the beginning of national life they started the agitation for public education. The constitution of 1776 provided for the establishment of schools and a state university by the legislature, and the state soon possessed a vigorous institution of higher learning and a large number of academies. By 1817, at the request of the legislature, Judge Archibald D. Murphy, a statesman with broad educational traditions, even formulated an elaborate plan for a complete system of public schools. This scheme failed, because it proposed to 'maintain,' as well as educate, the children of the poor. But the suggestions of the Murphy committee shortly brought about the establishment of a 'literary,' or common school fund (1825), the income of which was to be used for the support of public schools. Eventually this fund was enlarged by most of North Carolina's share of the 'surplus revenue' money, which was distributed by the national government among the several states in 1837, and, early in the educational development of 1835–60, enabled North Carolina to maintain by far the best system of public instruction in the South.

In the case of the other Southern commonwealths,

which were admitted after the union had been formed, there was similarly a very gradual growth of sentiment for universal education. While each state had its own peculiar obstacles, the educational development in them all was sufficiently like that already described in the five original states to make further details unnecessary. In every state of the South there was appearing an alliance between far-sighted statesmen and educators and the great middle class of citizens for the purpose of establishing common schools for all white children, and the old ecclesiastical and exclusive idea of education was beginning to fade. By the close of the first half century of national existence, a public system had not actually materialized in any of the states, but most of them had begun to create 'literary funds,' subsidize schooling for the poor, and enact 'permissive' laws for establishing public schools. Except in Virginia and South Carolina, provisions had been made for a general administrative organization in state, county, and district; and in North Carolina the common school system awaited only a first hint of the great educational awakening (1835–60) to become full-fledged. Moreover, most of the larger cities—Baltimore, Charleston, Savannah, Louisville, Nashville, Memphis, Mobile, New Orleans—had already organized a regular system of public schools, and all of the older commonwealths had made some attempt at supporting a state institution of higher learning, which was virtually the head of a public school system. The various denominations had begun to found colleges in some numbers, but even these institutions were not so strictly ecclesiastical as William and Mary started out to be, and assumed a wider function than

There was a similar gradual growth of sentiment for universal education in the other Southern states before the great educational awakening.

merely training for the ministry, while the aristocratic and classical 'grammar' schools had largely given way to the 'academies,' which were non-sectarian, democratic, and more comprehensive in their curriculum.

In colonial New York during Dutch days (New Netherlands), the organization of schools, like that in Holland, was parochial.

The Parochial Schools and Further Development in the Colony and State of New York.—A second main type of educational organization appears in colonial New York, or New Netherlands, as it was called during Dutch days (1621–1674). In contrast to the *laissez faire* attitude of Virginia, the foundation of schools was parochial. Instead of the chance endowment of schools wherever the benefactors happened to be located, a school was founded in connection with every church. This arrangement grew out of the Calvinistic conception of universal education, which formed an essential part of the social traditions in Holland during the seventeenth century. Long before the Dutch came to America, the parochial school, as a means of preserving the Reformed faith, had become an indispensable part of church organization. But the Dutch state also had concerned itself with the facilities for education. The Reformed Dutch Church was granted the right to examine teachers, enforce subscription to the creed, and, in the case of the elementary schools at least, largely determine the appointments, but the legal support and control of education were vested in the civil authorities.[1] Hence there early arose in New Amsterdam and the villages of New Netherlands a parochial school system and a distribution of control between church and state very

[1] For an interesting and clear account of Dutch education both in the Netherlands and the colonies, read Kilpatrick, *The Dutch Schools of New Netherland* (Washington, 1912).

similar to that in Holland. Besides the ordinary elementary branches, these parochial schools of the New Netherlands taught the 'true principles of Christian religion,' and the catechism and prayers of the Reformed Church. Thus the Dutch schools differed from those in the Anglican colonies of the South, which stressed secondary education, in being chiefly elementary, although some attempt at conducting a Latin school was also made in New Amsterdam from 1652 on. However, after the English took permanent possession of New York (1674), the parochial school of the city was limited to the support of the Reformed Church, and, as a result of its long refusal to adopt the English language, its possible influence toward the realization of universal education was completely lost. While the Dutch schools of the villages generally retained the joint control and support of the local court and church, with a constantly increasing domination of the former, as a whole the English occupation of New York would seem to have set public education back about one hundred years.

These Dutch schools taught the catechism and prayers of the Dutch Reformed Church, and, unlike those of the Anglican South, were chiefly elementary.

But when the English took possession, the ideal of universal education was replaced by the *laissez faire* organization of schools.

At any rate, during the eighteenth century New York seems to have fallen into the *laissez faire* support of education that we have seen prevailing in the Southern colonies. The upper classes largely sought their education abroad or through tutors and the clergy, although in 1754 King's College (now Columbia University) was founded, and during the century a number of secondary schools were organized and granted gratuities by the legislature. And the few elementary schools that existed were either private or maintained by some church or philanthropic society. As already shown,[1]

The upper classes sought their education abroad or through tutors, although King's College and a number of secondary schools were founded, and a few elementary schools were maintained privately.

[1] See pp. 43ff.

However, after the population had been welded by the Revolution, public education developed rapidly. 'The University of the State of New York' was organized (1787), a land endowment was created in each township (1789), and $50,000 per annum for five years was voted (1795) to encourage elementary education, and later the same sum was arranged for by land endowment.

this was the period distinguished for the schools founded by the Society for the Propagation of the Gospel. At the close of the Revolution, however, the various elements of the population had been welded together in the common struggle, and a sentiment for public education began to prevail over vested interests and sectarian jealousies. A series of broad-minded governors—the Clintons, Lewis, Tompkins, and Marcy—constantly reminded the legislature of its duty to establish common schools. In 1787 a system of public education was theoretically organized under the management of a Board of Regents, with the title of 'The University of the State of New York,' but it did not include elementary schools. Two years later lands in each township were set apart for the endowment of common schools, and in 1795 it was enacted that the sum of $50,000 for five years should be distributed for the encouragement of elementary education in counties where the towns would raise by taxation half as much as the amount of their share. This arrangement was not carried on beyond the five years, but in 1805 the proceeds from 500,000 acres of land were appropriated for a common school fund, which was not to be used until the interest reached $50,000 per annum.

A state superintendency of schools was established in 1812, and the first incumbent greatly advanced public education. After the office was combined

In 1812 further organization was enacted whereby a state superintendent of common schools was to be appointed, and the county unit replaced by a more democratic town and district basis. But it had been supposed that the state fund would provide for the entire support of the schools, and there still remained an obstinate opposition to local taxes. The towns, however, were gradually persuaded to raise the amount required to secure their share of the state donation. Much progress was brought about through the first superintendent, Gideon Hawley, and while, after eight years of service, he was removed by political manipulation and the office combined with the secretaryship of state, each of his successors undertook to distinguish the educational side of his administration by some marked advance or improvement in the common schools. But for a generation the academies and colleges remained under supervision of the regents, and, except for state appropriations to academies, no one undertook to extend the public system into secondary and higher education. Moreover, the professional training of teachers in the academies was encouraged by the state, and thereby the organization of normal schools was delayed. Hence, while New York started the first system of public education adjusted to the political and social conditions of the new nation, and probably had the most effective schools of the times, not until the great period of common school development (1835–1860) were its people fully willing to contribute for a general public school system, make it entirely free, or develop it consistently in all directions.

with the secretaryship of state in 1820, each of his successors strove to promote the educational side of his work.

However, the public system was not extended to the secondary field, and the state appropriations for academies delayed the foundation of high and normal schools.

New York City.—Meanwhile, an interesting development of educational facilities was taking place in New York City. In 1805 the opportunities offered in the private, church, and charity schools were seen by certain of the most prominent citizens to be totally inadequate for a city of seventy-five thousand inhabitants, and a 'Free School Society' was founded to provide for the boys who were not eligible for these schools. The president was De Witt Clinton, afterward governor, and, as we

The Free School Society of New York City was founded in 1805 to provide education for boys not eligible for the private and church schools, and through it educational sentiment was trained until a city board of education was established by the legislature (1842) and the Public School Society eventually merged in it (1853).

have seen,[1] in 1806 the first school was opened, from motives of economy, upon the monitorial basis. The state fund did not reach a sufficient amount to be available until 1815, but special gifts were made to the school society from time to time by the legislature, the city, and private individuals, and there was a rapid increase in the number of the society's schools during the first quarter of a century. In 1826 the legislature authorized the organization to charge a small tuition fee and change its name to the 'Public School Society.' While the fee system was soon found to injure the efficiency of the work and was abolished within six years, the new title persisted, as it did not suggest pauperism in the way the old name had. In 1828 the society was allowed the benefit of a small local tax. For quite a time the work of the association was unhindered, but in 1820–25 a vigorous effort was made to obtain a share of the state appropriation for the sectarian schools of the Bethel Baptist Church. This move was finally defeated, but the Roman Catholics made a more successful appeal fifteen years later by indicating that the society, while nominally nonsectarian, was really Protestant. To settle this dispute, the legislature in 1842 established a city board of education, and after eleven years the institutions of the Public School Society were merged in this city system. Thus was the way prepared for a public school system in New York City, and this development was typical of the training of educational sentiment through quasi-public societies that took place in Buffalo, Utica, Oswego, and several other cities.

In Pennsylvania the provision

Development in Pennsylvania.—As a colony Pennsylvania developed a church school organization, similar

[1] See p. 59.

to that of New Netherlands, except that it was carried on in connection with a number of creeds, and that the municipality was seldom a coördinate factor. Under Penn's 'Frame of Government' in 1683 ample provision was made for the enforcement of universal education, but the whole effect was lost the following year by modifying it so as to apply only 'to those having the means to do so.' The proprietary laws were continued in the royal colony, and the chief result of this legislation was the establishment of institutions of their own by the different religious sects. Pennsylvania was more heterogeneous in population than New York, as the tolerant attitude of the government had attracted a large variety of German sects, Swedes, Dutch, English, Welsh, Scotch and Irish Presbyterians, and Roman Catholics, and each was devoted to its own ecclesiastical schools. In 1715 all Protestant religious bodies were authorized to conduct schools and to receive bequests and hold land for their support, and, although this was vigorously opposed by the supreme judiciary in England, it became law by the lapse of time. Before this, in 1689, a 'Friends' Public School' had been started, which later (1711) was known as the 'Penn Charter School' and became the center of education in Philadelphia. While itself a secondary school, it established branch elementary schools over the city upon different arrangements. Some charged a fee and some were free; some were for boys and some for girls. In keeping with the conclusions of various 'Yearly Meetings' (1722, 1746, etc.), the Friends likewise provided elementary, and to some extent secondary, schools in close proximity to all meeting-houses throughout the colony.

made for universal education by Penn resulted only in the establishment of parochial institutions by the different sects.

The Friends started in Philadelphia a secondary school (1689), which established branch elementary schools in various parts of the city.

A similar parochial organization was developed by the other sects, especially the Lutherans, Mennonites, and Moravians.

Similarly, the German sects, Presbyterians, Episcopalians, and Catholics established their own distinctive parochial schools. The Lutheran congregations, for example, each set up a school alongside of the church as early as possible; the Mennonites included in their system the famous schools of Christopher Dock, who in 1750 produced the first elaborate educational treatise in America; and the Reformed Church, as we previously noted,[1] started a species of charity schools through the help of the S. P. G. There was also some attempt at secondary and higher education, especially in the case of the well-known Moravian institutions at Bethlehem, Nazareth, and Lititz, and the Presbyterian Log College at Neshaminy, which became the cradle of Princeton, Washington and Jefferson, Hampden-Sydney, and Union Colleges. A somewhat broader spirit was manifest in the voluntary 'neighborhood' schools of western Pennsylvania, in the attempts at universal education of the Connecticut colonists in the Wyoming Valley, and in the 'academy' set up at Philadelphia through Franklin,[2] to train public men and teachers, and fuse the various nations in a common citizenship. But, as a whole, parochial education prevailed and exerted the largest influence in Pennsylvania during the eighteenth century. While these schools did much to further the modern idea of the elementary school, the national, sectarian, and class jealousies that ensued kept the authorities from a consideration of universal education and greatly delayed the establishment of a public system of schools.

Attempts at a broader common school also arose in the west, the Wyoming Valley, and Philadelphia, but parochial education prevailed.

[1] See pp. 47f.

[2] See p. 47 and Graves, *History of Education during the Transition*, pp. 292f.

Despite the broad vision of Franklin and other leaders, a state system arose only gradually through 'poor schools.'

The state system only very gradually arose through a prolonged stage of 'poor schools.' The new constitution (1790) of the state provided: "The legislature shall, as soon as conveniently may be, provide by law for the establishment of schools throughout the State, in such manner that the poor may be taught gratis." Men of broad vision, like Franklin, Benjamin Rush, and Timothy Pickering, had striven hard to have popular education introduced, but the general sentiment of the times could not reach beyond providing free education for the poor. Moreover, although this moderate constitutional provision was a compromise, it was not for some years (1802, 1804, and 1809) that the legislature passed acts to make it effective. Even then public institutions to fulfill the legislation were not established, but the tuition of poor children was paid for at public expense in private, church, and neighborhood schools. The result of this was that most poor parents were too proud to declare themselves paupers, and the proceeds of sixty thousand acres of land appropriated for 'aiding public schools' went to subsidize private institutions. But the idea of common schools continued to develop, and governors and other prominent men constantly called attention to the need of universal education. Philadelphia was the first municipality to be converted, and in 1818, under a special act of the legislature, it became 'the first school district of Pennsylvania,' with the power to provide a system of education on the Lancasterian plan[1] at public expense. After three or four years this special legislation was extended to five more counties, and in 1824 a general law for free schools in any community was enacted, though soon repealed.

[1] See pp. 59f.

Finally, in 1828, 'the Pennsylvania Society for the Promotion of Common Schools,' after demonstrating the ineffectiveness of the 'pauper school' law in a series of memorials, succeeded in having a state school fund established, and six years later 'an act to establish a general system of education by common schools' was passed.

In 1834 a system was established under the secretary of state, which permitted districts levying local taxes to share in a state fund, and the appropriation was greatly increased by the following year. But it was not until the educational awakening that most of the districts took advantage of this permissive law.

This law established a state system of schools under the general superintendency of the secretary of state. For this system it appropriated $75,000 per annum from the income of the state school fund, and permitted the wards, townships, and boroughs, which it constituted school districts, to share in this, provided they levied local taxes for schools. The northern counties, settled mostly by New England colonists, and the western portion of the state, with its large element of Scotch-Irish Presbyterians, ardently favored this encouragement of universal education, but the law was only 'permissive' and was bitterly opposed by the Quaker and German inhabitants of 'old' Pennsylvania, who feared that their own parochial schools would be replaced. The wealthy classes were also hostile to the new law, on the ground that they ought not to be taxed to educate other people's children. In a vigorous campaign to repeal the act, however, the opponents of the law were defeated the following year (1835), and the desire to establish public schools was greatly increased by the enlargement to $400,000 of the annual state appropriation, in which the school districts might participate only on condition of local taxation. Even then not more than one-half the districts took advantage of the opportunity, and it was several years before most of them claimed their share. Hence, while the battle was won by 1835, the consummation of public education in Pennsylvania did not take place until the great awakening of common schools had swept over the country.

Early Education in New Jersey and Delaware.—The two remaining 'middle' colonies, New Jersey and Delaware, were settled by a variety of nationalities and sects,—Swedes, Finns, Dutch, Quakers, Anglicans, and Scotch Presbyterians. This extreme cosmopolitanism made any real attempt at a general system of public education more impossible than in Pennsylvania and New York. As in those colonies, the parochial schools of the Dutch, the Quakers, the Germans, and the Presbyterians accomplished something for public education, but much of the school organization was *laissez faire*, as in Virginia. After the formation of the union, New Jersey and Delaware met with the same kinds of hindrance to the development of common schools as did Pennsylvania, and they were even slower in getting a system established. In both commonwealths a state school fund was started early in the nineteenth century, but it was not distributed for about a dozen years, and then it was used mostly for the education of paupers in subsidized private schools. Some 'permissive' legislation for the organization of school districts and commissioners and the establishment of public schools was also passed, but it accomplished little before the middle of the century.

The organization of colonial schools in New Jersey and Delaware was *laissez faire*, as in Virginia, and what legislation for public education passed under the state government was permissive.

Decline of Education in Massachusetts.—The third type of colonial school organization appeared first in Massachusetts. As compared with the *laissez faire* and the parochial methods, governmental activity here pre-

As a result of its homogeneous and democratic society, the colony of

Massachusetts was the first to develop a school organization through governmental activity.

vailed. Accordingly, Massachusetts may be said to have inaugurated the first real system of public education. The character of the schools in this colony developed from its peculiar form of society and government. It was democratic, concentrated, and homogeneous, as compared with the cosmopolitan and sectarian social structure in the Middle colonies, or the class distinctions and scattered population of the South. While there were some servants and dependents in the Massachusetts Bay Colony and a distinction was made between 'freemen' and others, there were at no time rival elements that were unable to combine. The settlements were not a mere confederation, but the blending of all elements into a single organism, where the individuality of each was merged in a new social whole. This condition was a result of the radical ingrained religious conviction that every one was a child of God, capable of becoming a vital and useful member of society, and that the community was obligated to give him training to that end in the home, church, and school. Out of this Calvinistic attitude sprang a spirit of coöperation and helpfulness, a general participation of all townsmen in local government, and the Massachusetts type of school organization. Common schools seem to have been supported in most towns from the first by voluntary or compulsory subscriptions, and before the close of the first quarter of a century there had been established by the colony at large an educational system in which every citizen had a working share. Because of the exclusiveness and unity in matters theological, the schools, while religious and moral, could hardly be considered sectarian. The first educational act of the colony, passed in 1642, was similar to the old English apprenticeship law in its provision for industrial education, and, while it was broadened so as to include some literary elements and a rate to procure materials was established, no school is mentioned in it. But in 1647 each town of fifty families was required, under a penalty of £5, to maintain an elementary school, and every one of a hundred families a 'grammar' (secondary) school.[1] These schools might be supported in part by tuition fees, as well as by the town rate, and the obligation seems to have still rested on the parents to see that the children did 'resort' to the school, but all the germs of the present common school system in the United States would appear to have been present in the colony of Massachusetts before the middle of the seventeenth century.

In 1642 the colony passed a law to provide an industrial education, which had some literary elements; and in 1647 each town of fifty families was required to maintain an elementary school, and each of a hundred families a 'grammar' school.

This generous support of public education, however, was followed by a period of decline for about a century and a half. The causes for this decadence of local interest in education have been carefully investigated,[2] and found to be rather complicated. In the first place, the complete domination of Calvinism gradually disintegrated and was replaced by a toleration of several creeds. The non-Puritans, who were constantly increasing in numbers, were obliged by the law of 1638 to preserve an outward conformity to the Calvinistic regime under penalty of banishment, but by 1662 a compromise was granted, whereby persons not conforming in every respect might be admitted to all church privileges, except communion, and the persecu-

However, owing to the growth of diversity in religion, the lowering of intellectual standards, and the dispersion of population, first 'moving,' then 'divided,' and finally 'district' schools were established in place of the town schools.

[1] See Graves, *History of Education during the Transition*, pp. 173f

[2] See Updegraff, *Origin of the Moving School in Massachusetts*, Chaps. V–X.

tion of Quakers, Baptists, and other sects was largely abandoned. In 1670 came the successful secession of the Old South Church from the original church of Boston, as the result of a quarrel concerning the compromise just mentioned, and within a decade the Baptists were permitted to build a meeting-house in Boston. By 1692 recognition had been largely granted to all Protestant beliefs, and to be a 'freeman,' or voter on all colonial questions, it was no longer necessary to be a member of a Puritan church. While every town was still required to support by tax an orthodox pastor, by 1728 the Episcopalians, Quakers, and Baptists were permitted to pay their assessments to their own ministers, and the alliance of the state with a despotic church, which had made possible the system of public education, was largely broken. Moreover, there was a decided lowering of intellectual standards upon the part of the colonists. The hard struggle to wring a living from an unpropitious soil, and the disturbances due to wars, Indian skirmishes, and the difficulties of pioneer life greatly lessened their feeling of need for a literary training. Another reason for the educational decline was the dispersion of the population in the towns, as the best land near the center was more and more taken up. The intervening hills, streams, swamps, and poor roads, together with the fear of Indians and wild animals, greatly hindered those on the outskirts in reaching the church and school of the town. As a result of these different tendencies, the towns, most of which had been eager to establish schools even before being compelled to do so, began to seek various methods of evading the school law without incurring the fine. The minister was at times made the nominal schoolmaster, or a teacher was even employed during the session of the 'General Court' (*i. e.* legislature) and discharged upon adjournment. Laws were enacted against these subterfuges, greater vigilance was exercised, and the fine was increased first to £10 (1671) and then to £20 (1683), with a progressive increase where the number of families ran over one hundred (1712). Thus the fine came to be sufficient to support a schoolmaster, and it was made more and more unprofitable for a town to disobey the law.

Under these circumstances it became advantageous to many citizens, especially those at the center of a town, to have the entire support of the school come through general taxation rather than partially by means of tuition fees. But the people in the more distant portions of the town refused to vote a rate from which they themselves obtained no profit. They demanded that, in return for their taxes, the public school should be brought nearer to them. Probably they were influenced in this stand by the fact that private 'dame' schools, and possibly elementary schools, had for some time been opened in various parts of the town conveniently near their homes. Another factor that may have aided in suggesting this solution was the legal recognition of various remote settlements within the town, known as 'parishes' or 'districts,' through the grant of self-government, separate church organizations, and other privileges similar to those of the town as a whole, though on a smaller scale. At any rate, we find that, in the early part of the eighteenth century, wherever a rate was adopted as the sole means of school support, it was agreed that, instead of holding the town school for twelve months in the center alone, opportunities should be offered for a fraction of that period in various portions of the town. When the compromise took the form of having one town master teach in different districts through the year, the result was known as a 'moving school,' but when separate schools under different masters or mistresses came to be taught at the same time, the town school was said to be 'divided.' These divisions were allowed more and more control of their schools by the town until they practically became autonomous. Before the time of the Revolution 'divided schools' were recognized as a regular institution, and, together with other customs that had grown up during the eighteenth century, they were given legal sanction and denominated 'district schools' in the law of 1789. By 1800 the districts were not only allowed to manage their own share of the town taxes, but were authorized to make the levy themselves; in 1817 they were made corporations and empowered to hold property for educational purposes; and in 1827 they were granted the right to choose a committeeman, who should appoint the teacher and have control of the school property.

This decline into the district system reached its lowest point in 1827.

Thus, as Martin describes it, the year 1827 "marks the culmination of a process which had been going on for more than a century,—the high-water mark of modern democracy, and the low-water mark of the Massachusetts school system."[1] The district system did in its earlier stages bind the families of a neighborhood into a corporation whose intent was the most vital of human needs,—education, and the people came to feel the necessity of supporting it by their own generous contributions. But in the course of time the districts became

[1] *Evolution of the Massachusetts School System*, p. 92.

involved in private and petty political interests, and had but little consideration for the public good. The choice of the committeeman, the site, and the teacher caused much unseemly wrangling, and as each received only what it paid in, the poor district obtained only a weak school and that for but a short term. The increasing expense of the district system had also made it impossible for any except the larger towns to support the old-time 'grammar' school, and this part of the old school requirements had fallen into disuse before the close of the eighteenth century. To meet the needs of secondary education, the policy of endowing 'academies' with wild lands in Maine had gradually grown up, and this custom was legalized in 1797. Seven academies,—four in Massachusetts proper and three in the province of Maine, had originally been endowed with a township apiece, and some fourteen more had been chartered by towns at an early date, and empowered by the state to hold educational funds. By the time of the educational awakening there were some fifty of these private secondary institutions subsidized by the state, although managed by a close corporation. The first public high school had been established in Boston (1821), but this type of secondary school had not begun to have any influence as yet. Into such a decadence had the liberally supported system of public education fallen before the rapid development in common schools began and the influence of Horace Mann and other reformers [1] was felt. Hence during the first quarter of the nineteenth century public education in Massachusetts had been quite surpassed by New York, which had largely

Moreover, the increasing expense of the system brought into existence the policy of state endowment of academies in the place of the town 'grammar' schools.

Hence, by the beginning of the nineteenth century, Massachusetts had fallen behind New York in the progress of public education.

[1] See pp. 167ff.

outgrown its *laissez faire* attitude and was now leading all the states in the development of schools.

In Connecticut the colonial laws concerning education were very similar to those of Massachusetts, and just before the Revolution a decadence into the district system also began to appear. The educational development in Massachusetts was likewise typical of the other New England states, except Rhode Island.

Similar History of Other New England States.—The development of common schools in Massachusetts may be considered typical of New England in general, with the exception of Rhode Island. During the colonial period, Connecticut by the middle of the seventeenth century, and Vermont before the Revolution, had very closely copied the governmental activity of Massachusetts in organizing schools. The section of the Hartford colony law (1650) on 'children' reminds one strongly of the Massachusetts act of 1642, while the section on 'schools' is an almost *verbatim* repetition of the Massachusetts law of 1647. Similar provisions were made in the New Haven colony before the two were merged in the colony of Connecticut in 1661. By the close of the century Connecticut had also granted lands, gratuities, and taxes for the support of its chief 'grammar' schools, and had established a fine of £5 upon any town neglecting to maintain an elementary school, and double the amount in the case of a Latin school. Likewise, by 1766 the foundations of a district system had been laid through recognizing the divisions in a certain town. In 1794 these districts were given a separate existence legally and allowed to locate their own schoolhouses and levy taxes. The results of this step constituted one of the greatest problems for Henry Barnard during the great period of educational development. Similarly, in Vermont before statehood was well under way, provision had been made for town and district schools, county 'grammar' schools, and even a state university, and some legal steps taken to see that the towns, districts, and counties lived up to the statutes. In the beginning of the second quarter of the nineteenth century a state school fund and school commissioners were established, but they were abolished within a few years, and the schools of Vermont were in a parlous condition when the awakening found them. New Hampshire was part of Massachusetts until 1693, and Maine was until 1820, and their development of popular education contains no new features.

Because of its idea of freedom, Rhode Island objected to legislation concerning education, but the chief towns voluntarily maintained ungraded schools for the poor.

The Early Organization of Education in Rhode Island.—But Rhode Island would have none of the common schools and centralization of education, and until well into the nineteenth century followed more nearly the random organization of schools in Virginia. The colony was dominated by the idea of freedom in thought and speech, for which it had been founded in 1636, and as legislation involving the regulation of schools seemed to be an interference, if not actual compulsion, it would tolerate nothing of the sort for almost two centuries. Schools were, however, organized within the first century in the chief towns of the colony,—Newport (1640), Bristol (1683), Providence (1684), and Portsmouth (1716). These schools were voluntarily maintained through the rent and sale of local school lands, rent of the schoolhouses and their cellars, subscriptions, taxation, income from wharves, lotteries, and tuition fees, and the management of them was vested in the town meetings. But these institutions could hardly be considered common schools, for they were ungraded and intended for the poor. The idea of a free public school for all classes was first suggested in 1767 in the report of Moses Brown, one of a committee to formulate a plan of education and bring it before the town meeting, but it was

In 1798 a permissive law for free schools in any town was passed, but Providence alone availed itself of it. Not until 1828 was the basal law for common schools passed, and the system was meager until the awakening.

naturally not adopted. In 1798, however, the Mechanics and Manufacturers' Association, under the leadership of John Howland, and supported by educators and men of wealth, after a struggle of two years brought about a law that permitted each town in the state to maintain at public expense 'one or more free schools.' Providence availed itself of this act and thus started a public school system in 1800, but no other municipality paid any attention to the law, and it was repealed in 1803. The basal state law for common schools was not passed until 1828, when $10,000 was appropriated and each town was required to supplement its share by such an amount as should annually be fixed in town meeting. While this amount was increased in 1839 to $25,000, and subsequently to much larger sums, the state school system was but poor and meager until the influence of the educational awakening was felt, and Henry Barnard [1] had done his work for the state (1843–49).

The Extension of Educational Organization to the Northwest.—It is thus evident that by the close of the first half century of the republic, there was everywhere slowly growing up a sentiment for public education. The development of common schools had, however, been greatly hindered in the Southern states by the separation of classes in an aristocratic organization of society. Yet the superior class had shown no lack of educational interest in their own behalf and had through the facilities offered reared a group of intellectual leaders, some of whom, like the far-sighted Jefferson, had caught the vision of universal education. The great diversity of nationality and creed in the Middle states, on the other

[1] See p. 183.

hand, had fostered sectarian jealousies and the traditional practice of the maintenance of its own school by each congregation. This had proved almost as disastrous to the rise of a system of public schools, although Pennsylvania and even more New York had well begun the establishment of a public system. In both sections of the country public education was at first viewed as a species of poor relief, and the wealthy were unable to see any justice in being required to educate the children of others. As a result, the young 'paupers' at times had their tuition paid in private schools, and these institutions were not infrequently allowed to share in public funds. The New England states, however, as a result of the homogeneity of their citizens, had early adhered to a system of public schools for all, organized, supported, and supervised by the people. While the efficiency of their common schools was eventually crippled by the grant of autonomy to local districts and the arising of petty private and political interests, they had initiated this unique American product,—a public system for all, dependent upon local support and responsive to local wishes.

This growth of a 'common schools consciousness' was destined, as the result of a great educational awakening, to increase rapidly about the middle of the nineteenth century in the Middle and Southern, as well as the New England states. But before describing this development further, it is important to see the effect of the ideals of these three sections of the country when introduced into a new part of the United States by emigrants from the older commonwealths. The new domain referred to was those large tracts of unsettled territory, belonging, according to claims more or less overlapping, to six or seven of the original states, and finally (1781), in settlement of these disputes, ceded to the federal government, with the understanding that the territory should be 'formed into distinct republican States.' After much discussion and various acts of Congress for half a dozen years, the famous 'Ordinance of 1787' was passed for the government of this 'Northwest Territory.' By the act the entire territory was divided into townships, six miles square, after the New England system, and of the thirty-six sections into which each township was subdivided, section sixteen was reserved for the support of public schools. Two townships of land were also dedicated for the establishment of a university. This policy of educational endowment was later extended to the vast territory purchased from France in 1803 and known as 'Louisiana,' and to all the other territory afterward annexed to the United States.

Despite the federal land endowment, in the first three states carved out of the Northwest Territory public education took form but slowly, and in its history there is a record of the efforts to win over the settlers from states where public education was not in vogue.

This federal land endowment gave an additional stimulus to the establishment of public education in the four commonwealths—Ohio, Indiana, Illinois, and Michigan—that were admitted from the Northwest Territory before 1840. But the final system of public education in these new states took form but slowly for various reasons. The settlers were poor; incessant Indian wars, the wilderness, wretched roads, and lack of transportation facilities tended to repel immigrants and leave the country sparsely settled; the large tracts of school land were slow in acquiring value, and, to attract settlers, were often leased at nominal rates or sacrificed at a small price; and social distinctions and sectarian jealousies persisted among the immigrants. As a whole, immigration from the earlier commonwealths had followed parallels of latitude, and the northern parts of Ohio, Indiana, and Illinois were occupied mostly by people from New England and New York, and the southern by former inhabitants of Virginia, Kentucky, Tennessee, Louisiana,[1] and other states where the public school system was not yet as well developed. In Michigan, however, because of its northerly location, the great influx throughout the state had come from New York, New England, and northern Ohio.

But Michigan, whose settlers had been used to common schools, showed early the germs of a public system, although its state organization did not appear until the awakening.

Consequently, the history of public education in the first three of the new states seems to be in each case largely a record of a prolonged struggle to introduce common schools among those of the people who had come from states not yet committed to this ideal, but Michigan, whose inhabitants had migrated from states where public education was in vogue, showed the germs of a public system even before statehood was conferred. The history of the common schools in Ohio, Indiana, and Illinois is very similar in general outline. Each one started off by claiming two townships of land for a university [2] and the sixteenth section for schools, and the state constitution committed it to equal school opportunities for all. But not until the close of the first quarter of the nineteenth century [3] was a system of

[1] Of course, Ohio was first settled in the southeast by that very important band of New Englanders led by Manasseh Cutler, but the southwest was decidedly Southern in the sympathies of its population, and even the southeast became more cosmopolitan through later immigrations.

[2] Ohio secured an extra township of land for the Symms settlement in the southwest, on the ground that it was so far removed from the Cutler colony.

[3] Ohio and Indiana in 1824, and Illinois in 1825.

common schools, with the organization of districts, appointment of school officers, and local taxation provided by the legislature. Even then the acts were largely 'permissive,' the tax was not exacted from anyone who objected, and for some time various laws allowed public funds to be paid to existing private schools for the tuition of the poor. The complete system with a state superintendent was first organized in Ohio by 1836, but a similar stage of development was not reached by the other two states until after the great period of common school development (1835–60) had passed over the country. Michigan, on the other hand, as early as 1817 established a 'catholepistemiad,' which was to include a university and a system of schools of all grades, and a dozen years later in its revision of the school laws provided for a department of education at the university and a state superintendency of schools. While under this territorial law of 1829 tuition fees were to be required, except from the poor, by the first state constitution in 1837 the school lands were taken over from the wasteful management of the towns, and a public school was required to be open for three months in every district. The state superintendency was also established, and before 1840 Michigan was well started with a complete system of common schools.

Thus by the time of the awakening, while few states had organized systems of public education, the movement for common schools

Condition of the Common Schools Prior to the Awakening.—Thus, while some of the New England states, New York, and Ohio possessed the only definitely organized systems of public education, the movement for common schools had made some progress in all sections of the country even before the educational awakening spread through the land. A radical modification had taken place in the European institutions with which education in the United States began. To meet the demands of the new environment, education had become more democratic and less religious and sectarian. Wealth had become much greater and material interests had met with a marked growth. The old aristocratic institutions had begun to disappear. Town and district schools had been taking the place of the old church, private, and 'field' schools, and in some of the cities the foundation for public education was being laid by quasi-public societies or even through local taxation. The academies had replaced the 'grammar' schools, and the colleges had lost their distinctly ecclesiastical character. State universities were starting in the South and Northwest. All these evidences of the growth of democracy, nonsectarianism, popular training, and the social movement in education were destined to be greatly multiplied and spread before long. Such an awakening will be found to be characteristic of the great development of common schools that took place in the decades around the middle of the nineteenth century. But, before pursuing the subject further, we must direct our attention to some new reforms in method and content that were being introduced by Pestalozzi into education in Europe and were destined to produce a great stimulus in the public systems of the United States.

had made some progress everywhere in elementary, secondary, and higher education.

SUPPLEMENTARY READING

I. Sources

Clews, Elsie W. *Educational Legislation and Administration of the Colonial Governments.*

Hening, W. W. *The Statutes-at-large of Virginia.*

HINSDALE, B. A. *Documents Illustrative of American Educational History* (*Report of the U. S. Commissioner of Education*, 1892–93, pp. 1225–1414.)

MASSACHUSETTS. *Colonial Records.*

II. AUTHORITIES

BARNARD, H. *American Journal of Education*, Vol. XXVII, pp. 17ff.

BOONE, R. G. *Education in the United States.* Parts I and II.

BOONE, R. G. *History of Education in Indiana.*

BOURNE, W. O. *History of the Public School Society of the City of New York.*

BROWN, E. E. *The Making of Our Middle Schools.* Chaps. III–XIV.

BRUMBAUGH, M. G. *Life and Works of America's Pioneer Writer on Education.*

CARLTON, F. T. *Economic Influences upon Educational Progress in the United States, 1820–50* (*Bulletin of the University of Wisconsin*, 1908).

CUBBERLEY, E. P. *Changing Conceptions of Education.*

CURRY, O. H. *Education at the South.*

DEXTER, E. G. *History of Education in the United States.* Chaps. I–VI.

HINSDALE, B. A. *Horace Mann and the Common School Revival.* Chap. I.

JACKSON, G. L. *The Development of School Support in Colonial Massachusetts.*

JOHNSTON, R. M. *Early Educational Life in Middle Georgia.*

KILPATRICK, W. H. *The Dutch Schools of New Netherland and Colonial New York.*

MCCRADY, E. *Education in South Carolina prior to and during the Revolution* (*Collections of the Historical Society of South Carolina.* Volume IV).

MARTIN, G. H. *Evolution of the Massachusetts Public School System.* Lects. I–III.

MAYO, A. D. *Report of the United States Commissioner of Education.* 1893–94, XVI; 1894–95, XXVIII; 1895–96, VI–VII; 1897–98, XI; and 1898–99, VIII.

Monroe, P. and Kilpatrick, W. H. *Colonial Schools (Monroe Cyclopaedia of Education).*

Palmer, A. E. *The New York Public School.*

Pratt, D. J. *Annals of Public Education in the State of New York.*

Randall, S. S. *History of the Common School System of the State of New York.* First and Second Periods.

Smith, W. L. *Historical Sketch of Education in Michigan.*

Smith, C. L. *History of Education in North Carolina.*

Steiner, B. C. *History of Education in Connecticut.*

Steiner, B. C. *History of Education in Maryland.*

Stockwell, T. B. *History of Public Education in Rhode Island.*

Suzzallo, H. *The Rise of Local School Supervision in Massachusetts.*

Updegraff, H. *The Origin of the Moving School in Massachusetts.*

Wickersham, J. P. *History of Education in Pennsylvania.* Chaps. I–XVI.

CHAPTER V

OBSERVATION AND INDUSTRIAL TRAINING IN EDUCATION

The social and psychological tendencies in Rousseau were greatly developed by Pestalozzi.

Pestalozzi as the Successor of Rousseau.—Having outlined the various phases and influences of philanthropic education and surveyed the rise of the common school in America, we may now turn again to the more immediate development of the movements that found their roots in Rousseau. These received their first great growth through Pestalozzi. In the second chapter it was noted how Rousseau's 'naturalistic' doctrines logically pointed to a complete demolition of the artificial society and education of the times. A pause at this point would have led to anarchy. If civilization is not to disappear, social destruction must be followed by reconstruction. Of course the negative attitude of the *Emile* was itself accompanied by considerable positive advance in its suggestions for a natural training, but this advice was often unpractical and extreme and its main emphasis was upon the destruction of existing education. Hence the happiest educational results of Rousseau's work came through Pestalozzi, who especially supplemented that reformer's work upon the constructive side. Rousseau had shattered the eighteenth century edifice of despotism, privilege, and hypocrisy, and it remained for Pestalozzi to continue the erection of the more enduring structure he had started to build upon the ruins. Thus Pestalozzi became the first prominent educator to help Rousseau develop his negative and somewhat inconsistent 'naturalism' into a more positive attempt to reform corrupt society by proper education and a new method of teaching. He therein enlarged for education the social and psychological tendencies begun by Rousseau.

Pestalozzi was inspired by the example of his mother and grandfather to elevate the peasantry through the ministry, law, improved agriculture,

Pestalozzi's Industrial School at Neuhof.—But to understand the significance of the experiments, writings, and principles of this widely beloved reformer, one must make a brief study of his life and surroundings. *Johann Heinrich Pestalozzi* was born at Zürich in 1746. After the death of his father, he was brought up from early childhood almost altogether by his mother. Through her unselfishness and piety, and the example of his grandfather, pastor in a neighboring village, Pestalozzi was inspired to relieve and elevate the degraded peasantry about him. He first turned to the ministry as being the best way to accomplish this philanthropic purpose. But he broke down in his trial sermon, and then took up the study of law, with the idea of defending the rights of his people. In this, too, he was destined to be balked; strangely enough, through the influence of Rousseau. In common with several other students of the University of Zürich, Pestalozzi was greatly impressed by the *Social Contract* and the *Emile*, which had recently appeared, and he ruined his possibilities for a legal and political career through a radical criticism of the government. Then, in 1769, he undertook to demonstrate to the peasants the value of improved methods of agriculture. He took up, after a year of training, a parcel of waste land at Birr, which he called *Neuhof* ('new farm'). Within five years the experiment proved a lamentable failure. Meantime a son had been born to him, whom he had undertaken to rear upon the basis of the *Emile*, and the results, recorded in a Father's *Journal*, suggested new ideas and educational principles for the regeneration of the masses. He began to hold that education did not consist merely in books and knowledge, and that the children of the poor could, by proper training, be taught to earn their living and at the same time develop their intelligence and moral nature.

and philanthropic education at Neuhof (Birr).

Hence the failure of his agricultural venture afforded Pestalozzi the opportunity he craved to experiment with philanthropic and industrial education. Toward the end of 1774 he took into his home some twenty of the most needy children he could find. These he fed, clothed, and treated as his own. He gave the boys practical instruction in farming and gardening on small tracts, and had the girls trained in domestic duties and needlework. In bad weather both sexes gave their time to spinning and weaving cotton. They were also trained in the rudiments, but were practiced in conversing and in memorizing the Bible before learning to read and write. The scholastic instruction was given very largely while they were working, and, although Pestalozzi had not as yet learned to make any direct connection between the occupational and the formal elements, this first attempt at an industrial education made it evident that the two could be combined. Within a few months there was a striking improvement in the physique, minds, and morals of the children, as well as in the use of their hands. But Pestalozzi was so enthusiastic over the success of his experiment that he greatly increased the number of children, and by 1780 was reduced to bankruptcy.

The *Leonard and Gertrude*.—Nevertheless, his wider

purpose of social reform by means of education was not allowed to languish altogether, for a friend shortly persuaded him to publish his views. *The Evening Hour of a Hermit*,[1] a collection of one hundred and eighty aphorisms, was his first production. This work embodied most of the educational principles he afterward made famous, but it could be understood by few of the people, and he was advised to put his thought into more popular form. So in 1781 he wrote his well-known story of *Leonard and Gertrude*. This work, with subsequent additions, gives an account of the degraded social conditions in the Swiss village of 'Bonnal' and the changes wrought in them by one simple peasant woman. 'Gertrude' reforms her drunkard husband, educates her children, and causes the whole community to feel her influence and adopt her methods. When finally a wise schoolmaster comes to the village, he learns from Gertrude the proper conduct of the school and begs for her continued coöperation. Then the government becomes interested, studies the improvements that have taken place, and concludes that the whole country can be reformed in no better way than by imitating Bonnal. The *Leonard and Gertrude* appealed especially to the romanticism of the period, and constituted Pestalozzi's one popular success in literature.

When his educational experiment was closed, he wrote out his views in the *Leonard and Gertrude*.

His School at Stanz and the Observational Methods.— During the last decade of his life at Neuhof, Pestalozzi was busy warding off poverty and starvation, and found no time for writing or educational work. But in 1798

At fifty-two he took charge of a throng of orphan children in the Ursuline convent at Stanz.

[1] *Die Abendstunde eines Einsiedlers*. A translation of the entire work can be found in Barnard, Vol. VI, pp. 169–179, while its essence is given by de Guimps, *Pestalozzi*, pp. 75–78.

a turn in political fortunes gave him another opportunity to continue his educational experiments. In that year Switzerland came under control of the French revolutionists, and the independent cantons were united in a Helvetic Republic under a 'directorate' like that in France. As this movement promised reform, Pestalozzi enthusiastically supported it. He was in turn offered patronage by the new government, but he asked only for a school in which he might carry on his philanthropic work in education. This opportunity was given him at the village of Stanz. The Catholic community in this place had refused to yield to what they considered a foreign and atheistic invasion, and most of the able-bodied adults had been slaughtered. That left the government with a throng of friendless children for whom they felt bound to provide. Pestalozzi, being asked to take charge of them, started an orphan home and school in an Ursuline convent. Here he soon gained the confidence and love of the children, and produced a most noticeable improvement in them physically, morally, and intellectually.

Through experience and observation, rather than books, he taught the children religion and morals, number, language, geography, history, and natural history.

He found it impossible to obtain any assistants, books, and materials, but he felt that none of these conventional aids could be of service in the work he desired to do. Hence he sought to instruct the children rather by experience and observation than by abstract statements and words. This was the real beginning of his influential method of teaching through 'observation,' which was destined thereafter to be more stressed than his idea of intellectual training in connection with manual labor. Religion and morals, for example, were never taught by precepts, but through instances that arose in the lives of the children he showed them the value of self-control, charity, sympathy, and gratitude. In a similarly concrete way the pupils were instructed in number and language work by means of objects, and in geography and history by conversation rather than by books. While they did not learn their natural history primarily from nature, they were taught to corroborate what they had learned by their own observation. With regard to this whole method Pestalozzi said:

> "I believe that the first development of thought in the child is very much disturbed by a wordy system of teaching, which is not adapted either to his faculties or the circumstances of his life. According to my experience, success depends upon whether what is taught to children commends itself to them as true through being closely connected with their own observation. As a general rule, I attached little importance to the study of words, even when explanations of the ideas they represented were given." [1]

He sought to reduce observation to its lowest terms in reading by means of his 'syllabaries,' and hoped similarly to simplify all education.

In connection with his observational method, Pestalozzi at this time began his attempts to reduce all perception to its lowest terms.[2] It was while at Stanz, for example, that he first adopted his well-known plan of teaching children to read by means of exercises known as 'syllabaries.' These joined the five vowels in succession to the different consonants,—'ab, eb, ib, ob, ub,' and so on through all the consonants. From the phonetic nature of German spelling, he was able to make the exercises very simple, and intended thus to furnish a necessary practice in basal syllables. In a similar way he hoped to simplify all education to such an extent that schools would eventually become unnecessary, and that

[1] See *How Gertrude Teaches Her Children*, I.

[2] The resulting elements he soon came to call the 'A B C of observation' (*A B C der Anschauung*). See p. 139.

each mother would be able to teach her children and continue her own education at the same time.

He combined study with manual labor.

Pestalozzi was, moreover, able to continue at Stanz his principle of intellectual development in conjunction with industrial training. While not altogether successful in his efforts at a correlation, Pestalozzi, more than at Neuhof, now "sought to combine study with manual labor, the school with the workshop," for, said he:

> "I am more than ever convinced that as soon as we have educational establishments combined with workshops, and conducted on a truly psychological basis, a generation will necessarily be formed which will show us by experience that our present studies do not require one-tenth of the time or trouble we now give to them."

Being forced to give up at Stanz, he obtained with difficulty a position at Burgdorf.

The 'Institute' at Burgdorf and the 'Psychologizing of Education'.—From these experiments and concrete methods that Pestalozzi started at Stanz eventually developed all his educational contributions. But before the close of a year the convent was required by the French soldiers for a hospital. As soon as he recovered from the terrific physical strain under which he had labored, Pestalozzi was forced to seek another place in which to continue his educational work. But, while he had a most unusual sympathetic insight into the minds of children and had been developing educational practice in two important directions, he had, according to the orthodox standards for securing a position to teach, "everything against him; thick, indistinct speech, bad writing, ignorance of drawing, scorn of grammatical learning." He would probably have been unable to obtain a school, had it not been for certain influential friends in the town of Burgdorf. They secured a position for him, first in the school for the tenants and poorer people, and later in the elementary school of the citizens.

In Burgdorf, Pestalozzi was obliged, on account of the social position of many of his pupils, to suspend his experiment of combining industrial with intellectual training. Thus to a large extent his direct contributions to the present day social movement in education ceased, although, as will later be seen, his special efforts in this direction were greatly enlarged and perpetuated by Fellenberg. He continued, however, the other great feature of his work, his experiments with the 'observational' method, and thus helped develop the modern psychological movement in education. He "followed without any plan the empirical method interrupted at Stanz," and "sought by every means to bring the elements of reading and arithmetic to the greatest simplicity, and by grouping them psychologically, enable the child to pass easily and surely from the first step to the second, and from the second to the third, and so on."[1] He further worked out and graduated his 'syllabaries,' and invented the idea of large movable letters for teaching the children to read. Language exercises were given his pupils by means of examining the number, form, position, and color of the designs, holes, and rents in the wall paper of the school, and expressing their observations in longer and longer sentences, which they repeated after him. For arithmetic he devised boards divided into squares upon which were placed dots or lines concretely representing each unit up to one hundred. By means of this 'table of units'[2] the pupil obtained a

Here he had to suspend his experiment of combining industrial with intellectual training, but continued and developed his observational method through

the 'syllabaries,'

descriptions of the wall paper of the school,

the 'table of units,'

[1] See footnote 1 on p. 125.

[2] An illustration of this table is given in Krüsi, *Pestalozzi*, p. 172. This

clear idea of the meaning of the digits and the process of addition, and practiced his knowledge further by counting his fingers, beans, pebbles, and other objects. Pestalozzi further explained that "after the child has come to a full understanding of the combination of units up to ten, and has learned to express himself with ease, the objects are again presented, but the questions are changed: 'If we have two objects, how many times one object?' The child looks, counts, and answers correctly." In that way the pupils learned to multiply, and the meaning of division and subtraction was similarly acquired. The children were also taught the elements of geometry by drawing angles, lines, and curves.

and drawing angles, lines, and curves;

Likewise, the development of teaching history, geography, and natural history by this method of observation must have been continued at Burgdorf. As a result of these experiments, says Pestalozzi, "there unfolded itself gradually in my mind the idea of the possibility of an 'A B C of observation' to which I now attach great importance, and with the working out of which the whole scheme of a general method of instruction in all its scope appeared, though still obscure, before my eyes." And the underlying principle of his system he shortly formulated most tersely in the statement, "I wish to psychologize instruction." [1] By this, he showed, is meant the harmonizing of instruction with the laws of intellectual development, together with the simplification of the

and thus evolved his 'A B C of observation,' and his stated wish to 'psychologize education.'

system was probably not completed until Pestalozzi settled at Yverdon, and much of the credit for the scheme should go to Krüsi and Schmid.

[1] *Ich will den menschlichen Unterricht psychologisieren.* This formula was made by him when asked for a written statement of his system by the 'Friends of Education,' a society that was striving to propagate his views.

elements of knowledge and their reduction to a series of exercises so scientifically graded that even the lowest classes can obtain the proper physical, mental, and moral development. And sense perception or observation, he holds, when connected with language for expressing the different impressions, is, therefore, the foundation of education.

Pestalozzi's 'institute' at Burgdorf was immensely successful; and,

Despite a want of system and errors in carrying out his method, Pestalozzi seems to have produced remarkable results from the start. At the first annual examination the Burgdorf School Commission wrote him that "the surprising progress of your little scholars of various capacities shows plainly that every one is good for something, if the teacher knows how to get at his abilities and develop them according to the laws of psychology." And the reformer soon met with even greater success in a school of his own. In January, 1801, the government granted him the free use of the 'castle,' or town hall, of Burgdorf and a small subsidy for his 'institute.' Pupils poured in; a number of progressive teachers, including Krüsi, Tobler, Buss, and Niederer,[1] came to assist him; many persons of prominence visited the school and made most favorable reports upon its methods; and during the following three years and a half the Pestalozzian views on education were systematically developed and applied.

[1] Hermann Krüsi, a young schoolmaster of Gais, had, during a famine in Appenzell, brought a troop of starving children to Burgdorf at the invitation of Fischer, a friend of Pestalozzi. Fischer died shortly afterward, and Krüsi joined Pestalozzi's venture. Through Krüsi, the services of Tobler, "a private tutor whose youth had been much neglected," and of Buss, "a bookbinder, who devoted his leisure to singing and drawing," were also secured for the institute. Niederer was a clergy-

to explain his method in detail, he wrote *How Gertrude Teaches Her Children.*

How Gertrude Teaches Her Children.—Pestalozzi was also able at Burgdorf to undertake a detailed statement of his method by the publication in October, 1801, of his *How Gertrude Teaches Her Children.* This work does not mention Gertrude, but consists of fifteen letters to his friend, Gessner. The first three letters contain biographical details, especially concerning the meeting with his assistant teachers. Then follows an account of his general principles; of the specific teaching of language, drawing, writing, measuring, and number by means of observation; of the elementary books that he contemplates writing,—the *A B C of Observation* and the *Book for Mothers;* [1] of the reform in elementary education and of the need of judgment as well as knowledge; and of moral and religious development. Like all of Pestalozzi's works, *How Gertrude Teaches Her Children* is quite lacking in both plan and proportion, and is filled with repetitions and digressions. It contains, however, the foundation of his system and of most modern reform in elementary education, and has to be studied to reveal its values. It has already been quoted several times directly, but the following summary of its principles, made by Pestalozzi's biographer, Morf, after a most careful study of this unsystematic work, may serve to give an idea of Pestalozzi's educational creed. He had vaguely come to believe:

man and philosopher, who gave up his parochial duties to work with Pestalozzi.

[1] The *Book for Mothers* was later written under Pestalozzi's direction by Krüsi. It completely failed in its purpose, however, since the average mother was unable to break from the ideals and habits of her own school-days. The *A B C of Observation* also appeared, and during this period Pestalozzi and his assistants likewise produced a variety of books applying the new method to various school subjects.

"1. Observation is the foundation of instruction.

"2. Language must be connected with observation.

"3. The time for learning is not the time for judgment and criticism.

"4. In each branch, instruction must begin with the simplest elements, and proceed gradually by following the child's development; that is, by a series of steps which are psychologically connected.

"5. A pause must be made at each stage of the instruction sufficiently long for the child to get the new matter thoroughly into his grasp and under his control.

"6. Teaching must follow the path of development, and not that of dogmatic exposition.

"7. The individuality of the pupil must be sacred for the teacher.

"8. The chief aim of elementary instruction is not to furnish the child with knowledge and talents, but to develop and increase the powers of his mind.

"9. To knowledge must be joined power; to what is known, the ability to turn it to account.

"10. The relations between master and pupil, especially so far as discipline is concerned, must be established and regulated by love.

"11. Instruction must be subordinated to the higher end of education."

But in 1804 the government took back the 'castle,' and Pestalozzi soon transferred his 'institute' to Yverdon, where his success was greater than ever.

The 'Institute' at Yverdon and the Culmination of the Pestalozzian Methods.—While this productive work at Burgdorf was at its height, a change in the political situation overthrew everything. In 1804 the cantonal government demanded back the 'castle,' although it turned over to Pestalozzi an old convent at Münchenbuchsee. For a few months the reformer made a fruitless attempt to coöperate in his new location with Fellenberg, whose industrial school in the neighboring Hofwyl will be discussed later in this chapter.[1] When, however, despite

[1] See pp. 153ff.

their similarity of purpose, a marked difference of temperaments made a union of the work of Pestalozzi and Fellenberg impossible, the former transferred his school to Yverdon in 1805, and was soon followed by most of his assistants. The 'institute' here sprang into fame almost immediately, and increased in numbers and prosperity for several years. Children were sent to Yverdon from great distances, and teachers thronged there to learn and apply the new principles at home. Visitors and sightseers, including kings, nobles, generals, statesmen, and educators came from all parts of Europe and America. Pestalozzi was decorated by the czar of Russia, and presented with distinctions from half a dozen other monarchs. A flourishing girls' school grew up near the institute under the direction of associates, and for a short time Pestalozzi himself conducted a school for orphans in the neighborhood, while Conrad Naef of Zürich came to Yverdon and founded a celebrated institution for the deaf and dumb upon the Pestalozzian principles.

There he elaborated the 'syllabaries' the 'table of units,' and devised the 'table of fractions' and the 'table of fractions of fractions';

The work of the institute at Yverdon was a continuation and culmination of the observational methods started at Stanz and Burgdorf. It was a great center of educational experimentation, and nearly every advanced practice characteristic of present elementary education was first undertaken there. His general method of teaching all subjects was through observation connected with language. The children were taught to observe correctly and form the right idea of the relations of things, and so to have no difficulty in expressing clearly what they thoroughly understood. The simplification introduced through the 'syllabaries' and 'table of units' was further elaborated. A 'table of fractions' was also devised for teaching that subject concretely. It consisted of a series of squares, which could be divided indefinitely and in different ways. Some of the squares were whole, while others were divided horizontally into two, three, or even ten equal parts. The pupil thus learned by observation to count the parts of units and form them into integers. There was further developed a 'table of fractions of fractions,' or compound fractions,[1] in which the squares were divided, not only horizontally, but vertically, so that the method of reducing two fractions to the same denominator might be self-evident. It was in this number work that the Pestalozzians were most radical. By means of various devices Krüsi, and afterward Schmid [2] even more, attained great clearness, accuracy, and rapidity in arithmetic. The work was often done aloud without paper, and many of the students became most apt in calculation.

he taught drawing, writing, and geometry through elements of form taken from objects;

Similarly, in order to draw and write, the pupil was first taught the simple elements of form. The consecutive exercises for building up form from its elements, however, Pestalozzi was not happy in determining, but Buss successfully worked out an 'alphabet of form.' Objects, such as sticks or pencils, were placed in different directions, and lines representing them were drawn on the board or slate until all elementary forms, straight or curved, were mastered. The pupils combined these elements,

[1] This table can be found in the Holland, Turner, and Cooke edition (Syracuse, 1898) of *How Gertrude Teaches Her Children*, p. 217.

[2] Joseph Schmid was a Tyrolese shepherd boy, who had come to Yverdon as a pupil, but because of his brilliancy was soon promoted to be an assistant master. His *Exercises on Numbers and Forms* was one of the best known books based upon the Pestalozzian methods.

instead of copying models, and were encouraged to design symmetrical and graceful figures. This also paved the way for writing, for, said Pestalozzi, "in endeavoring to teach writing, I found I must begin by teaching drawing." The children wrote on their slates, beginning with the easiest letters and gradually forming words from them, but soon learned to write on paper with a pen. Writing was, however, taught in connection with reading, although begun somewhat later than that study. Constructive geometry was also learned through drawing. Much use was made of squares, which were divided into smaller squares or rectangles, and thus sense impression preparatory to geometry was furnished. The pupils were taught to distinguish, first vertical, horizontal, oblique, and parallel lines; then they learned right, acute, and obtuse angles, different kinds of triangles, quadrilaterals, and other figures; and finally discovered at how many points a certain number of straight lines may be made to cut one another, and how many angles, triangles, and quadrilaterals can be formed. To make the matter concrete, the figures were often cut out of cardboard or made into models. Thus the pupils were led up to theoretical geometry, which was made more valuable and interesting by their working out the demonstrations for themselves, instead of learning them from a book.

nature study, geography, and history from actual observation;

In nature study, geography, and history the concrete observational work was similarly continued. Trees, flowers, and birds were viewed, drawn, and discussed. The pupils began in geography by acquiring the points of the compass and relative positions, and from this knowledge observed and described some familiar place.

The valley of the Buron near at hand was observed in detail and modeled upon long tables in clay brought from its sides. Then the pupils were shown the map for the first time and easily grasped the meaning of its symbols. Pestalozzi inspired the scientist, Karl Ritter, with a great love for geography and a desire to work it out psychologically. Ritter had already been trained in principles similar to Pestalozzi's in Salzmann's school at Schnepfenthal,[1] but his method in geography seems to have been influenced mostly by Pestalozzi. Like the Swiss reformer, he held to the necessity of providing children with first-hand experiences by beginning with home geography. Hence, instead of the 'arbitrary and unmethodical collection of all facts ascertained to exist throughout the earth,' which constituted the old 'encyclopedic' type of geography, Ritter presented a work based on principles indicated by the title,—*The Science of the Earth in Relation to Nature and the History of Man; or General Comparative Geography as the Foundation of the Study of and Instruction in the Physical and Historical Sciences*. The principles underlying this elaborate work, of which some nineteen volumes were published by the time of his death, virtually made the science of geography. Nor was Pestalozzi sufficiently acquainted with music to apply his method to it. This was, however, done by his friend, Nägeli, a Swiss composer of note, who reduced it to its simplest tone elements and then combined and developed these progressively into more complex and connected wholes. Pupils were thus led to discover pleasing combinations and develop musical inventiveness. In religious and moral training, as at Stanz, Pes-

music from the simplest tone elements; and religion and morality from concrete examples.

[1] See pp. 31f.

talozzi sought by concrete examples to quicken the germ of conscience into action and develop it by successive steps. The love of God he believed could be taught better through the child's love for his mother [1] and other human beings than through dogma and catechism, and the significance of obedience, duty, and unselfishness through being required to wait before having his desires fulfilled, and so realizing that his own is not the only will or pleasure in the world.

But for various reasons the institute at Yverdon broke up, after twenty years, and Pestalozzi died two years later.

With all these achievements, however, the institute at Yverdon was slowly dying. Pestalozzi was never a practical administrator, and he was now an old man. The death of his wife deprived him of most of the mental balance that remained to him. He came to depend almost entirely upon his assistant, Schmid, who was most despotic and drove several of the best teachers from the institute. Disputes and lawsuits became common, and the finances of the institution went from bad to worse. The constant interruptions of visitors also demoralized the school. Finally, in 1825, after an existence of a score of years and with a reputation throughout the civilized world, the institute was closed. Pestalozzi retired to Neuhof, then in possession of his grandson. Two years later he died and was buried near his old home beside the school of the little village.

Pestalozzi makes explicit Rousseau's 'naturalism' by defining education as the natural development of human capacities,

Pestalozzi's Educational Aim.—After this account of Pestalozzi's personality, experiments, and writings, we are ready to discuss his aim in education and to understand the principles underlying his method of 'observation' and in what sense they were a continuation of Rousseau's 'naturalism.' In his first writing, *The*

[1] See *How Gertrude Teaches Her Children*, XIV and XV.

Evening Hour of a Hermit, he held that "all the beneficent powers of man are due to neither art nor chance, but to nature," and that education should follow "the course laid down by nature." So in all his works he constantly returns to the analogy of the child's development with that of the natural growth of the plant. For example, he writes:

"Sound education stands before me symbolized by a tree planted near fertilizing waters. A little seed, which contains the design of the tree, its form and proportions, is placed in the soil. See how it germinates and expands into trunk, branches, leaves, flowers, and fruit. The whole tree is an uninterrupted chain of organic parts, the plan of which existed in its seed and root. Man is similar to the tree. In the new-born child are hidden those faculties which are to unfold during life. The individual and separate organs of his being form themselves gradually into unison, and build up humanity in the image of God."

Consequently, Pestalozzi defines education as "the natural, progressive, and harmonious development of all the powers and capacities of the human being," and insists that "the knowledge to which the child is to be led by instruction must, therefore, be subjected to a certain order of succession, the beginning of which must be adapted to the first unfolding of his powers, and the progress kept exactly parallel to that of his development." This belief in the observance of development from within is in keeping with Rousseau's naturalism, and was afterward enlarged upon by Froebel in his stressing of the innate. In contrast to such an education in harmony with nature, Pestalozzi saw that the traditional practices of the times gave the pupil a mere ability to read words, a memory knowledge of mathematics, and a superficial

and contrasting this with the formal education of the day.

culture through the classics that was purely formal and ineffective for real development. He declares:

> "Our unpsychological schools are essentially only artificial stifling machines for destroying all the results of the power and experience that nature herself brings to life. . . . After the children have enjoyed the happiness of sensuous life for five whole years, we make all nature around them vanish before their eyes; tyrannically stop the delightful course of their unrestrained freedom; pen them up like sheep, whole flocks huddled together in stinking rooms; pitilessly chain them for hours, days, weeks, months, years, to the contemplation of unnatural and unattractive letters, and, (contrasted with their former condition), to a maddening course of life."

This need for allowing the powers of the child to develop gradually in keeping with nature and the complete absence of anything of the sort in the schools of the period had been pointed out by Rousseau, but largely in a negative way. He talked blindly in his 'naturalism' about an abandonment of all society and civilization and a return to nature, but he failed to make his educational doctrine concrete and explicit and to apply it to the school. Pestalozzi further modified and extended the Rousselian doctrine by recommending its application to all children, whatever their circumstances and abilities. Where Rousseau evidently had only the young aristocrat in mind in the education of Emile, Pestalozzi held that poverty could be relieved and society reformed only through ridding each and every one of his degradation by means of mental and moral development. Accordingly, he was the stanch advocate of universal education, as shown by the protest implied in the following simile:

He further extended Rousselianism by applying it to all children.

"As far as I am acquainted with popular instruction, it appears to me like a large house, whose uppermost story shines in splendor of highly finished art, but is occupied by only a few. In the middle story is a great crowd, but the stairs by which the upper one may be reached in an approved and respectable manner are wanting; if the attempt be made in a less regular way, the leg or arm used as a means of progress may be broken. In the lowest story is an immense throng of people, who have precisely the same right to enjoy the light of the sun as those in the upper one; but they are left in utter darkness and not even allowed to gaze at the magnificence above."

His general method was training in 'observation' through the surrounding material, analysis into its simplest elements, and expression in words.

His General Method and Its Applications.—Pestalozzi's general method of giving free play to this natural development of the powers of all and so for reforming social conditions was to train his pupils through 'observation.'[1] He felt that clear ideas could be formed only by means of careful sense perceptions, and he was thoroughly opposed to the mechanical memorizing with little understanding that was current in the schools of the day. In all studies, therefore, he strove to direct the senses of the pupils to outer objects and to arouse their consciousness by the impressions thus produced. While such 'object lessons' did not exist in the traditionalized schools, Pestalozzi insisted that the material for them is all about the children, and that it can best be obtained in the home and school and in the ordinary occupations, surroundings, and experiences of life. His method in general seems to have been to analyze each subject into its simplest elements, or 'A B C,' and to develop it by graded exercises based as far as possible upon the study of objects rather than words. Yet Pestalozzi felt that "experiences must be clearly expressed in words, or

[1] I. e. *Anschauung*.

otherwise there arises the same danger that characterizes the dominant word teaching,—that of attributing entirely erroneous ideas to words." Accordingly, as shown in the summary of *How Gertrude Teaches Her Children*,[1] in all instruction he would connect language with 'observation.'

This received special applications to language, arithmetic, drawing, writing, geometry, geography, natural science, history, music, and morality.

The application of this method of natural development by means of analysis, observation, and verbal expression to the various studies constituted the most far-reaching work of Pestalozzi. The special applications of this general method that were worked out by him and his followers in the most common subjects of the curriculum have been described in detail in the account of his work at Stanz, Burgdorf, and Yverdon. Language was taught, not by abstract rules, but by conversation concerning objects, as speaking was held to precede grammar, reading, spelling, and composition. The language training began with single elements or sounds, learned through the 'syllabaries'; from these words were built up; and from words, sentences. As sounds were the elements in language, numbers were the basis of arithmetic. Here again observation was used, and numbers and their relations were taught the pupil through objects. For this purpose the various tables of units, fractions, and compound fractions were devised. Similarly, from the rudiments of form were taught drawing, writing, and constructive geometry. For the study of geography, nature, and history, elements were found in the locality that could be combined until the whole world and all the relations of man were worked out. Music was reduced to its simplest elements and progressively developed, and moral and religious

[1] See p. 131.

training was given through the ordinary concrete relations and experiences of life.

The Permanent Influence of Pestalozzi.—It is easy to exaggerate the achievements of this almost sainted reformer of Switzerland. Pestalozzi's methods were neither very original nor well carried out. His chief merit lay in developing and making positive the suggestions offered by Rousseau, and in utilizing them in the work of the schools. Even in this he failed somewhat in practicality and consistency. He was often unable to work out his own methods. While he stated his views in general most convincingly, we have seen that many of the details had to be managed by his assistants and followers. Occasionally, when he undertook to apply the methods himself, he was strangely inconsistent. Although strongly opposed to all verbal and *memoriter* teaching, in language work he made the mistake of shaping the sentences for his pupils and having them repeat after him; he insisted upon teaching reading and spelling by pronouncing every possible variety of syllable; and in geography, history, and nature study he required the pupils to commit mere lists of important places, facts, or objects arranged in alphabetic order. Moreover, as can be seen both in his educational experiments and his writings, Pestalozzi was groping and never possessed full vision. He did not grasp definite educational principles in a scientific way, but, like Rousseau, obtained his ideas of teaching from sympathetic insight into the minds of children. His writings for the most part record his empirical efforts at an effective training, and are revelations of methods of teaching in the concrete rather than the abstract. His works are also poorly arranged,

Pestalozzi lacked in originality, practicality, and consistency, and was often repetitious, inaccurate, and lacking in comprehensiveness,

repetitious, and inaccurate, and there was little organization or order in his schools.

But his work contained the germ of modern pedagogy and educational reform.

The inconsistency, incompleteness, and lack of breadth in Pestalozzi's work, however, are of small import when compared with its influence upon society and education. The value of his achievements rests, not in their adequacy or finality, but in the fact that they contained the germ of all modern pedagogy and educational reform. In the eighteenth century caste ruled through wealth and education, while the masses, who supported the owners of the land in idleness and luxury, were sunk in ignorance, poverty, and vice. The schools for the common people were exceedingly few, the content of education was largely limited by ecclesiastical authority, and the methods were traditional and verbal. The teachers generally had received little training, and were selected at random. Often it was only the old soldier, widow, servant, or workman who gathered the children for an hour or two on Sundays to learn the rudiments. Ordinarily the pay was wretched, no lodgings were provided for the teacher, and he had often to add domestic service to his duties, in order to secure food and clothing. In the midst of such conditions appeared this most famous of modern educators, who never ceased to work for the reformation of society. As Voltaire, Rousseau, and others had held that the panacea for the corrupt times was rationalism, atheism, deism, socialism, anarchy, or individualism, Pestalozzi found his remedy in education. Like Rousseau, he keenly felt the injustice, unnaturalness, and degradation of the existing society, but he was not content to stop with mere destruction and negations. He saw what education might do to purify social conditions and to elevate

He held education to be a panacea for social ills, and he has thus become one of the greatest exponents of the social and psychological movements in education.

the people by intellectual, moral, and industrial training, and he burned to apply it universally and to develop methods in keeping with nature. He would make Rousseau's 'naturalism' specific and extend it to all. In this he may be considered one of the greatest exponents of the social movement in modern education. His efforts to evolve a natural method of teaching were likewise fruitful, and mark the greatest stimulus given to the modern psychological movement in education. His experiments have stimulated educational theorists, instead of accepting formal principles and traditional processes, to work out carefully and patiently the development of the child mind and to embody the results in practice. From him have come the prevailing reforms in the present teaching of language lessons, arithmetic, drawing, writing, reading, geography, elementary science, and music. In harmony with his improved methods, Pestalozzi also started a different type of discipline. His work made clear the new spirit in the school by which it has approached the atmosphere of the home. He found the proper relation of pupil and teacher to exist in sympathy and friendship, or, as he states it, in 'love.' This attitude constituted the greatest contrast to that of the brutal schools of the times, and introduced a new conception into education.

From him have come many modern reforms in teaching language, arithmetic, drawing, writing, reading, geography, elementary science, and music.

What, then, if Pestalozzi is right in saying: "My life has produced nothing whole, nothing complete; my work cannot, then, either be a whole, nor complete"? If he never produced a closed and perfected system, so much the better. It is not merely the form of his experiments nor even the results, but the fact that he was ready to experiment, and did not depend upon tradition, that made the work of Pestalozzi suggestive and fruitful afterward.

His system was more effective, because it was not closed and perfected

In fact, whenever his practice was most fixed, it was least effective; and wherever his spirit has since prevailed, the most intelligent practice has resulted. The nineteenth century was suffused with his ideals, and his methods have become the basis of much subsequent reform. His work has constantly grown more significant as the years have passed, and the indebtedness of modern educational method to him will be more evident when we have seen the part he played in developing the practice of Herbart and Froebel.

Pestalozzi's methods were spread by his disciples throughout Europe,—Switzerland,

The Spread of Pestalozzian Schools and Methods through Europe.—The 'observational' methods of Pestalozzi and institutions similar to his were soon spread by his assistants and others throughout Europe. Strange to say, as a result of their familiarity with his weaknesses and the conservatism resulting from isolation, the Swiss were, as a whole, rather slow to incorporate the Pestalozzian improvements. Zürich was, however, an exception to the general rule. This city was naturally more progressive and had previously been a seat of reform in matters religious.[1] Here Zeller of Würtemberg, who had visited Burgdorf and helped conduct a Pestalozzian training school at Hofwyl,[2] was early invited to give three courses of lectures in aid of the establishment of a teachers' seminary based upon the principles of Pestalozzi. A large number of teachers, clergymen, and persons of prominence heard these lectures, and thus increased the body of those disseminating the new educational reforms. Krüsi, after leaving the institute at

[1] See Graves, *A History of Education during the Transition*, pp. 189f.

[2] See p. 155.

Yverdon, also founded a number of schools and carried Pestalozzianism into various parts of Switzerland. He finally, in 1833, became the director of a teachers' seminary at his native village of Gais. Near this institution he founded two Pestalozzian schools under the management of his daughter, and during the last decade of his life contributed largely to the Pestalozzian literature. Many other disciples eventually started or reorganized schools in various parts of Switzerland upon the principles of Pestalozzi, and, before the middle of the nineteenth century, his 'observation' methods were in general use, and educational conditions had been greatly changed in Switzerland.

Prussia

But the reforms in method never secured the hold upon the country of their origin that they did in Germany. The innovations were most remarkable in Prussia, and the elementary education there has come to be referred to as the 'Prussian-Pestalozzian school system.' The name was first used by the great educational leader, Diesterweg, in his address at the centennial celebration of Pestalozzi's birth, but it so aptly indicates the influence of the Swiss reformer that it has remained ever since. By the beginning of the nineteenth century Pestalozzianism began to find its way into Prussia. In 1801 the appeal of Pestalozzi for a public subscription in behalf of his project at Burgdorf was warmly supported. In 1802 Herbart's account of *Pestalozzi's Idea of an A B C of Observation* attracted much attention. A representative was sent from Prussia to Burgdorf to report upon the new system in 1803. Meanwhile the Pestalozzian missionaries were fast converting the land. Plamann, who had visited Burgdorf, in 1805 established a Pestalozzian school in Berlin,[1] and published several books applying the new methods to language, geography, and natural history. The same year Grüner opened a similar school at Frankfurt, which was later the means of starting Froebel upon an educational career. Zeller was coaxed away from Würtemberg, and in the seminary at Königsberg lectured to large audiences, and organized a Pestalozzian orphanage there. A similar institution for educating orphans was opened at Potsdam by Türck. In 1808, two of Pestalozzi's pupils, Nicolovius and Süvern, were made directors of public instruction in Prussia, and sent seventeen brilliant young men to Yverdon to study for three years. Upon their return these vigorous youthful educators zealously advanced the cause. The greatest impulse, however, was given the movement by the philosopher, Fichte. In the course of his *Addresses to the German Nation*, 1807–1808, he described the work of Pestalozzi and declared:

> "To the course of instruction which has been invented and brought forward by Heinrich Pestalozzi, and which is now being successfully carried out under his direction, must we look for our regeneration." [2]

In this position Fichte was ardently supported by King Frederick William III, and even more by his noble queen, Louise, who now felt that only through these advanced educational principles could a restoration of the territory and prestige lost to Napoleon at Jena be effected. Throughout his reign the king took the keenest

[1] Froebel taught in this school while studying at the University of Berlin. See p. 222.

[2] The *Reden an die Deutsche Nation* number fourteen in all. This indorsement of Pestalozzi's principles occurs in the tenth.

interest in the Pestalozzian schools, and the queen frequently went to visit the institutions of Zeller. A similar spirit was animating the other states of Germany. As early as 1803, Bavaria sent an educator named Müller to Burgdorf to study the methods, and upon his return he started a school at Mainz. Saxony authorized Blochmann, a former pupil of Pestalozzi, to reorganize its schools upon the new basis. Through Denzel, Würtemberg introduced the new methods, and during the first decade of the century many Pestalozzians were appointed seminary directors and school inspectors. Denzel also organized the school system for the duchy of Nassau. The Princess Pauline of Detmold and other rulers were likewise eager to improve the education of their realms by the introduction of the new principles. Everywhere in Germany the greatest enthusiasm prevailed among teachers, state officials, and princes. Thus in place of the reading, singing, and memorizing of texts, songs, and catechism, under the direction of incompetent choristers and sextons, with unsanitary buildings and brutal punishment, all Germany has come to have in each village an institution for training real men and women. Each school is under the guidance of a devoted, humane, and seminary-bred teacher, and the methods in religion, reading, arithmetic, history, geography, and elementary science are vitalized and interesting. As a result, the German schools have for the past three or four generations been considered models, and have been visited by educators and distinguished men from every land.

and other states of Germany,

In France the spread of Pestalozzianism was at first prevented by the military spirit of the time and by the apathy in education, and later, when the reaction oc-

France,

curred, the schools came under ecclesiastical control and had little influence upon the people. Nevertheless, there were evidences of interest in the new doctrines. General Jullien came to Yverdon to study the methods, and issued two commendatory reports, which induced some thirty French pupils to go to Pestalozzi's institute. Chavannes also published a treatise upon the Pestalozzian methods in 1805. Three years later the philosopher, de Biran, founded a Pestalozzian school under the management of a certain Barraud, whom he had sent to study under Pestalozzi. These efforts, however, had little effect upon education, and the Pestalozzian principles did not make much headway in France up to the revolution of 1830. After that time they rapidly became popular, especially through Victor Cousin. This famous professor, who was later minister of public instruction, issued in 1835 a *Report on the State of Public Instruction in Prussia*, which showed the great merit of Pestalozzianism in the elementary schools of that country. The other great minister, Guizot, had likewise recommended the Prussian schools as the best type for the reform movement, and had shown himself most zealous in training teachers for their vocation after the ideals of Pestalozzi. Spain, Spain at first took kindly to the new methods. A few schools were founded on these principles, and a number of pupils sent to Pestalozzi through the government, but a reaction soon occurred and education was Russia, turned over to the ecclesiastical authorities. In Russia the czar showed himself interested in Pestalozzi's work, a school similar to the 'institutes' was founded, and a former assistant of Pestalozzi became tutor to the royal princes, but probably nothing permanent was accomplished. Schools were also established before long in Italy, Denmark, and Holland by Pestalozzians, but none of them met with much success, and continental Europe in general adopted the new principles indirectly from Germany.

and England.

In England the influence of Pestalozzi was large, but the use made of his methods was not altogether happy. The private school opened by Mayo after his return from Yverdon employed object teaching in several subjects, and a popular textbook, entitled *Lessons on Objects*, was written by his sister, Elizabeth.[1] This book of Miss Mayo's consisted of encyclopedic lessons on the arts and sciences arranged in definite series, and much beyond the comprehension of children from six to eight years old, for whom it was intended. Together with several texts of a similar sort, it had a wide influence in formalizing object teaching and spreading it rapidly in this form. As we have seen,[1] the Mayos were also interested in infant schools, and when 'The Home and Colonial School Society' was organized in 1836, they combined the Pestalozzian methods with those of the infant school. Thus through the model and training schools of this society formalized Pestalozzianism was extended through England and America.

In the United States Pestalozzianism was introduced by William McClure through Joseph Neef;

Pestalozzianism in the United States.—Pestalozzianism began to appear in the United States as early as the first decade of the nineteenth century. It was introduced not only from the original centers in Switzerland, but indirectly in the form it had assumed in Germany, France, England, and other countries. The instances of its appearance were sporadic and seem to have been but

[1] See pp. 68f.

little connected at any time. The earliest presentation was that made from the treatise of Chavannes in 1805 by William McClure. This gentleman was a retired Scotch-American merchant and a man of science, who had, upon the invitation of Napoleon, gone to visit the orphanage at Paris directed by Joseph Neef, a former teacher at Burgdorf. Mr. McClure afterward spent much time at the institute in Yverdon, and by his writings, articles, and financial support did much to make the new principles known in the United States. In 1806 he induced Neef to come to America and become his "master's apostle in the new world". Neef maintained an institution at Philadelphia for three years and afterward founded and taught schools in Louisville, Kentucky, and other parts of the country. In 1823 he went with McClure and Owen to New Harmony, Indiana, where an attempt was made to unite Pestalozzianism with the principles of the 'infant school'.[1] But his imperfect acquaintance with English and with American character and his frequent migrations prevented his personal influence from being greatly felt, and the two excellent works that he published upon applications of the Pestalozzian methods were given scant attention.[2]

a large number of articles and translations were published on the subject; and applications were made by

A large variety of literature, describing the new education, and translating the accounts of Chavannes, Jullien, Cousin, and a number of the German educationalists, also appeared in the American educational journals from 1820 to 1860. *The American Journal of Education*, edited by William Russell, 1826–1831, and its successor,

[1] See p. 65.

[2] For a further account of Neef's work, see *Education*, Vol. XIV, pp. 449–461, or W. S. Monroe's *Pestalozzian Movement*, Chaps. III–VI.

Colburn, Guyot, Parker, Mason, and others.

The American Annals of Education, edited by William C. Woodbridge, 1831–1839, were especially active in giving descriptions and personal observations of the Pestalozzian schools in Europe. Both in articles for his *American Journal of Education* (1855–1881) [1] and in his practical work, Henry Barnard lauded the Pestalozzian methods. Returned travelers, like Professor John Griscom, published accounts of their visits and experiences at Yverdon and Burgdorf, and such lecturers as the Reverend Charles Brooks began to suggest the new principles as a remedy for our educational deficiencies. Pestalozzi's objective methods and the oral instruction resulting from them were used in various subjects by a number of educators. For example, the methods advocated in arithmetic were introduced into America by Warren Colburn. He spread 'mental arithmetic' throughout the country, and in his famous *First Lessons in Arithmetic on the Plan of Pestalozzi*, published first in 1821, he even printed the 'table of units.' The formalized 'Grube method' of arithmetic, which is for the most part based upon Pestalozzi's principle of reducing every sense perception to its elements, also became very popular in the United States about 1870, and remained a fetish for almost a generation. The Pestalozzi-Ritter method in geography was early presented in the United States through the institute lectures and textbooks of Arnold Guyot, who had been a pupil of Ritter and came to America from Switzerland in 1848. The promotion of geographic method along the same lines was later more successfully performed by Francis Wayland Parker in his training of teachers and his work on *How to Teach Geography*. Colonel Parker

[1] See pp. 184ff.

has also had several successful pupils, who are to-day largely continuing the Pestalozzian tradition. The Pestalozzian method in music was brought into the Boston schools and elsewhere about 1836 by Lowell Mason, who was influenced by the works of Nägeli. In several of the subjects taught in their school, Bronson Alcott and his brother urged and practiced the methods of Pestalozzi, and David P. Page, as principal of the New York State Normal School, utilized the spirit and many of the methods of the Swiss reformer.

The most influential movements, however, were brought about by Horace Mann's *Seventh Annual Report*

The most influential propaganda of the Pestalozzian doctrines in general, however, came through the account of the German school methods in the *Seventh Annual Report* (1843) of Horace Mann,[1] and through the inauguration of the 'Oswego methods' by Dr. Edward A. Sheldon. Mann spoke most enthusiastically of the success of the Prussian-Pestalozzian system of education and hinted at the need of a radical reform along the same lines in America. The report caused a great sensation, and was bitterly combated by a group of thirty-one Boston schoolmasters and by conservative sentiment throughout the country. Nevertheless, the suggested reforms were largely effected, and were carried much further by the successors of Mann in the secretaryship of the Massachusetts State Board of Education.[2] Dr. Sheldon, on the other hand, caught his Pestalozzian inspiration from Toronto, Canada, where he became acquainted with the formalized methods of the Mayos through publications of the Home and Colonial School Society.[3] He resolved to introduce the principles of Pestalozzi into the Oswego schools, of which he was at that time superintendent, and

and by Sheldon's 'Oswego methods.'

[1] See p. 173. [2] See pp. 256ff. [3] See pp. 68f. and 149.

in 1861 secured from the society in London a Miss M. E. M. Jones, an experienced Pestalozzian, to train his teachers in these methods. There was some criticism of the Oswego methods on the ground of formalism, but after a year and a half of the experiment, a committee of distinguished educators, who had been invited to inspect the work, pronounced the Oswego movement in general a success. Superintendent Sheldon had from the first admitted a few teachers from outside to learn the new methods, and in 1865 the Oswego training school was made a state institution. This was the first normal school in the United States where object lessons were the chief feature, and where classes were conducted by model teachers and practice teaching was afforded under the supervision of critic teachers. The excellent teachers graduated from this institution caused the Oswego methods to be widely known throughout the country. A large number of other normal schools upon the same basis sprang up rapidly in many states, and the Oswego methods crept into the training schools and the public systems of numerous cities. As a consequence, during the third quarter of the nineteenth century, Pestalozzianism, though somewhat formalized, had a prevailing influence upon the teachers and courses of the elementary schools in the United States.

After Pestalozzi had to give up the attempt to combine industrial training with intellectual, it was taken up by his friend, Fellenberg.

Pestalozzi's Industrial Training Continued by Fellenberg.—Such was the wide influence of Pestalozzi upon education. But while throughout his work he maintained and made new applications of his observational methods, his principle of combining industrial training with intellectual education, which he had begun so successfully at Neuhof and Stanz, could not be continued at

Burgdorf.[1] His pupils there came chiefly from aristocratic families and were not obliged to support themselves by manual labor. However, Pestalozzi still hoped to save enough of the income from the school payments of the rich to found a small agricultural school for the poor on this plan and connect it with the 'institute.' And although most of those who thronged about him, including teachers, failed to understand how effective an instrument for training the young could be made of manual labor under skillful supervision, the lesson of Pestalozzi was not altogether lost upon true philanthropists. It foreshadowed a new light that was destined to be thrown upon education. The opportunity for carrying out this aim came through his friend, *Philipp Emanuel von Fellenberg* (1771–1844).

Fellenberg obtained a large estate, upon which he opened a school to train teachers in the Pestalozzian method.

Fellenberg belonged to a wealthy and noble family of Berne. His father was cultivated and learned, and his mother religious and well educated. He had been prepared for a diplomatic career, but a more unselfish view of life had been presented to him by his mother's counsel: "The rich have always helpers enough, help thou the poor." The altruistic impulse thus given him, and an interest in the experiments of Pestalozzi, who was a friend of his father, were decidedly strengthened by his marriage to the granddaughter of an influential and philanthropic friend of the great Swiss reformer. Like Pestalozzi, Fellenberg believed that an amelioration of the wretched moral and economic conditions in Switzerland could be accomplished only through education. To secure the means for an experiment in this direction, he persuaded his father to purchase for him an estate of six

[1] See p. 127.

hundred acres at Hofwyl, just nine miles from Burgdorf. Here Pestalozzi urged him to undertake his favorite idea of industrial education, and when that educator removed to München-Buchsee, just a ten minute walk from Hofwyl, the attempted union of their efforts mentioned earlier in the chapter [1] was made. As a result of the marked difference in the temperament of the two men, so close a coöperation did not prove feasible, and Pestalozzi soon withdrew, but their friendship remained unbroken and Fellenberg even sent one of his sons to Yverdon to be educated. After the departure of the great educator, Fellenberg decided to continue the experiment, and in 1806, with the aid of Zeller,[2] who had been sent him by Pestalozzi, he opened a school to train teachers in the Pestalozzian method.

Later, with the aid of Wehrli, he combined Pestalozzi's observational work and industrial training in an 'agricultural institute' for poor boys.

The Agricultural School and Other Institutions at Hofwyl.—Fellenberg especially desired, however, to combine Pestalozzi's observational work and his older principle of industrial training in an 'agricultural institute' for poor boys. This plan was not fully realized until he secured in 1808 as an assistant the young and enthusiastic Jacob Wehrli. Wehrli soon convinced Fellenberg of his ability to change the most unmanageable vagabonds into industrious members of society, but some experimentation with four young paupers was necessary before the school was well started. The work was so arranged that each old pupil, as fast as he was trained, took charge of a newer one as an apprentice, and the school from the first became a sort of family. The chief feature of the institute was agricultural occupations, including drainage and irrigation, but from the requirements of farm

[1] See pp. 131f.

[2] See pp. 144, 146, and 147.

life it was natural to develop other employments and to train cartmakers, blacksmiths, carpenters, locksmiths, shoemakers, tailors, mechanics, and workers in wood, iron, and leather. Workshops for these trades were established upon the estate, and the pupils in the agricultural institute were enabled to select a training in a wide range of employments, without neglecting book instruction. By this means, too, they could support themselves by their labor while being educated. Through the institute also a considerable number of the pupils were trained to be directors of similar institutions or to become rural school-teachers. Fellenberg thought it important that all who were to teach in the common schools should have a thorough acquaintance with the practical labor of a farm, the means of self-support, and the life and habits of the majority of their pupils.

And, in order to interest wealthy young men in the education of the poor and hold them longer, he established a 'literary institute.'

But the work of Fellenberg did not stop there. From the beginning he had felt that the wealthy should understand and be more in sympathy with the laboring classes, and learn how to direct their work more intelligently. Hence he began very early an agricultural course for landowners, and many young men of the wealthy classes came to show a striking interest in his deep-soil ploughing, draining, irrigating, and other means of educating the poor. But these wealthier youths remained at the institute so short a time that he could not extend his ideals very widely. To retain them longer at Hofwyl, in 1809 he opened a 'literary institute,' which, besides the usual academic studies, used Pestalozzi's object lessons and strove to develop physical activities. Moreover, the pupils in the literary institute had to cultivate gardens, work on the farm, engage in carpentering, turning, and other mechanical occupations, and in many ways come into touch and mutual understanding with the poorer boys in the agricultural institute. The wealthy learned to dignify labor, and the poor, instead of envying those in the higher stations of life, became friendly and desirous of coöperating with them. Eventually there arose an independent community of youth, managing its own affairs outside of school, arranging its own occupations, games, and tours, choosing its own officers, and making its own laws. Within this little world was provided a training for society at large, with its various classes, associations, and corporations, which Fellenberg seems to have regarded as divinely ordained. Likewise, in 1823, a school for poor girls was opened by his wife, and four years later he started a 'real,' or practical, school for the middle classes, which was intermediate between the two 'institutes.'

A 'real' school was also started for the middle classes, and a school for poor girls was opened.

Fellenberg's Educational Aim and Course.—Thus Pestalozzi's principle of observation as the groundwork of memory was strengthened by Fellenberg's emphasis upon actual doing. Manual activity Fellenberg felt to be a necessary complement to sense perception and object teaching. "For what has been done," said he, "and done with thought, will be retained more firmly by the memory, and will bring a surer experience than that which has been only seen or heard." Even more than with Pestalozzi, the pupil was to be treated not as a mere recipient, but as an agent capable of collecting, arranging, and using his own ideas. From various letters of Fellenberg we have definite information concerning the details of the curriculum at Hofwyl. Besides the vocational training, the course in the agricultural institute included reading, writing,

Fellenberg strove to combine observation with actual doing.

The studies in the agricultural institute, the school for girls, the course for teachers, and the literary institute.

arithmetic, religion, drawing, singing, history, geography, natural history, botany, and geometry, or about the same range of subjects as was dealt with in Pestalozzi's 'institute.' The curriculum in the school for girls must have been very similar, except that the industrial work consisted of the household arts,—cooking, washing, cleaning, spinning, and knitting. In the course for teachers, beside manual labor on the farm, special training was given in grammar, religion, drawing, geography, history of Switzerland, agriculture, and 'anthropology,' which included physiology, hygiene, and first aid to the injured. Those who seemed qualified for a more thorough course were allowed to elect work in the literary institute. The professional training consisted in a thorough study of the subject-matter they were to teach, lessons on communicating instruction, and practice teaching under inspection, followed by criticism and discussion. The education for the higher classes in the literary institute included some of the usual work in the classics, but stressed the modern languages, sciences, drawing, music, and practical work. The physical training was given through gymnastics, military exercises, swimming, riding, walking, and skating. As in the other courses, religious studies also had an important place.

Industrial Training in the Schools of Europe.—The educational institutions of Fellenberg were well managed and proved very successful. The number of pupils in the agricultural institute soon increased from a mere family circle to over one hundred and fifty, and the idea of education through industrial training spread rapidly.

While the schools at Hofwyl disappeared after the death of Fellenberg,

While, after the death of Fellenberg in 1844, the schools at Hofwyl, through mismanagement and political changes, gradually declined, their principles became embodied in education everywhere. Various types of industrial education came to supplement academic courses, and extend the work of the school to a larger number of pupils. Thus the tendency of modern civilization to care for the education of the unfortunate through industrial training has sprung from the philanthropic spirit of Pestalozzi and his practical collaborator, Fellenberg, and their endeavors to furnish educational opportunities for all. The poor, the defective, and the delinquent have, through vocational training, been redeemed and given a chance in life, and many children have been kept in school that would inevitably have fallen by the wayside. Public schools, special industrial schools, orphanages, institutions for the deaf and blind, reformatories, and even prisons have yielded rich harvests because of Pestalozzi's first sowing.

their industrial principles spread through Europe,—

Movements of this sort have been apparent in all advanced countries. The industrial institutions rapidly increased in Switzerland, beginning in 1816 with the school in the neighboring district of Meykirch. In 1832 a cantonal teachers' association was formed at Berne, with Fellenberg as president and Wehrli as vice president, to reform the methods of organization and instruction current in Switzerland. Every canton soon had its 'farm school,' in which, wrote Henry Barnard, "the school instruction occupies three hours in the summer and four in winter; the remainder of the day being devoted to work in the field or garden, or at certain seasons of the year and for a class of pupils, in some indoor trade or craft." Industrial training was also introduced into most of the Swiss normal schools. In Germany the industrial work

Switzerland,

Germany,

suggested by Pestalozzi and Fellenberg came into successful operation in many of the orphanages and most of the reform schools. A most striking example of the latter was the 'House of Redemption,' opened in 1833 near Hamburg. Here boys and girls of criminal tendencies were given an industrial training and then apprenticed, and comparatively few ever lapsed into evil ways after leaving the school. Later industrial education was taken up by the *Fortbildungsschulen* ('continuation schools') of the regular system.[1] At the reform and continuation

France,

schools of France industrial training has long formed the distinctive element in the course. Educators and statesmen of England, especially Lord Brougham, likewise early commended the work of Fellenberg, and industrial training shortly found a foothold in that country. There

and England.

was opened in 1835 at Queenswood Hall, Hampshire, the famous George Edmondson school, which was provided with agricultural and trade departments, including blacksmithing and printing. In 1839 the Battersea Training Establishment was opened upon the same basis as the Swiss normal schools. At the well-known Red Hill school and farm for young criminals, established in 1849, and other similar institutions, vocational training has also produced remarkable results.

In the United States 'manual labor' institutions were started to enable students to earn their way through college and to preserve their health;

Industrial Institutions in the United States.—The industrial work of the Pestalozzi-Fellenberg system began to appear in the United States about the close of the first quarter of the nineteenth century. After that, for twenty years or so, there sprang up a large number of institutions of secondary or higher grade with 'manual labor' features in addition to the literary work. The primary

[1] See p. 288, footnote 2.

object of the industrial work in these institutions was to enable students to earn their way through school or college and recruit sectarian ranks during a period of strong denominational controversy. The other great argument for this training was that it secured physical exercise for those under the strain of severe intellectual labor. It was the first serious academic recognition of the need of a 'sound mind in a sound body,' and did much to overcome the prevailing tendency of students toward tuberculosis and to furnish a sane substitute for the escapades and pranks in which college life abounded. The first of these manual labor institutions were established in the New England and Middle States between 1820 and 1830, and within a dozen years the manual labor system was adopted in theological schools, colleges, and academies from Maine to Tennessee. The success of this feature at Andover Theological Seminary, where it was begun in 1826 for 'invigorating and preserving health, without any reference to pecuniary profit,' was especially influential in causing it to be extended. Much impetus was also given the movement through the writings and addresses of Rev. Elias Cornelius, secretary of the American Educational Society, who perceived the terrible inroads made upon health by education without systematic exercise. From 1830 to 1832 many articles and lectures describing and commending the Fellenberg system were read before learned societies and published in the leading educational journals. The 'Society for Promoting Manual Labor in Literary Institutions,' founded in 1831, appointed a general agent to visit the chief colleges in the Middle West and South, call attention to the value of manual labor, and issue a report upon the subject.

but, as material conditions improved, the industrial features were given up.

Little attention, however, was given in the literary institutions to the pedagogical principles underlying this work. As material conditions improved and formal social life developed, the impracticability of the scheme was realized, and the industrial side of these institutions was given up. This physical phase was then replaced by college athletics. By 1840–50 most of the schools and colleges that began as 'manual labor institutes' had become purely literary.

Industrial education has also been adopted for the solution of peculiar racial problems, for the training of defectives and delinquents, and for increasing the efficiency of the public system.

A further movement in industrial education was found in the establishment of such schools as Carlisle, Hampton, and Tuskegee, which adopted this training as a solution for peculiar racial problems. But the original idea of Pestalozzi, to secure redemption through manual labor was not embodied in American institutions until the last quarter of the century. After 1873, when Miss Mary Carpenter, the English prison reformer, visited the United States, contract labor and factory work in the reformatories began to be replaced by farming, gardening, and kindred domestic industries. At the present time, moreover, the schools for delinquents and defectives in the New England, Middle Atlantic, Middle West, and most of the Southern states, have the Fellenberg training, though without much grasp of the educational principles involved. Finally, within the last decade there has also been a growing tendency to employ industrial training or trade education for the sake of holding pupils longer in school and increasing the efficiency of the public system. In so far as it has tended to replace the more general values of manual training, once so popular, with skill in some particular industrial process, this modern movement represents a return from the executive occupational work started by

Froebel [1] to the philanthropic practice of Fellenberg and Pestalozzi.

Hence it was largely through the practical development of this great disciple at Hofwyl that Pestalozzi has had a marked influence upon the social, as well as upon the psychological, movement in modern education.

SUPPLEMENTARY READING

I. Sources

FELLENBERG, P. E. von. *Letters from Hofwyl.*

NEEF, F. J. N. *Sketch of a Plan and Method of Education* and *The Method of Instructing Children Rationally in the Arts of Reading and Writing.*

PESTALOZZI, J. H. *The Evening Hour of a Hermit*, *Letters on Early Education*, *Leonard and Gertrude*, and *How Gertrude Teaches Her Children.*

II. Authorities

BACHMAN, F. P. *The Social Factor in Pestalozzi's Theory of Education* (*Education*, Vol. XXII, pp. 402–414).

BARNARD, H. *American Journal of Education.* Vol. III, pp. 591–596; X, 81–92; XIII, 323–331; XV, 231–236; XXVI, 359–368.

GRAVES, F. P. *Great Educators of Three Centuries.* Chap. IX.

GREEN, J. A. *Pestalozzi's Educational Writings.*

GREEN, J. A. *Life and Work of Pestalozzi.*

GUIMPS, R. de. *Pestalozzi, His Aim and Work.* (Translated by Crombie.)

HAMILTON, C. J. *Henri Pestalozzi* (*Educational Review*, Vol. III, pp. 173–184).

HÈRISSON, F. *Pestalozzi, élève de J. J. Rousseau.*

HOLMAN, H. *Pestalozzi.*

HOYT, C. O. *Studies in the History of Modern Education.* Chap. III.

[1] See pp. 237ff and 244f.

KELLOGG, A. M. *Life of Pestalozzi.*

KING, W. *The Institutions of De Fellenberg.*

KRÜSI, H. *Pestalozzi, His Life, Work, and Influence.*

MISAWA, T. *Modern Educators and Their Ideals.* Chap. VI.

MONROE, W. S. *Joseph Neef and Pestalozzianism in the United States* (*Education*, Vol. XIV, pp. 449–461).

MONROE, W. S. *The Pestalozzian Movement in the United States.*

MORF, H. *Zur Biographie Pestalozzi's.*

MUNROE, J. P. *The Educational Ideal.* Pp. 179–187.

PARKER, S. C. *History of Modern Elementary Education.* Chaps. XIII–XVI.

PAYNE, J. *Lectures on the History of Education.* Lect. IX.

PINLOCHE, A. *Pestalozzi and the Foundation of the Modern Elementary School.*

QUICK, R. H. *Educational Reformers.* Pp. 354–383.

SHELDON, E. A. *The Oswego Movement.*

CHAPTER VI

THE COMMON SCHOOL REVIVAL IN NEW ENGLAND

During the second quarter of the nineteenth century there took place a remarkably rapid advance in public education, which has been generally known as 'the common school revival.'

Location, Time, and Scope of the Revival.—The interest in the improved methods of Pestalozzi and other reformers that was manifesting itself everywhere in the United States during the second quarter of the nineteenth century seems to have been but one phase of a much larger movement. This awakening has been generally known as 'the common school revival,' [1] which first became influential during the latter part of the decade between 1830 and 1840. It had its storm center in New England, since this portion of the United States had especially fallen into an educational decadence, but everywhere it greatly furthered the cause of public education, which had as yet not made a marked advance in any state.

As we have found in Chapter IV, half a dozen of the states had started an organization of common schools, and in a dozen others permanent school funds had been started, an influential minority of leading citizens were constantly advocating universal education, and pub-

[1] 'Revival' is an unfortunate term that has come to be accepted through long usage. It belongs to mediæval philosophy, and, if we hold to evolution and progress, it scarcely conveys our meaning. While its general use is recognized, it has been avoided here and in other chapters as far as possible. It more nearly affords an accurate description of the movement in New England than in the other parts of the country, since educational conditions there had actually retrograded.

lic interest in the matter was evidently increasing. But the consummation of a regular system was still much hindered by sectarian jealousies, by the conception of public schools as institutions for paupers and the consequent custom of allowing private schools to share in public funds, and by the unwillingness of the wealthy to be taxed locally for the benefit of other people's children. While these obstacles had not been apparent in Massachusetts and Connecticut, the systems in these states were further hampered by the division into autonomous districts and by the interference of petty politics, and had, in consequence, sadly declined. Educational ideals were everywhere in evident need of expansion and further democratization, and school methods and curricula, as well as organization, cried aloud for radical revision. As a result of the reform movement, a great work had been accomplished before the middle of the century, and its influence was felt up to the close. The common schools rapidly increased, and high schools, the true American product in secondary education, began to be introduced everywhere. Appropriations for public education were multiplied, and salaries became large enough to attract better teachers to the public schools. Normal schools were established to give an adequate training, and paid supervision became part of the system. Text-books and methods were greatly improved. As the demand for an awakening was most felt in New England, and the movement was most in evidence there and was stimulated by the work of several of the greatest reformers, we shall here limit the discussion to that part of the country and reserve the account of progress elsewhere during this period for a later chapter.

Early Leaders in the Awakening.—In this awakening the most conspicuous figure is probably Horace Mann, but there were several leaders in the field before him, many were contemporaneous, and the work was expanded and deepened by others of distinction long after he withdrew from the scene. For a score of years before Mann appeared, definite preparation for the movement had been in progress, and the labors of the individuals and associations engaged in these endeavors should be briefly noted. Many of the efforts seem to have aimed at an improvement in methods through the creation of an institution for training teachers, thus anticipating one of the greatest achievements of Mann. As early as 1816 Denison Olmstead, at that time principal of a 'union' school at New London, in his master's oration at Yale urged that a seminary for the gratuitous training of schoolmasters be opened, and proposed a curriculum of review work, methods, school organization, and government, but met with little response. Seven years later, J. L. Kingsley, a professor in Yale, made a forceful argument in the *North American Review* for a similar proposition. In 1823 William Russell, principal of an academy in New Haven, published his *Suggestions on Education*, in which he held that better preparation should be made for teaching through the establishment of a professional school. Two years after this, the Rev. T. H. Gallaudet issued a series of able articles on normal instruction, including an experimental school, which were republished and given a wide circulation. About this time also actual attempts at a private normal school were made by the Rev. Samuel R. Hall at Concord, Vermont (1823), Andover, Massachusetts (1830), and Plymouth, New Hampshire (1837).

While Horace Mann was the most conspicuous figure, the movement began a score of years before his time.

Many efforts were made to establish an institution for training teachers;

several associations were founded in the interest of common schools; there was great activity on the part of educational journals; and there were published a number of reports upon first-hand investigation of education in Europe.

Likewise, there were several associations, like the 'American Institute of Instruction,' founded in the interest of common schools during this period. A number of educational journals, moreover, published articles on schoolbooks, the methods of Lancaster, Pestalozzi, Neef, Fellenberg, the infant and Sunday schools, physical education, European school systems, and a variety of other timely topics and reforms. Among these progressive publications were the *Academician*, published in New York by Albert and John W. Pickett, 1818–1820; the *Teacher's Guide and Parent's Assistant*, issued at Portland, Maine, 1826–1827; the *American Journal of Education*, edited by William Russell from 1826 to 1830, and then continued from 1831 to 1839, as the *American Annals of Education* under the editorship of William C. Woodbridge, and the *Quarterly Register*, published 1828–1843 by the 'American Educational Society.' The latest European ideas were also reported from first-hand observation by a number who had gone abroad to investigate. The most influential of these reports was *A Year in Europe*, written in 1819 by Professor John Griscom, who was a lecturer before several New York associations, including the Public School Society.[1] Almost as widely read were the reports of William C. Woodbridge, who visited Europe in 1820–1824; of Professor Calvin E. Stowe of Lane Theological Seminary, Cincinnati, in 1836; and of Alexander D. Bache, first president of Girard College, Philadelphia, in 1839.

But the greatest contributions before Mann were made by

Work of James G. Carter.—All these movements indicate the educational ferment that was going on. But the predecessor of Mann, who accomplished most for the

[1] See p. 98.

common schools, and influenced that reformer most directly was *James G. Carter* (1795–1849). Henry Barnard declares that to Carter "more than to any other one person belongs the credit of having first attracted the attention of the leading minds of Massachusetts to the necessity of immediate and thorough improvement in the system of free or public schools." Carter was a practical teacher and wrote continually in the newspapers, especially on the need of a normal institution to improve instruction in the public schools. These popular appeals, which he began about 1824, proved very successful. His constructive *Outlines of an Institution for the Education of Teachers*, which was widely circulated and reviewed, has earned him the title of 'father of the normal schools.'

James G. Carter,

After being elected to the legislature, he accomplished much by his zeal and his skill in parliamentary tactics. Through him a bill was passed in 1826 to reform the decadent system of Massachusetts. By it each town as a whole was required to choose a regular committee, instead of the ministers and selectmen, to supervise the schools, choose text-books, and examine, certify, and employ the teachers. The act was strenuously opposed by many districts, on the ground that it deprived them of their accustomed rights of local autonomy, and the following year the districts were allowed, as a sop, to choose a committeeman, who should appoint the teachers. The effect of the law of 1826 was largely spoiled by this compromise, but the enactment proved a first step toward the centralization and supervision of schools. In 1826 an effort was also made to place secondary education, which was largely conducted by academies, more under public control. A law was passed, requiring each town of five hundred fami-

who constantly advocated normal schools, and obtained legislation for school committees elected by the town, for the support of high schools, and for a State Board of Education.

lies to support a free English high school, and every one of four thousand inhabitants to maintain a classical high school, in which pupils could be fitted for college. Next, in 1834, Carter succeeded in getting a state school fund established from the proceeds of the sale of lands in the province of Maine and the state's claims against the federal government for military services. By this act the income was distributed only to those towns which raised one dollar of taxation for every child of school age, and made the returns required by the state. But Carter's greatest and most fruitful victory was won in 1837, when he managed to procure the passage of the bill for a State Board of Education, after it had been once defeated, by inducing the house to discuss it in 'committee of the whole.'

To the surprise of most people, Horace Mann, and not Carter, was chosen secretary of the new state board, but he proved, both by heredity and training, to be peculiarly fitted.

Horace Mann as Secretary of the Massachusetts Board.—By reason of his merits as an educator, his persistent efforts in behalf of educational reform, and his advocacy of the bill, it was assumed by most people that Carter would be chosen as secretary of the new board. To their surprise, a lawyer named *Horace Mann* (1796–1859), at that time president of the senate, was selected for the post, but the choice is now known to have been most fortunate. By both heredity and training Mann was suffused with an interest in humanity and all phases of philanthropy, especially education. He possessed a happy combination of lofty ideals, intelligence, courage, enthusiasm, and legislative experience, which equipped him admirably for leadership in educational reform. The law proposed for the new Board of Education numerous duties in the way of collecting and spreading information concerning the common schools and of making suggestions for the improvement and extension of public education, but it provided no real powers. It was obvious that the permanence and influence of the board would depend almost wholly upon the intelligence and character of its secretary, and the peculiar fitness of Horace Mann can alone account for his selection.

Aids and Obstacles to Mann's Reforms.—At any rate, during the twelve years he held the secretaryship, Mann subserved the interests of the state most faithfully. To awaken the people, the new secretary at once started upon an educational campaign through the state, and during each year of his tenure he made an annual circuit for this purpose. Besides the regular trips, Mann held himself subject to calls from everywhere, within the state and out, for educational meetings, lectures, and addresses; and when, after seven years, teachers' institutes were introduced into Massachusetts, he constantly served as an efficient lecturer and instructor. An even more effective means of disseminating Mann's reforms was found in the series of *Annual Reports*, which he issued from the first, and in the publication of his *Massachusetts Common School Journal*, begun in the second year of his administration. The *Reports* were by law to give information concerning existing conditions and the progress made in the efficiency of public education each year, and to discuss the most approved organization, content, and methods for the common schools, in order to create and guide public opinion most intelligently. While practically every educational topic of importance at the time is dealt with, his suggestions as a whole maintain a definite point of view and a connected body of practical doctrine. Sometimes they seem commonplace, but it must be remembered that

His chief means of developing educational sentiment were his campaigns through the state,

his *Annual Reports* and *Common School Journal*,

they were not so then, and that the work of Mann did much to render them familiar. While addressed to the State Board, they were really intended for the citizens of Massachusetts in general, and their influence was felt far beyond the confines of the state. They vitally affected school conditions everywhere in New England, and were read with great interest in all parts of the United States, and even in Europe. *The Journal*, on the other hand, was issued semi-monthly and consisted of only sixteen pages to each number. It was devoted to spreading information concerning school improvement, school law, and the proceedings of the State Board, and it urged upon school officials, parents, and children their duties toward health, morals, and intelligence, but was not as valuable as some of the educational journals that had preceded it.

his encouragement of school libraries,

Another medium in the improvement of educational facilities was Mann's general establishment of school libraries by state subsidy throughout Massachusetts. But probably the most permanent means of stimulating the awakening and propagating the reforms led by Horace Mann was the foundation by Massachusetts of the first public normal schools in this country.

and his establishment of the first three state normal schools.

A devoted friend of Mann offered to donate ten thousand dollars for this purpose, in case the state would supply a like amount. This generous proposal was accepted by the legislature in 1838. It was decided to found three schools, so located that all parts of the state might be equally served. The course consisted in a review of the common branches from the teaching point of view, work in educational theory, and training in a practice school under supervision. Despite the hostility of conservatives, incompetent teachers, and sectarian dogmatists, these schools, while not largely attended, were a great success from the start.

The arduous and unremitting labors of Mann in instituting and promoting the various means of school reform must have made the greatest inroad upon his strength and financial resources. He was frequently afflicted with insomnia for weeks, and his income never amounted to a living wage. But a more trying obstacle that the reformer had to contend with was the dense conservatism and bitter prejudices often animating people that he felt ought eagerly to have supported him. The Board and its secretary were for years violently assailed by reactionaries of all types. Attempts were early made in the legislature to abolish the Board of Education or to have its duties and powers transferred to the governor and council, but after a fierce fight this type of opposition ceased. Mann's controversy with the Boston schoolmasters was also sharp, but decisive. His *Seventh Annual Report* (1843) gave an account of his visit to foreign schools, especially those of Germany, and praised with great warmth the 'Pestalozzian'[1] instruction without text-books, the enthusiastic teachers, the absence of artificial rivalry, and the mild discipline in the Prussian system. The report did not stigmatize the conservatism of the Boston schools or bring them into comparison with those of Berlin, but the cap fitted. The pedagogues were disquieted, and proceeded to answer savagely. But when the smoke of battle had cleared away, it was seen that the leaders of the old order had been completely routed. A more insidious attack was that led by the ultra-orthodox. The old schools of the Puritans, with their dogmatic reli-

His arduous labors seriously injured his health; and he was bitterly opposed by

politicians,

Boston school principals,

and the ultra-orthodox,

[1] See p. 139f

gious teaching, had been steadily fading for more than a century before the new board had been inaugurated,[1] but many narrow people were inclined to charge this disappearance to the reformer, whose liberal attitude in religion was well known. Throughout the contest, however, Mann held that the Bible should be read in the public schools, but that it should be without comment. The assaults, which culminated with articles in the sectarian press and with polemic sermons, were vigorously and successfully repelled by the secretary and others, including many of the more sensible orthodox people. However, while these different controversies wore Mann out and probably led ultimately to his resignation, they had much to do with making his reputation as a great educator. They have even caused us at times to forget that he was but a striking figure in a general movement. Men like Carter were in the field long before him, and his co-worker, Barnard, served the cause of the common schools for half a century after Mann withdrew.

but these difficulties were the making of his reputation.

The Educational Suggestions and Achievements of Mann.—Mann's general positions and specific recommendations concerning education may easily be gathered from his *Lectures*, *Reports*, and *Common School Journal*. His foremost principle was that education should be universal and free. Girls should be trained as well as boys, and the poor should have the same opportunities as the rich. Public schools should afford education of such a quality that the wealthy would not patronize private institutions because of their superiority. This universal education, however, should have as its chief aim moral character and social efficiency, and not mere erudition, culture, and

Mann advocated a universal and free education of the highest order, of which the chief aim should be moral character and social efficiency.

[1] See pp. 105f.

accomplishments. But while the public school should cultivate a moral and religious spirit, this could not be accomplished, he felt, by inculcating sectarian doctrines. The main objection urged to the private school system in his *First Report* was its tendency "to assimilate our modes of education to those of England, where Churchmen and Dissenters, each sect according to its creed, maintain separate schools in which children are taught from their tenderest years to wield the sword of polemics with fatal dexterity."

He also stressed a proper material equipment for the schools.

But Mann was mainly a practical, rather than a theoretical, reformer. To the material side of education, he gave serious attention. He declared that school buildings should be well constructed and sanitary. This matter seemed to him so important that he wrote a special report upon the subject during his first year in office. He carefully discussed the proper plans for rooms, ventilation, lighting, seating, and other schoolhouse features, and insisted that the inadequate and squalid conditions which existed should be improved. In his *Fourth Report* also he considered many of the physical evils, especially those arising from pupils of all ages being in the same room. He found that in many cases this was the result of a multiplication of districts, and suggested 'union' schools or consolidation as a remedy. As to methods, he maintained that instruction should be based upon scientific principles, and not upon authority and tradition. Pestalozzi's inductive method of teaching received his approval, for he felt that the pupils should be introduced at first hand to the facts of the humanities and sciences. The work should be guided by able teachers, who had been trained in a normal school, and should be imparted in a spirit of

He held that methods should be improved, and the teachers should be trained.

mildness and kindness through an understanding of child nature. The teachers, who should be men as well as women, ought also to supplement their training and experience by frequently gathering in associations and institutes. In the matter of the studies to be pursued, Mann was inclined to be over-practical. In discussing educational values, he failed to see any reason "why algebra, a branch which not one man in a thousand ever has occasion to use in the business of life, should be studied by more than twenty-three hundred pupils, and bookkeeping, which every man, even the day laborer, should understand, should be attended to by only a little more than half that number." Similarly, he holds that of all subjects, except the rudiments, physiology should receive the most attention, and he writes an extended essay upon its use and value. He exaggerates the importance of this subject, possibly as a result of his devotion to phrenology; but in his whole espousal of subjects that will prepare for concrete living, he seems close to Spencer's test of "what knowledge is of the most worth." [1]

He exaggerated the importance of practical studies.

Mann was not an educational philosopher, but an educational missionary.

In order that these various reforms might be realized, Mann insisted frequently that the state should spare no labor or expense. But in a republic he felt that "education can never be attained without the consent of the whole people." "All improvements in the school suppose and require a corresponding and simultaneous improvement in public sentiment." It was such a general elevation of ideals, effort, and expenditure that Horace Mann sought, and for which he began his crusade. He was a man of action, and not a philosopher. Nor was he the only reformer of the times, as we have been prone to

[1] See pp. 327ff.

believe in our admiration for his moral earnestness and great devotion. But it was just such ethical characteristics as his that were needed to achieve the desired reforms, and that largely account for the numerous practical results accomplished during his time. And the evident progress made in this period covers a wide range. During the twelve years of Mann's secretaryship, the appropriations made for public education in Massachusetts were more than doubled. Through this rise in enthusiasm for public education, the proportion of expenditure for private schools in the state was reduced from seventy-five to thirty-six per cent of the total cost of schools. The salaries of masters in the public schools were raised sixty-two per cent, and, although the number of women teachers had grown fifty-four per cent, the average of their salaries was also increased fifty-one per cent. The school attendance enormously expanded both absolutely and relatively to the growth of population, and a full month was added to the average school year. When Mann's administration began, but fourteen out of forty-three towns had complied with the high school law of 1826, but, by the middle of the century, fifty new high schools had been established, and the opportunities for secondary education under public control, which had been declining for half a century, were greatly enlarged. While the time for a full appreciation of skilled school superintendents had not yet arrived, the efficiency of supervision was largely increased by making the compensation of the town visiting committees, established through Carter, compulsory by law. The first state normal schools at last appeared, and raised immensely the standards of teaching. Teachers' institutes, county associations,

He was not the only reformer of the times, but his achievements were extensive,—

he doubled the appropriations for public education; he increased the number and salary of the teachers, the length of the school year, and the opportunities for secondary education; and brought about skilled supervision and professional training.

and public school libraries were given general popularity.

Quite as marked was the improvement effected in the range and serviceability of the school studies, in text-books, methods of teaching, and discipline. While not a remarkable educationalist himself, Mann rendered practical and brought into use many of the contributions made to educational theory by others, and thereby anticipated many of the features of later educational practice. The word method of reading took the place of the uneconomical, artificial, and ineffective method of the alphabet, and the Pestalozzian object methods and oral instruction were introduced. The connection between physical and mental health and development became better understood. Thus during this educational awakening the people of Massachusetts renewed their faith in the common schools. Mann was assisted by many progressive educators and teachers of the times and a sympathetic Board of Education, but under his leadership a practically unorganized set of schools, with diverse aims and methods, was welded into a well-ordered system with high ideals. The experiment of state school administration under the control of a board and secretary proved to be so satisfactory that until 1908 it retained vogue in Massachusetts. Even now the only change is in the way of wider powers and centralization and the recognition of the responsibility and dignity of the executive officer by changing his title to 'state commissioner.'[1]

Henry Barnard's Part in the Educational Awakening.—But there was another important contribution to

[1] In 1908, after the state commission on the investigation of industrial education made its report, it was merged in the State Board, and provision was made for the appointment of a 'commissioner' with enlarged powers.

the awakening made by a New Englander, which was of a rather different nature from that connected with the influence of Horace Mann. Before that reconstruction of the common schools, which was responsible for the best elements in our national civilization, could be at all complete, it was necessary that America should have a better comprehension of what was being done in education elsewhere. The United States had for two centuries been undergoing a gradual transition from the institutional types transplanted from England and the Continent in colonial days, and was coming more and more to blossom out into democracy and the people's schools, but for a long time there was little knowledge of what was being done by the other countries that had by this time adopted similar ideals. Conceptions of universal and democratic education and of improved organization and methods had slowly developed in Prussia and other German states, and had extended to France and even to Holland, Denmark, and Sweden. A literature connected with the advanced theories of such reformers as Rousseau, the philanthropinists, Pestalozzi, and Fellenberg had likewise grown up in Europe. It was very important that America, now keenly alive to the need of educational reorganization, should become acquainted with all this, that the new world might secure the advantages of comparison, corroboration, and expansion of view from the work of older civilized peoples. For this it did not need to imitate slavishly or adopt wholesale, but it might find in the example of other lands suggestions to be modified and adapted to its needs.

A different contribution that was needed for the awakening was a systematic exposition of European education.

Much of this enlargement of vision, we have seen,[1]

[1] See pp. 168 and 173.

had been going on before the awakening was well under way, especially through the reports of Americans that had inspected the educational systems of Europe or had visited places where the educational experiments of the various reformers were conducted. It has likewise been indicated that a number of treatises on foreign schools, methods, and organization had been published in a series of educational journals that had sprung up in the United States. A few European accounts, like that of Cousin,[1] had also been translated. Suggestions of elaborate systems of popular instruction for one state or another had several times been published. The Moravians had brought in the educational ideals of Comenius;[2] Lancaster had come to this side of the Atlantic to exploit his system further;[3] and Neef had introduced the methods of his master, Pestalozzi, into Pennsylvania and elsewhere;[4] and Mann himself, while hampered by an imperfect knowledge of modern languages, had been profoundly influenced by Europe.[5] But the time was now ripe for a more extensive and systematic exposition of European education and its application to popular education in America, and for a really capable scholar to bring these world views within the grasp of all classes of teachers and educational authorities.

This was the chief work of the scholarly Henry Barnard, although he also performed several

Barnard as Secretary of the Connecticut State Board.— This effective literary representative of the awakening appeared at length in *Henry Barnard* (1811–1900), who is fully worthy of a place in the educational pantheon of America. While still in his teens, Barnard had made a

[1] See pp. 148 and 150.
[2] See Graves, *History of Education during the Transition*, pp. 272ff.
[3] See pp. 53ff. [4] See p. 150. [5] See p. 173.

brilliant record at Yale for general scholarship, and a position as assistant librarian during his last two years in college did much to afford him a wide grasp of bibliography. After graduation, he had obtained a valuable experience in teaching, and, by travelling extensively in America and Europe, he had formed a broad acquaintance with educational institutions, libraries, galleries, and social conditions in all the leading states and nations.

practical services for educational administration.

Although Barnard's real work was found in his accounts of European schools and education, he frequently occupied important places in educational administration and performed many direct services for American schools. For this mission his first opportunity came in his native state. Two years after his return to Connecticut, he began his part in the educational awakening as secretary of the new State Board of Commissioners of Common Schools, and undertook to do a work similar to that of Mann in Massachusetts. The public schools of the state certainly stood in need of reforms. Throughout the eighteenth century Connecticut schools had been among the most efficient in the country, but since the income from the Western Reserve lands had begun, in 1798, and especially after this had been increased by the United States deposit fund in 1836, public education had steadily declined. A state tax was still maintained, but all local effort was paralyzed through lack of exercise. No doubt, too, this unwillingness to tax the locality had been increased by the transferal of the entire management of the common schools from the town to the 'school society,' which was a species of district, almost identical with the parish of each Puritan or Congregational church. The re-

As secretary of the Connecticut State Board, he undertook reforms similar to those of Mann in Massachusetts by means of his *Reports* and *Connecticut School Journal*,

sults of this ruinous policy had been revealed in an investigation made by the legislature. The report of a committee showed that not one-half of the children of school age were attending the common schools, that the teachers were poorly trained and supervision was neglected, that there was little attention given to courses of study, buildings, or equipment, and that there was little general education beyond elementary work.

Add to this the fact that the masses of the people supposed that Connecticut still led in popular education and were perfectly satisfied, and it can be seen how desperate was the situation to be overcome. The board had little authority, except to inspect, report, and stimulate the common schools through its secretary. In his reports, however, Barnard made suggestions for a complete plan of reformed public education, gave practical advice concerning school buildings, distribution of school money, the need of local taxation, uniform schoolbooks, grading of schools, a public seminary for secondary instruction, the duties of school visitors, and the professionalization and permanency of teachers. In these documents and in the *Connecticut Common School Journal* that he established, he began his rich collection of material bearing upon popular education at home and abroad. But Barnard was more a scholar and literary man than an educational statesman like Mann. He succeeded in getting the legislature to pass several reforms and a general revision and codification of the school laws, and in arousing several towns to amend their educational plans, but the crucial difficulty of the 'school societies' could not be touched and seems to have been carefully avoided in all his discussions. He did, however, force the conservatives

and, while he did not make an attack upon the 'school societies,' the conservatives legislated him out of office.

to throw off the mask of indifference and meet him with open opposition. At the end of four years they succeeded in legislating him out of office and in undoing all his reforms.

Commissioner of Common Schools in Rhode Island.— This gave Barnard an opportunity to pursue his favorite investigations, and for about a year and a half he was engaged in collecting material for a history of education in the United States. Then he was persuaded by the governor of Rhode Island to become the first Commissioner of Common Schools for that state. While he found in Rhode Island a better educational sentiment and less opposition than in Connecticut, the actual condition of the decentralized and individualistic schools was far worse.[1] But, through his assemblies of teachers and parents and his educational treatises, he soon began to convince the people of the unwisdom of district organization, untrained teachers, short terms, irregular attendance, poor buildings and ventilation, and meager equipment. He also continued to publish his collection of educational material through the foundation of the *Rhode Island School Journal.* As a result of his efforts, when failing health compelled him to resign in 1849, the state no longer regarded wilfulness and personal opinion as praiseworthy independence, and he could honestly claim that Rhode Island had at the time one of the best school systems in the United States.

After collecting material for a history of education in the United States for a year and a half, he became the first Commissioner of Common Schools for Rhode Island, and there wrought radical reforms and published educational material in his *Rhode Island School Journal.*

State Superintendent of Schools in Connecticut.— But the *clientèle* that Barnard had built up in Connecticut continued his reforms and constructive work after his departure, and improved upon them. In 1851, they even

[1] See pp. 111f.

In 1851 he was recalled to Connecticut, and was enabled to carry out and extend his reforms.

succeeded in having him recalled virtually to his old duties. He was designated as 'State Superintendent of Common Schools,' as well as 'Principal of the State Normal School,' which had been established through the efforts of his adherents. The state had now learned its error in mingling politics with education, and Barnard was able to carry out his reforms unmolested. Through the normal school he sent out a great body of trained teachers for the schools. He revised the school code, checked the power of the 'school societies,' or districts, consolidated and simplified the organization and administration of public education, made a more equitable distribution of the school fund, and encouraged local taxation. But his most distinctive work, as might be expected, was on the literary side. He prepared a valuable series of documents upon foreign education, normal schools, methods of teaching, school architecture, and other topics, and a long report upon *The History of Legislation in Connecticut Respecting Common Schools up to 1838.* This last document was not merely a record of legislation, but a detailed and interesting history of education in Connecticut, together with a sketch of educational effort in all the other states that had made any progress

He also prepared documents upon foreign education and other topics, and a history of education in Connecticut.

While still there, he founded his *American Journal of Education*,

Barnard's American Journal of Education.—It was, too, during the last days of his Connecticut superintendency that Henry Barnard suggested the establishment of a national journal of education. He first broached the matter to the 'American Association for the Advancement of Education' at its meeting in Washington, December, 1854. But the association soon found itself unable to pursue this enterprise for lack of financial support, and in May of the next year Barnard undertook it upon his own responsibility. In a general circular he announced his intention to supply the need of "a series of publications, which should, on the one hand, embody the matured views and varied experience of wise statesmen, educators, and teachers in perfecting the organization, administration, instruction, and discipline of schools in every grade through a succession of years, under widely varying circumstances of government, society, and religion; and, on the other hand, expose real deficiencies, excite to prudent and efficient action, and serve as a medium of free and frequent communication between the friends of education in every portion of these great fields."

This was the beginning of the epoch-making work known as *Barnard's American Journal of Education.* It was planned to run the journal for five years only, but the period of publication was extended from time to time through the editor's realization of its importance. The work was somewhat interrupted upon occasions by other duties, but it continued for more than a generation, until at length thirty-one large octavo volumes, averaging about eight hundred pages each, had been issued. In addition, fifty-two special treatises reprinted from articles in the journal brought the material together in a connected way. Besides giving nearly all his time to editing this *magnum opus*, Barnard sank his entire fortune of $50,000 in its publication. Even then the returns were so small that the plates were kept from being consigned to the melting-pot, to meet his indebtedness, only at the eleventh hour by the formation of an organization of friends to save them. This great treasury of material includes every phase of the history of education from

which eventually issued thirty-one large volumes; and fifty-two special treatises were reprinted from the material

The work includes accounts of

educational history, of contemporaneous educational systems, of professional training of teachers, and of a variety of other themes.

the earliest times down into the latter half of the nineteenth century. It furnishes accounts of all contemporaneous systems in Europe and America, descriptions of institutions for the professional training of teachers, and essays upon courses of study for colleges and technical schools, the education of defectives and delinquents, physical education, school architecture, great educators, and a large variety of other themes. While it is always most reliable in its treatises upon foreign educational activity, of even greater value is its practical grasp of educational life in America from the beginning. It contains the greatest collection of interesting monographs upon the development of educational ideals and organization in the various states, and is the most complete description in literature of the educational life of a nation.

First United States Commissioner of Education.— Barnard was at various times offered the presidency of institutions of higher learning, but, with the exception of brief periods in the headship of the University of Wisconsin (1859–1861) and of St. John's College, Maryland (1866–1867), he always declined to serve in this capacity. He must have learned that he was adapted neither by health nor temperament to an administrative position, and his interest was chiefly in the common schools and educational literature. In fact, even the connection with the University of Wisconsin appealed to him mostly because of what he hoped he might be able to do for popular education and for the training of teachers through the accompanying office of Agent of the Board of Normal Regents. His work at St. John's College had barely started, when he was appointed the first United States Commissioner of Education. This office Barnard had been constantly trying to have established ever since he had found, as Secretary of the Connecticut Board, how absolutely lacking the federal government was in school statistics and educational documents. Upon several occasions he is recorded to have brought the matter before a national organization of teachers. He hoped especially to have the government, with its larger influence and greater means, perform the sort of service that he afterward undertook at his own expense in the *American Journal of Education.* In this way facilities might be secured to collect and publish reliable educational statistics, and to issue a library of independent treatises, which should, when complete, form an encyclopædia of education.

He had hoped to have the government undertake this work of publication through a commissionership of education, and, when he was called to this office, he suspended his *Journal* and used the product of his investigations in his annual reports.

The bureau was not created for many years, and then through the immediate initiative of another, but when Henry Barnard was called as first commissioner in 1867, he organized the office practically upon the lines he had previously suggested. He suspended his *Journal* and used the product of his investigations in the annual reports of the office. His wide experience with European and American educational institutions and systems, together with his splendid library, enabled him to fill his publications with rich material and accomplish the work rapidly. He started that searching inquiry into the administration, management, and instruction of educational institutions of every grade, and into all educational societies, school funds, legislation, architecture, documents, and benefactions that have since been maintained by the Bureau of Education. However, within three years a change in the national administration brought a new incumbent into the commissionership. Barnard then gave his

But three years later he was displaced in the office, and returned to his *Journal*.

literary efforts once more to his beloved *Journal*, and until his death a generation later it absorbed his entire attention.

This was his life work and marked him as the representative of the literary side of the educational awakening.

Value of Barnard's Educational Collections.—Hence an experience of more than thirty years in the inspection and administration of schools in America and illuminating visits to Europe proved only introductory and auxiliary to Barnard's real life work of collecting a great educational compendium. By temperament, native ability, and habit, he proved himself well fitted to be the leading representative of the much desiderated literary side of the awakening. Through his work American education was, in its period of greatest development, granted the opportunity of looking beyond the partial and local results of the first half century of national life. It was enabled to modify and adapt to its own uses the educational theories, practices, and organizations of the leading civilized peoples, and to bring together for a comparative view sections and states that were widely separated. Those who have criticized *Barnard's American Journal of Education* on the ground of its being confused, unskillful, and careless in its editorship, have failed to understand his true purpose.

It is not a systematic account, but a great *thesaurus* of material.

The editor did not intend to build a universal encyclopædia of education, but to do all "with special reference to the conditions and wants of our own country." To that end he often found it necessary to condense important works or to present highly scientific methods and profound philosophic systems in popular form. Nor was it possible to classify and work out a connected and complete historical account, when there were no reliable records or collections of materials in existence. It was necessary that some one should first gather the information from newspapers, pamphlets, memorials, monographs, and plans, and publish it as it was found. In this way he accomplished a more valuable work than if he had published a systematic history of education in the United States. The *Journal* was his crowning work and a means of international repute. The expositions of Vienna and Paris, as well as those in this country, decorated him with medals, and he was lauded by educators in every land. This great *thesaurus* of information and enlightenment, in connection with the virile efforts of Mann and other practical leaders in education throughout the country, has made the American educational awakening one of the most fruitful in history, and has enabled it to become both an inspiration and a guide in the remarkable development of the common schools and state educational systems that has since taken place.

SUPPLEMENTARY READING

I. Sources

BARNARD, H. *American Journal of Education.*

MANN, H. *Annual Reports of the Secretary of the Massachusetts Board of Education* (1838–1849), *Common School Journal*, and *Lectures on Education.*

MANN, MARY. *Lectures and Annual Reports on Education of Horace Mann* (Vol. II of *Atkinson's Life and Works of Horace Mann*).

SUPERINTENDENTS AND COMMISSIONERS OF EDUCATION. *Annual Reports* of schools in the various states of New England.

II. Authorities

BOWEN, F. *Mr. Mann and the Teachers of the Boston Schools* (*North American Review*, Vol. LX, pp. 224–246).

BOONE, R. G. *History of Education in the United States.* Chaps. VII–VIII.

BROWNING, O. *Henry Barnard* (*Encyclopædia Britannica*).

COMBE, G. *Education in America: State of Massachusetts* (*Edinburgh Review*, Vol. LXXIII, pp. 486–502).

DEXTER, E. G. *History of Education in the United States.* Chaps. VII–XIII.

GRAVES, F. P. *Great Educators of Three Centuries.* Chap. XIII.

HARRIS, W. T. *Horace Mann* (*Educational Review*, Vol. XII, pp. 105–119).

HINSDALE, B. A. *Horace Mann and the Common School Revival in the United States.*

MANN, MARY. *Life of Horace Mann.*

MARTIN, G. H. *Horace Mann and the Revival of Education in Massachusetts* (*Educational Review*, Vol. V, pp. 434–450).

MARTIN, G. H. *The Evolution of the Massachusetts Public School System.* Lects. IV–VI.

MAYO, A. D. *Horace Mann* and *Henry Barnard* (*Report of the United States Commissioner of Education*, 1896–1897. Vol. I, Chaps. XV and XVI).

MONROE, W. S. *The Educational Labors of Henry Barnard.*

PARKER, F. W. *Horace Mann* (*Educational Review*, Vol. XII, pp. 65–74).

WINSHIP, A. E. *Horace Mann the Educator.*

CHAPTER VII

DEVELOPMENT OF MODERN EDUCATIONAL PRACTICE

Froebel and Herbart as Disciples of Pestalozzi.—Before considering the educational development that took place later as a result of the awakening, it may now be well to take up some of the wider movements that have affected modern educational practice everywhere. In the discussion of naturalism, observation, and industrial training, we have noted great improvements taking place in educational practice and have witnessed the rise of the psychological tendency in education. The germs of this, as of other modern educational movements, were found in the suggestions of Rousseau, and were developed into more constructive and practical suggestions by the philanthropinists, Pestalozzi, and Fellenberg. The positions of Pestalozzi were somewhat vague and were based upon sympathetic insight rather than scientific principles, but, besides leaving a direct influence upon the teaching of certain subjects in the elementary curriculum, they became the basis of the elaborate systems of Herbart and Froebel. And the development of educational practice introduced by these latter educators has most profoundly affected the content and method of the course in all stages of modern training. Herbart and Froebel may be regarded as contemporary disciples and interpreters of the Swiss reformer, who was born a generation before, but they continued his work

Herbart and Froebel may be considered contemporary disciples of Pestalozzi.

along rather different lines. Each went to visit Pestalozzi, and it would seem from their comments upon what they saw that each found in the master the main principle which appealed to him and which he afterward developed more or less consistently throughout his work.

Froebel emphasized the aspect of education as natural development from within and stressed the child and his activities;

There were two very definite aspects to Pestalozzi's positions, which may at first seem opposed to each other, but are not necessarily contradictory. On the one hand, Pestalozzi seems to have held that education should be a natural development from within; on the other, that it must consist in the derivation of ideas from experience with the outside world. The former point of view would logically argue that every characteristic is innate and implicit in the child at birth in the exact form to which it is afterward to be developed, and that the teacher can at best only assist the child's nature in the efforts for its own unfolding.[1] This attitude Pestalozzi apparently borrowed from the psychology implied in Rousseau's naturalism. The other conception of education as sense perception, which is evident in Pestalozzi's observational methods,[2] depends upon the theory that immediate and direct impressions from the outside are the absolute basis of all knowledge, and holds that the contents of the mind must be entirely built up by the teacher. Some such naïve interpretation has been common since speculation began, especially among teachers, and had been formulated in Pestalozzi's day by Locke, Hume, and others. In the main, Froebel took the first of these Pestalozzian viewpoints and rarely admits the other, but

[1] This view is especially revealed in the quotations concerning his educational aim, given in Chapter V, pp. 137f.

[2] See pp. 139f.

the latter phase was developed by Herbart to the almost total disregard of the former. Hence the one educator laid emphasis upon the child's development and activities, and the other concerned himself with method and the work of the teacher.[1] The original contributions of both reformers to educational practice, however, were large, and are deserving of extended description. As Herbart began to formulate his principles somewhat before Froebel became interested in education, he will here be treated first.

Herbart in general adopted the view of education as impressions from without, and concerned himself mainly with method and the teacher.

The Early Career and Writings of Herbart.—*Johann Friedrich Herbart* (1776–1841) both by birth and by education possessed a remarkable mind and was well calculated to become a profound educational philosopher. All his traditions were intellectual. His paternal grandfather was rector of the gymnasium at Oldenburg, Herbart's native town, and his father was a lawyer and privy councilor there. Moreover, the mother of Herbart is known to have been 'a rare and wonderful woman,' who was able to assist her son in his favorite studies of Greek, mathematics, and philosophy. While still a youth in the

Herbart's traditions were all intellectual, and in the gymnasium and university he distinguished himself in Greek, mathematics, and philosophy.

[1] The *Ruling Principle of Method* by Antonio Rosmini-Serbati (1797–1855) represents a third possible development of Pestalozzi's theories. It seems to emphasize Pestalozzianism upon the emotional side, as do the doctrines of Herbart and Froebel upon the cognitional and volitional sides respectively. His professed aim was a natural development to moral perfection through obedience to law, human and divine, natural and revealed. The system also unites the ordered evolution of Froebel and the apperception of Herbart. Although it grew out of his subtle system of metaphysics, and is not fully emancipated from the scholastic effort to reduce all intellectual processes to categories, it professes to adopt the observational attitude of modern science and the psychological method. However, outside of Italy, there were few schools conducted upon his principles, and his theories have exerted little influence upon educational practice.

gymnasium, Herbart distinguished himself by writing essays upon moral freedom and other metaphysical subjects. At the University of Jena, under the inspiration of Fichte, he produced incisive critiques upon the treatises of that philosopher and of the other great idealist of the age, Schelling. He was also influenced here by the enthusiasm for Greek displayed by the advocates of 'new humanism.' This literary movement had its seat near Jena, at Weimar, the abode of Herder, Goethe, and Schiller. Herbart became an ardent student of the *Odyssey*, and among other writings produced a treatise on some musical aspects of the epics of Homer. Likewise, he continued his interest in mathematics, and his training in each of the three subjects was destined to play a part in his educational theories.

Each of the three subjects was destined to play a part in his educational theories.

Just before graduation, however, Herbart left the university to become private tutor to the three sons of Herr von Steiger-Reggisberg, Governor of Interlaken, Switzerland. During the period of almost three years (1797–1799) that he occupied this position, he obtained a most valuable practical experience. He was required by his patron to make bi-monthly a written report of the methods he used and of his pupils' progress in their studies and conduct. Five of these letters are still extant, and reveal the germs of the elaborate system that was afterward to bear the name of Herbart. The youthful pedagogue seems to have recognized the individual variations in children, and to have shown a due regard for the respective ages of his pupils, who were eight, ten, and fourteen years old. He also sought, by means of his beloved *Odyssey*, to develop in them the elements of morality and a 'many-sided interest.' This early experience, rather than his ingenious system of psychology and metaphysics, which he afterward developed in explanation, was the real foundation of his pedagogy, and furnished him with the concrete examples of the characteristics and individualities of children that appear in all his later works. He ever afterward maintained that a careful study of the development of a few children was the best preparation for a pedagogical career, and eventually made an experience of this kind the main element in his training of teachers.

but a practical experience as a private tutor was the real foundation of his pedagogy.

While still in Switzerland, Herbart met Pestalozzi and was greatly attracted by the underlying principles of that reformer. He paid a visit to the institute at Burgdorf in 1799, and during the next two years, while at Bremen completing his interrupted university course, he undertook to advocate and render more scientific the thought of the Swiss educator. It was at this time that Herbart wrote a sympathetic essay *On Pestalozzi's Latest Writing, 'How Gertrude Teaches Her Children,'* and made his interpretation of *Pestalozzi's Idea of an A B C of Observation.* In the former work, Herbart describes what he saw at Burgdorf and defends some of the methods, which had been severely criticized. He also suggests supplementing the observational work of Pestalozzi with a study of triangles. He carries this idea further in the latter treatise, and attempts, as a result of his mathematical bent, to found the methods of Pestalozzi upon a definite theory of mechanics. While in Bremen also he made public addresses in which he tried to explain and expand the Pestalozzian practice.

Having met Pestalozzi at Burgdorf, he undertook to interpret and supplement that reformer's principles in two essays.

The Moral Revelation of the World **and** ***The Science of Education.***—Following this period, from 1802 to 1809,

While lecturing at Göttingen, Herbart made a further exposition of Pestalozzi, and formulated his own *Moral Revelation of the World* and his work on *The Science of Education.*

Herbart lectured[1] on pedagogy at the University of Göttingen. While here, among other pedagogical works, he formulated his final position *On the Point of View in Judging the Pestalozzian Method of Instruction*, and published his ideas *On the Moral Revelation of the World as the Chief Function of Education.*[2] By this time he seems to have largely crystallized his own system. Pestalozzi had by his later works made evident the faults in his methods, and Herbart no longer strives to conceal their vagueness and want of system. In both of the Göttingen treatises he further insists upon 'educative instruction,' or real ethical training. Sense perception, he holds with Pestalozzi, does supply the first elements of knowledge, but the material of the school course should be arranged with reference to the general purpose of instruction, which is moral self-realization.[2] His position on the moral aim of education was made even more explicit in his standard, though deeply metaphysical, work on *The Science of Education*,[3] which he produced shortly afterward (1806).

His Seminary and Practice School at Königsberg.— In 1809 Herbart was called to the chair of philosophy at

[1] His position was at first that of a *Privatdocent*, or instructor that does not receive a regular salary, but is given a percentage of the fees of the students attending his lectures.

[2] *Ueber die ästhetische Darstellung der Welt als Hauptgeschäft der Erziehung*. With Herbart, the essence of the moral judgment is 'æsthetic' at bottom, and is entirely without proof. It deals with such relations among volitions as please or displease. This work was originally intended as an appendix to the second edition of his *Pestalozzi's Idea of an A B C of Observation*, but it proved to be a forerunner of *The Science of Education*. It contains in outline all the positions systematically developed in the more elaborate treatise.

[3] The translation of the title, *Allgemeine Pädagogik*, adopted by Felkin, is used here

Königsberg, and there did a great work for educational theory and practice. He soon established his now historic pedagogical seminary and the small practice school connected with it. This constituted the first attempt at experimentation and a scientific study of education on the basis now generally employed in universities. The students, who taught in the practice school under the supervision and criticism of the professor, were intending to become school principals and inspectors, and, through the widespread work and influence of these young Herbartians, the educational system of Prussia and of every other state in Germany was greatly advanced. In his numerous publications at Königsberg, Herbart devoted himself chiefly to works on a system of psychology as a basis for his pedagogy, but he also wrote a number of minor essays and letters upon education.

As Kant's successor at Königsberg, he established his famous pedagogical seminary and practice school, and developed a system of psychology as a basis for his pedagogy.

The Matured System in His *Outlines of Educational Doctrine*.—The conservatism and opposition to free inquiry in Prussia, however, eventually became too restrictive for a man of Herbart's progressive temperament. After serving nearly a quarter of a century in Königsberg, he accepted a call to a professorship of philosophy at Göttingen and the last eight years of his life were spent in expanding his pedagogical positions and lecturing with great approval at his old station. Here, in 1835, he issued the first edition of his *Outlines of Educational Doctrine*.[1] This treatise gives an exposition of his educational system when fully matured. It contains brief references to his mechanical metaphysics and psychology,

Late in life, he returned to Göttingen, and made the final exposition of his system in his *Outlines of Educational Doctrine*.

[1] The title is that used in Lange and De Garmo's translation. In 1835 he published his *Umriss pädagogischer Vorlesungen*, but six years later he embodied it in the new edition of his *Umriss der allgemeinen Pädagogik*.

but is as practical, sensible, and well organized a discussion of the educational process as has ever been published. The work proved to be his swan's song, for, shortly after the new edition appeared, Herbart died at the height of his reputation.

While Herbart's psychology was an afterthought, some knowledge of it will assist in understanding his educational principles.

Herbart's 'Ideas' and 'Apperception Masses.'— Herbart's metaphysical psychology grew out of his interest in philosophy, and was probably an afterthought to his educational doctrines. It seems to have been largely developed to afford a scientific basis for the method of pedagogical procedure that he had worked out of his experience as a tutor and his acquaintance with the Pestalozzian practice. But some explanation of his elaborate psychology may serve to make clearer his educational principles. With the possible exception of Kant's educational theories, Herbart's was the first real system of education that was related to a psychology invented by the founder. His psychological positions have now been almost entirely abandoned or reconstructed, but the idea of justifying educational practice through an appeal to some system of psychology, and as a logical deduction from the laws of development in the child's mind, has been productive of a marked advance in pedagogy. Herbart's system of psychology was largely an outgrowth of his own introspection. For the most part he holds that the mind is built up by the outside world, and he is generally supposed to have left no place for instincts or innate characteristics and tendencies.[1] With him the simplest elements of con-

[1] In this, however, both the devotees of Herbart, such as De Garmo was, or those more critical, like Adams, have overlooked the 'empirical' part of his *Psychology* and the whole of his *Applications of Psychology.*

sciousness are 'presentations,' or ideas, which result from the varying states into which the soul is thrown in endeavoring to maintain itself against external stimuli. They are atoms of mind stuff thrown off from the soul as the product of its contact with environment.

The main function of the soul is thus to become the parent of ideas, and the mind, which is simply the aggregate of the ideas, is gradually constructed by this 'psychological mechanism.'[1] Once produced, the ideas become existences with their own dynamic force, and constantly strive to preserve themselves. They struggle to attain as nearly as possible to the summit of consciousness, and each idea tends to draw into consciousness or heighten those allied to it, and to depress or force out those which are unlike. Hence in the constant interaction between ideas present at the same time in consciousness, 'similar' ideas fuse or combine into a homogeneous whole, and become more powerful in resisting all efforts to drive them out of consciousness; 'disparate' ideas, or those which cannot be compared, also combine, but form a complex or group rather than an indistinguishable unity; while 'contrary,' or hostile, ideas produce actual opposition, and each attempts to drive the other out of consciousness. For example, 'sweetness' and 'whiteness' would be 'disparate' ideas, since they are not of the same

He held that 'similar' ideas fuse, 'disparate' ideas combine, and 'contrary' ideas repel;

In these works he leaves as much room for the innate as could be asked, for he admits that the 'psychological mechanism' never works itself out completely. In the body, which is somehow joined with the soul, are innate predispositions, which may retard or stimulate the ideas, and "the psychological mechanism is thus interfered with in *characteristic* fashion." W. H. Kilpatrick of Columbia University has probably been the first to point out Herbart's position in this matter.

[1] See p. 200, footnote 1.

class and might co-exist in our idea of an object, but 'whiteness' and 'blackness' are so 'contrary' that one would necessarily contradict and drive the other out. Each new idea or group of ideas is, therefore, retained, modified, or rejected, according to its degree of harmony or conflict with the previously existing ideas.[1] In other words, all new ideas are interpreted through those already in consciousness.

hence we have 'apperception,' or the interpretation of all new ideas through those already in consciousness.

This principle, which Herbart called *apperception*, is the central doctrine in his whole educational system, and he works it out mathematically [2] and constantly returns to it from many different angles. In accordance with 'apperception' the teacher can hope to secure interest and the attention of the pupil to any new idea or set of ideas and have him retain it, only through making use of his body of related knowledge. The educational problem thus becomes how to present new material in such a way that it can be 'apperceived' or incorporated with the old. Hence, too, the mind of the pupil, which is thus practically built up by environment, must be largely in the hands of the teacher, since he can make or modify his 'apperception masses,' or systems of ideas.

The aim of education is the attainment of character.

The Moral and Religious Aim of Education.—In keeping with this control of the pupil's destiny by his instructors, Herbart holds that the aim of education should be to establish the moral life or character. His *Outlines* opens with the statement:

[1] See p. 198, footnote.

[2] Herbart here reveals in full his interest and training in mathematics, and develops a complete mechanics of ideas. On the analogy of psychical tensions to physical forces, he works out a system of mental statics and dynamics that may be quantitatively determined.

"The term 'virtue' expresses the whole purpose of education. Virtue is the idea of 'inner freedom,' which has developed into an abiding actuality in an individual. Whence, as inner freedom is a relation between 'insight' and 'volition,' a double task is at once set before the teacher. It becomes his business to make actual each one of these factors separately, in order that later a permanent relationship may result." [1]

This comes through 'inner freedom' or the harmonization of conduct with 'insight.'

In other words, virtue is attained by the pupil when his perception of what is right and wrong is in complete accord with his deeds, and the aim of education should, therefore, be to instil such ideas as will develop both his understanding of the moral order and a conscientious spirit in carrying it out. "To induce the pupil to make this effort," Herbart admits, "is a difficult achievement. It is easy enough, by the study of the example of others, to cultivate theoretical acumen; the moral application to the pupil himself, however, can be successfully made only in so far as his inclinations and habits have taken a direction in keeping with his insight." To make clearer the meaning of this 'inner freedom' and the moral aim, Herbart formulates subsidiary ethical concepts, which, together with the main ideal, should from the first be incorporated into the pupil's stock of ideas. But even the attainment of moral living is not sufficient.

Morality and religion are both needed.

"It is necessary to combine moral education proper, which in everyday life lays stress continually on correct self-determination, with religious training. The notion that something really worthy has been achieved, needs to be tempered by humility. Conversely, religious education has need of the moral also to forestall cant and hypocrisy." [2]

[1] *Outlines* (Lange and DeGarmo edition), p. 7.

[2] *Op. cit.*, p. 14.

'Many-sided Interest' and the 'Historical' and 'Scientific' Studies.—The making of the *morally religious man* is, therefore, Herbart's idea of the end of education. His ultimate aim must, however, be attained through instruction, and since that medium has to deal with the human mind, the more immediate purpose must be based upon psychology, just as the final goal is dependent upon ethics. It is obvious to Herbart that existing instruction has not succeeded, because it is based upon a false theory. According to his psychology, he maintains that "what is customarily ascribed to the action of the various 'faculties,' takes place in certain groups of ideas." The mind is not possessed of certain powers or forces, but consists merely of an aggregate of ideas. Hence he has no sympathy with any doctrine of 'formal discipline.' Even 'will,' upon which man's character rests, is not to be regarded as an 'independent faculty.' "Volition has its root in thought," he claims, "not, indeed, in the details one knows, but certainly in the combination and total effect of the acquired ideas." A careful study must, accordingly, be made of each pupil's thought masses, temperament, and mental capacity and processes, to determine how instruction may furnish a 'moral revelation of the world.' In Herbart's judgment:

To produce the 'morally religious man' a study must be made of his thought systems, and such studies as will appeal to them and furnish 'a moral revelation of the world' must be given him.

> "Instruction in the sense of mere information-giving contains no guarantee whatever that it will materially counteract faults and influence existing groups of ideas that are independent of the imparted information. But it is these ideas that education must reach; for the kind and extent of assistance that instruction may render to conduct may depend upon the hold it has upon them." [1]

There is not much likelihood of the pupil's receiving

[1] *Op. cit.*, p. 23.

ideas of virtue that will develop into glowing ideals of conduct when his studies do not appeal to his thought systems and are consequently regarded with indifference and aversion. They must coalesce with the ideas he already has, and thus touch his life; *interest must be felt in order that will may be aroused.* But Herbart does not limit 'interest' to a temporary stimulus for the performance of certain school tasks; he advocates the building up by education of certain broad interests that may become permanent sources of appeal in life. Interest as an end or aim,—as a permanent product of education, should be paramount and the direct result of interest as a means. Instruction must be so selected and arranged as not only to relate itself to the previous experience of the pupil, but as also to reveal and establish all the relations of life and conduct in their fullness. To expand the mental horizon and open every avenue of approach to his ideas, interests, and will, it is necessary that the pupil should be given as broad instruction as possible. In this way only can a wide range of ideas be furnished and the necessary 'many-sided interest' created.

There is needed a 'many-sided interest.' This will include interests of (1) 'knowledge,' which are divided into 'empirical,' 'speculative,' and 'æsthetic,' and of (2) 'participation,' which are divided

In analyzing the *many-sided interest*, Herbart further holds that ideas and interests spring from two main sources,—'experience,' which furnishes us with a knowledge of nature, and 'social intercourse,' from which come the sentiments toward our fellow men. Interests may, therefore, be classed as belonging to (1) 'knowledge' or to (2) 'participation.' These two sets of interests, in turn, Herbart divides into three groups each. He classes the 'knowledge' interests as (a) 'empirical,' appealing directly to the senses; (b) 'speculative,' seeking to perceive the relations of cause and effect: and (c) 'æsthetic,'

into 'sympathetic,' 'social,' and 'religious.'

resting upon the enjoyment of contemplation. The 'participation' interests are divided into (a) 'sympathetic,' dealing with relations to other individuals; (b) 'social,' including the community as a whole; and (c) 'religious,' treating one's relations to the Divine. After making this analysis of the six types of interest that are needed, he also dilates upon the dangers of one-sidedness in each case, and endeavors to "bring out more clearly the manifold phases of interest that must be taken into account." For Herbart, then, just as religious morality is the final aim of education, the more immediate purpose of instruction is 'many-sided interest.' "Instruction," he declares, "will form the circle of thought, and education the character. The last is nothing without the first. Herein is contained the whole sum of my pedagogy."

Corresponding to the two groups of interests, studies are divided into (1) 'historical,' including history, literature, and languages, and (2) 'scientific,' embracing sciences, mathematics, and industrial training.

Since character is thus to develop through the medium of instruction and the growth of concrete knowledge, which should be as broad as possible, the subject-matter of the curriculum should cover the entire range of known ideas. Hence, to correspond to the two main groups of interests, Herbart divides all studies into two main branches,—the (1) 'historical,' including history, literature, and languages; and the (2) 'scientific,' embracing mathematics, as well as the natural sciences. Although recognizing the value of both main groups of interests and studies, Herbart especially stressed the 'historical,' on the ground that history and literature are of greater importance as the sources of moral ideas and sentiments. "Other reasons aside," says he, "the need alone of counteracting selfishness renders it necessary for every school that undertakes the education of the whole man to place human conditions and relations in the foreground of instruction.

This humanistic aim should underlie the study of the 'historical' subjects, and only with reference to this aim may they be allowed to preponderate." And elsewhere, when dealing with moral development through literature and history, he argues:

"Give to children an interesting story, rich in incidents, relationships, characters, strictly in accordance with the psychological truth, and not beyond the feelings and ideas of children; make no effort to depict the worst or the best, only let a faint, half-unconscious moral tact secure that the interest of the action tends away from the bad towards the good, the just, the right; then you will see how the child's attention is fixed upon it, how it seeks to discover the truth and thinks over all sides of the matter, how the many-sided material calls forth a many-sided judgment, how the charm of change ends in preference for the best, so that the boy, who perhaps feels himself a step or two higher in moral judgment than the hero or the author, will cling to his view with inner approbation, and so guard himself from a coarseness he already feels beneath him." [1]

The best starting-point and source of material for this moral training through the 'historical' subjects, Herbart, with his 'new humanistic' devotion to Greek literature, felt was to be found in Homer's *Odyssey*. He was chiefly interested in the work of the secondary school, but his principles were applied especially to elementary education by his followers. Herbart has in this way greatly influenced both stages of education in the teaching of history and literature for moral training, and has effected a great improvement in the methods of teaching these subjects.

'Correlation,' 'Concentration,' 'Culture Epochs.'— But, while all the subjects, 'historical' and 'scientific,' are

[1] *Science of Education* (Felkin edition), p. 89.

But, while many-sided-ness is desirable, all studies must be unified, and scattering avoided.

needed for a 'many-sided interest' and the various studies have for convenience been separated and classified by themselves, they must be so arranged in the curriculum as to become unified and an organic whole, if the unity of the pupil's consciousness is to be maintained. Concerning this, Herbart holds:—

> "Scattering no less than one-sidedness forms an antithesis to many-sidedness. Many-sidedness is to be the basis of virtue; but the latter is an attribute of personality, hence it is evident that the unity of self-consciousness must not be impaired. The business of instruction is to form the person on many sides, and accordingly to avoid a distracting or dissipating effect. And instruction has successfully avoided this in the case of one who with ease surveys his well-arranged knowledge *in all of its unifying relations* and holds it together as *his very own*." [1]

Hence the Herbartians formulated 'correlation' and 'concentration,' and the 'culture epochs theory,'

This position of Herbart forecasts the emphasis upon *correlation*, or the unification of studies, so common among his followers. The principle was further developed by later Herbartians under the name of *concentration*, or the unifying of all subjects around one or two common central studies, such as literature or history. But the selection and articulation of the subject-matter in such a way as to arouse many-sidedness and harmony is not more than hinted at by Herbart himself. He specifically holds, however, that the *Odyssey* should be the first work read, since this represents the interests and activities of the race while in its youth, and would appeal to the individual during the same stage. He would follow this epic with the *Iliad*, the *Philoctetes* of Sophocles, the histories of Xenophon, Plato's dialogues, and other classics, in the order of the growing complexity of racial interests

[1] *Outlines*, p. 49

depicted in them.[1] This tentative endeavor of Herbart, in the selection of material for the course of study, to parallel the development of the individual with that of the race, was continued and enlarged by his disciples. It especially became definite and fixed in the *culture epochs theory* formulated by Ziller and others.[2]

The 'Formal Steps of Instruction.'—But to secure this broad range of material and to unify and systematize it, Herbart realized that it was necessary to formulate a method of instructing the child. Due sequence and order must be introduced to shape the material into a well-arranged structure. This plan of instruction he wished to conform to the development and working of the human mind, and in this connection introduced his distinction between *absorption and reflection*.[3] This twofold mental process is necessary in grasping all new knowledge, and the alternation between the two steps has sometimes been described as the 'breathing' of the mind. 'Absorption' is giving oneself up to acquisition or contemplation of facts or ideas, and 'reflection' is the unification or assimilation of the manifold knowledge gained by absorption. As these two stages are mutually exclusive, the pupil passes in psychical development from one to the other. On the basis of this description of mental activity and growth, Herbart worked out the outlines of his logical method in instruction, which he states as follows:—

In the educational process Herbart distinguished between 'absorption,' the acquisition of facts, and 'reflection,' the assimilation of knowledge thus gained;

"We prescribe the general rule: give equal prominence to absorption and reflection in every group of objects, even the smallest;

[1] Herbart's attitude on the development of interests in the race is most fully brought out in his *Science of Education*, Introduction and Chapter V, 1.

[2] See pp. 213f.

[3] See *Outlines*, §§ 66–67, and *Science of Education*, Bk. II, Chap. I, § 1

that is to say, emphasize equally clearness of the individual perception, association of the manifold, coördination of the associated, and progress through exercise according to this coördination."

and formulated the four steps in his method of instruction,—'clearness,' 'association,' 'system,' and 'method,' which have been expanded and modified by the Herbartians.

Of the four steps indicated in this method, (1) *clearness*, the presentation of facts or elements to be learned, is purely 'absorption'; (2) *association*, the uniting of these with related facts previously acquired, is mainly 'absorption,' but contains elements of 'reflection'; (3) *system*, the coherent and logical arrangement of what has been associated, is non-progressive or passive 'reflection'; and (4) *method*, the practical application of the system by the pupil to new data, is progressive or active 'reflection.'[1] The formulation of this method was made only in principle by Herbart, but it has since been largely modified and developed by his followers. It was soon felt that, on the principle of 'apperception,' the pupil must first be made conscious of the existing stock of ideas so far as they are similar to the material to be presented, and that this can be accomplished by a review of preceding lessons or by an outline of what is to be undertaken, or by both procedures. Hence Herbart's noted disciple, Ziller, divided the step of 'clearness' into *preparation* and *presentation*, and the more recent Herbartian, Rein, added *aim* as a substep to 'preparation.' The names of the other three processes have been changed for the sake of greater lucidity and significance by the later Herbartians, and the *five formal* (*i. e.* 'rational') *steps of instruction* are now generally given as (1) *preparation*, (2) *presentation*, (3) *comparison and abstraction*, (4) *generalization*, and (5) *application*.[2] Herbart also made numerous other sugges-

[1] See *Outlines*, §§ 66–67, and *Science of Education*, Bk. II, Chap. I, § 1.
[2] *Cf.* McMurry's *Method of the Recitation.*

tive analyses and interpretations of the mechanics of instruction.

Herbart clarified the 'psychologizing instruction' and the beginning with sense perception of Pestalozzi, through an original system of psychology and the principle of 'apperception,' and made all tend toward moral development.

The Value and Influence of Herbart's Principles.— On all sides, then, as compared with Pestalozzi, Herbart was most logical and comprehensive. Where Pestalozzi obtained his methods from a sympathetic insight into the child mind, Herbart sought to found his upon scientific principles. The former was primarily a philanthropist and reformer; the latter a psychologist and scientific educationalist. Pestalozzi succeeded in arousing Europe to the need of universal education and of vitalizing the prevailing formalism in the schools, but he was unable with his vague and unsystematic utterances to give guidance and efficiency to the reform forces he had initiated. While he felt the need of 'psychologizing instruction' and of beginning with sense perception for the sake of clear ideas, he had neither the time nor the training to construct a psychology beyond the traditional one of the times, nor to analyze the way in which the material gained by observation is assimilated. Herbart, on the other hand, did create a system of psychology that, although subsequent to, and possibly not altogether consistent with, his educational practice, had an immediate bearing upon it. While his psychological system is fanciful and mechanical, and applies better as an explanation of the process of instruction than as a description of human thought, it largely started the fruitful research in psycho-physics of modern times, and has worked well as a basis for educational theory and practice. Moreover, it undertook to show how ideas, which were the product of the Pestalozzian 'observation,' were assimilated through 'apperception,' and maintained the possibility of making all material tend toward moral development through 'educative instruction.' This, he held, could be accomplished by use of proper courses and methods. In determining the subjects to be selected and articulated, he considered Pestalozzi's emphasis upon the study of the physical world to be merely a stepping-stone to his own 'moral revelation of the world.' While the former educator made arithmetic, geography, natural science, reading, form study, drawing, writing, and music the object of his consideration, and is indirectly responsible for the modern reforms in teaching these subjects, Herbart preferred to stress history, languages, and literature, and, through his followers, brought about improved methods in their presentation. He also first undertook a careful analysis of the successive steps in all instruction, and by his methodical principles has done much to introduce order and system into the work of the classroom.

He made Pestalozzi's emphasis upon the physical world a stepping-stone, and, stressing history, languages, and literature, through his followers brought about improved methods of teaching them.

On the other hand, a great drawback to the Herbartian doctrines is found in their formalization and exaggeration. For these tendencies his enthusiastic and literal-minded followers, rather than Herbart himself, have probably been to blame. No man has suffered more from the elaborations and interpretations of dogmatic disciples than Herbart. He was himself too keen an observer and too sane a teacher to allow his doctrines to go upon all fours. He is ordinarily credited by Herbartians with a psychology that takes no account of heredity or the innate characteristics of each mind, but holds that the mind is entirely built up by impressions from the outside and is merely a product of environment. While this is the position at which he arrives by pure speculation in his 'rational' psychology, he recognizes in his 'empirical'

While Herbart's principles have tended toward formalization and exaggeration in the hands of his disciples, his own attitude was evidently more sane and flexible.

psychology that there must be certain native predispositions in the body which influence the soul in one direction or another.[1] This limitation of complete plasticity by the pupil's individuality, and of the consequent influence of the teacher, is also admitted in his educational doctrine, and he declares that, "in order to gain an adequate knowledge of each pupil's capacity for education, observation is necessary—observation both of his thought masses and of his physical nature. The study of the latter includes that of temperament, especially with reference to emotional susceptibility." [2] Again, while Herbart holds that every subject should, if possible, be presented in an attractive, interesting, and 'almost playlike' way, he does not justify that 'sugar-coated interest' which has so often put Herbartianism in bad odor. "A view that regards the end as a necessary evil to be rendered endurable by means of sweetmeats," says he, "implies an utter confusion of ideas; and if pupils are not given serious tasks to perform, they will not find out what they are able to do."[3] Often, he realizes, "even the best method cannot secure an adequate degree of apperceiving attention from every pupil, and recourse must accordingly be had to the voluntary attention; *i. e.* to the pupil's resolution."[4] Similarly, the notion of some Herbartians that the goal of teaching is attained with the securing of apperception and interest, and that effortful memorizing is never desirable, finds no sanction in the master's statement that "voluntary attention is most frequently demanded for memorizing, for which, apart from all else, the presence of interest is not always a per-

[1] See footnote on p. 198.

[2] *Outlines*, p. 22.

[3] *Op. cit.*, p. 96.

[4] *Op. cit.*, p. 71.

fectly favorable condition."[1] Again, 'correlation' between different subjects, as well as between principles within the same subject, was advocated by Herbart, but he felt that such ramifications should not be unlimited, and held it "an error to argue that one who is being initiated into one subject ought to combine with that subject a second, third, or fourth, on the ground that subjects one, two, three, and four are essentially interrelated."[2]

Further, while Herbart made some effort in shaping the course of study to parallel the development of the individual with that of the race, it was Ziller that erected this procedure into a hard and fast theory of 'culture epochs.' But most common of all has been the tendency of his disciples to pervert the attempt of Herbart to bring about due sequence and arrangement into an inflexible *schema* in the recitation, and to make the formal steps an end rather than a means. These steps may be used to enable the novice in teaching to prepare himself for class work by arranging the materials he wishes to present after an organized plan, but they do not represent definite fixed stages that must be followed without exception in every recitation, nor do they correspond to the steps taken in the inductive method of science or logical reasoning in general, as has sometimes been supposed. Moreover, there is reason to believe that Herbart did not intend that all these steps should be carried out in every recitation, but felt that they applied to the organization of any subject as a whole, and that years might even elapse between the various steps.[3] In this respect, as in

[1] *Op. cit.*, p. 71. [2] *Op. cit.*, p. 211.

[3] For a fair-minded criticism of the 'five-step method,' read Dewey's *How We Think* (New York, 1910), Chapter XV.

the others, the doctrines of Herbart should not be confused with the wooden interpretations of certain Herbartians.

The Extension of His Doctrines through Disciples in Germany.—Thus the theoretical foundations of Herbart were laid mostly in outline, but some of his disciples undertook to fill in, extend, and somewhat crystallize his ideas. They reduced his theories to practice and applied them to the content and methods of the elementary and secondary systems of Germany. At first the doctrines of Herbart were little known, but a quarter of a century after his death there sprang up two flourishing contemporary schools of Herbartianism. In its application of Herbart's theory, the school of Stoy for the most part held closely to the original form; but that headed by Ziller gave it a freer and more extreme interpretation, and contributed several important modifications and elaborations to the theories. *Tuiskon Ziller* (1817–1883), both as teacher in a gymnasium and as professor at Leipzig, did much to popularize and develop the Herbartian system. His great work, *The Basis of the Doctrine of Educative Instruction*, which was published in 1865, brought Herbartianism into prominence, and resulted in the formation of the society known as the 'Association for the Scientific Study of Education,' which has since spread throughout Germany. Ziller further emphasized Herbart's division of the curriculum into two groups of studies, and made clear the subordination of the 'scientific' studies to the 'historical.' He also elaborated the doctrines of 'correlation' and 'concentration,' and was the first definitely to formulate the 'culture epochs' theory. "Every pupil should," said he, "pass successively

A quarter of a century after Herbart's death, his system was popularized and greatly developed and fixed by Ziller;

through each of the chief epochs of the general mental development of mankind suitable to his stage of development. The material of instruction, therefore, should be drawn from the thought material of that stage of historical development in culture, which runs parallel with the present mental stage of the pupil." This theory of culture epochs, like the biological theory of 'recapitulation,' of which it is a pedagogical application, is now admitted by most educators to be thoroughly inconsistent. While it has occasioned much academic discussion, few educators, beside Ziller, have ventured to embody it completely in a course of study. But Ziller worked out all his principles practically in a curriculum for the eight years of the elementary school, which he centered around fairy tales, *Robinson Crusoe*, and selections from the *Old* and *New Testaments*. He, moreover, developed Herbart's 'formal stages of instruction' by dividing the first step and changing the name of the last.[1]

and a most influential Herbartian pedagogical seminary and practice school was started at Jena by the conservative Stoy, which since 1885 has been continued by the more original Rein.

Karl Volkmar Stoy (1815–1885), the founder of the other school, gave less attention than Ziller to the development of the Herbartian theories, and his numerous educational works were mainly a forceful restatement of the master's positions. On the other hand, in 1874 he established a most influential pedagogical seminary and practice school upon the original Herbartian basis at Jena, where he had become a professor. And eleven years later, *Wilhelm Rein* (1847–), who had been a pupil of both Stoy and Ziller, succeeded the former in the direction of the practice school, and introduced there the elaborate development that had taken place since Herbart's time. He adopted Ziller's 'concentration,' 'cul-

[1] See p. 208.

ture epochs,' and other features, but made them a little more elastic by coördinating other material with the 'historical' center in the curriculum. Rein had previously worked out a course of study for the eight years of the *Volksschule* (*i. e.* elementary school) in great detail, and, by his embodiment of this in the practice school, Jena became the great center of Herbartianism. Those studying the Herbartian methods there had each lesson illustrated through a visit to a class, followed by a thorough discussion of the principles and problems involved therein. Most of the prominent Herbartians in other countries, especially the United States, obtained their first interest through a residence at Jena.

Herbartianism has also been influenced by Lange, Frick, and others.

Other Germans to influence Herbartianism have been Lange and Frick. The *Apperception* of Karl Lange is an excellent combination of scientific insight and popular presentation. It treats the various problems of education on the basis that "all learning is apperceiving." Lange agrees in general with the Herbartian method, but warns against its possible mechanics and formalism. Otto Frick, director of the 'Francke Institutions' at Halle,[1] inclining more to the close interpretation of Stoy, devoted himself to applying Herbartianism to the secondary schools. An organic course for the 'gymnasium' (*i. e.* the classical secondary school) was outlined in the eighth number of the *Quarterly Magazine*, which he edited. A throng of other German schoolmasters and professors have further adapted the doctrines of Herbart to school practice, and while their theories differ very largely from one

[1] See Graves, *History of Education during the Transition*, pp. 300ff.; *Great Educators*, pp. 68ff.

another, from their common basis they are all properly designated 'Herbartian.'

The content and methods of education have, through this propaganda, been greatly modified.

In consequence of this continuous propaganda of the Herbartian doctrines, the content and methods of the school curricula in Germany have been largely modified. Herbart's emphasis upon the importance to the secondary schools of literary and historical studies as a moral training, especially through the medium of the Greek writers, has not, however, been as strongly felt as the adaptation of this idea to the elementary schools by the later Herbartians in the form of story and biographical material. Since the development of the empire, with its stimulus to improvement in elementary education, there has been a wide adoption of the Herbartian practice. History has attained a more prominent place in the curriculum, and is no longer auxiliary to reading and geography. It is regarded as a means of moral development, and the cultural features in the history of the German people are stressed more than the political. Ziller's plan for concentrating all studies about a core of history and literature, on the ground of thus producing 'a moral revelation of the world' for the pupil, is in evidence everywhere. A twofold course,—Jewish history through Bible stories, and German history in the form of legends and tales, appears in every grade of the elementary school after the first two, and even in these lower classes there is some attempt to utilize literature as a moral training through the medium of fairy stories, fables, moral tales, *Robinson Crusoe*, and the various contributions of the philanthropinists.[1]

In the elementary curriculum history has attained a more prominent place, and the cultural features of the subject are stressed.

Ziller's 'concentration' to produce a 'moral revelation' is seen in the course of Jewish and German history in the form of legends, and in the informal literary material of the lowest grades.

Herbartianism in the United States.—Next to the

[1] See pp. 28ff.

land of its birth, the United States has been more influenced by Herbartianism than any other country. The movement was fostered largely by American teachers who had taken the doctor's degree at Jena during the late eighties, and during the last decade of the nineteenth century it attained almost to the proportions of a cult. The movement centered chiefly in northern Illinois, and was especially strong in the normal schools. Much of the organization of the practice school at Jena was adopted with practically no modification in a large number of American normal schools. In 1892 'The National Herbart Society' was founded to extend the scope of these principles and to adapt them to American conditions, and included many prominent educators in its membership. The association started immediately to translate the works of Herbart and various German Herbartians, and since 1895 it has regularly published a *Year Book*. In this journal, during the first years of the society, it reproduced its discussions concerning apperception, interest, correlation, educative instruction, and other purely Herbartian themes. Besides these efforts, individual members of the organization have been active in discussing Herbartian principles and their embodiment in American methods of instruction. Charles DeGarmo, for sixteen years professor of Education at Cornell University, as early as 1889 published *The Essentials of Method*, which embodied the Herbartian theories, and gave them a wide popularity. He became the first president of the Herbart Society and editor of its publications, and has utilized Herbartian principles as the basis of a number of excellent text-books. Charles A. McMurry of the Illinois State Normal University, and his brother, Frank M.

In the United States Herbartianism was developed during the nineties by 'The National Herbart Society, and their translations and *Year Book*.

Individual members of the society, like DeGarmo and the McMurrys, also made important contributions.

McMurry of the Columbia Teachers College, both by books and articles, have done yeoman service for Herbartianism. In 1897 they published jointly *The Method of the Recitation*. Five years before Charles McMurry had brought out a *General Method*, and since then he has produced a number of works on special method, covering most subjects of the elementary curriculum.

Likewise, Herbartian features have frequently been adopted by other educators, as in the case of Parker, Jackman, and the Committee of Fifteen.

Moreover, many who would hardly consider themselves Herbartians have undertaken to modify and adapt these principles, especially correlation and concentration. Francis W. Parker of Chicago, among the phases of his educational practice, approached Ziller's principle of concentration so closely as to center the entire course of study around a hierarchy of natural and social sciences. But, as a rule, the more moderate type of correlation suggested by Herbart himself has been used, and such interrelations as those between arithmetic and manual training, history and literature, and geography and history have been developed by many educators. A correlation even of science and history was attempted by the late Wilbur S. Jackman, Colonel Parker's associate. The Committee of Fifteen, appointed by the National Education Association to report upon elementary education, show a strong Herbartian influence in their discussions of correlation, although they give the term a wider interpretation. Various other types of unification about a center of literature, history, or nature study, or, through combination with Froebelianism, of social activities, have been suggested.

The elementary curriculum has received important reforms

Largely as a result of the development of Herbartianism, a reform in the content of the curriculum has also become general in American elementary schools. This is especially noticeable in the increased amount and larger utilization of historical material. Beside the Herbartian, other factors were probably responsible for this development, but the work of the disciples of Rein undoubtedly played a leading part in encouraging a broader conception of the function of history. A wide appreciation of the growth of morality, culture, and social life in general, rather than merely the development of patriotism, became the object in studying this subject. English and German history, as well as the American, which alone was formerly taught, and sometimes Greek, Roman, and Norse, appear in the curricula of many elementary schools, and, instead of being confined to the two upper classes, historical material is often presented from the third grade up. Biographical and historical stories are largely employed in the lower classes, while in the upper some attempt is made to use European history as a setting for American, and throughout there is made as broad a study of social conditions as possible, rather than a mere account of wars and political changes. A similar development in the amount and use of literature also appears in the course of the elementary schools as a result of the Herbartian influence. Instead of brief selections from the best English and American writers, or even the poorer material that formerly appeared in the school readers, complete works of literature have begun to be studied in the elementary curriculum, and a wide and rapid survey of the great English classics has been encouraged in the place of merely reading for the sake of oral expression. Even in the lowest grades some attempt to introduce the classics of childhood has been made. While many committees and individual educators have

through the Herbartian movement.

A wide range of history from the cultural and social standpoint has come to be presented from the third grade up,

and a study of complete works of literature and a wide survey of the great English classics have taken the place of the former poor material in the elementary course.

assisted in this advance, the Herbartians have certainly been most prominent in the movement.

But Herbartianism itself has been abandoned for less dogmatic methods.

While in these ways all elementary, and to some extent secondary, schools have been affected, Herbartianism pure and simple has largely been abandoned for less dogmatic methods. Even the Herbart Society has ceased to exist as a propaganda, and has since 1902 been known as 'The National Society for the Scientific Study of Education.' But, although professed Herbartians are now almost unknown in the United States, no other system of pedagogy, except that of Pestalozzi, has ever had so wide an influence upon American education and upon the thought and practice of teachers generally.

Froebel's Early Life.—Let us now turn to Froebel, the other great successor of Pestalozzi, and to his development and extension of the master's principle of 'natural development.' *Friedrich Wilhelm August Froebel* (1782–1852) was born in Oberweissbach, a village in the Thüringian forest. The influence in his home was religious, but, owing to the preöccupation of his father and step-mother, he spent much time roving about the mysterious woods. Here he pondered upon the plants, animals, and various phenomena of nature, and there began within him a vein of mysticism and search for hidden unity. His formal schooling was very scattering, and at fifteen he was for two years apprenticed to a forester. His master was not able to afford him proper instruction, but the youth continued his religious communion with nature, and further enlarged his wood lore and practical acquaintance with plants. At length, Froebel's hunger for a knowledge of the natural sciences impelled him to enter the university at Jena. The atmosphere about this

Froebel's religious training and early life in the forest may have started his vein of mysticism and search for unity.

At the University of Jena he was affected by the idealistic philosophy,

institution was charged with the idealistic philosophy, the romantic movement, and the evolutionary attitude in science. Froebel could not have escaped the discussions upon Fichtian philosophy, which were current upon the street, at the table, and in every informal place of meeting, and he must have witnessed the academic growth of Fichte's pupil and colleague, Schelling. He must likewise have fallen under the spell of the Jena romanticists,—the Schlegels, Tieck, and Novalis, and possibly even of their friends and protectors, Goethe and Schiller. The advanced attitude in science at Jena may also have impressed the youth. While much of the science instruction failed to make clear that inner relation and mystic unity for which he sought, he must occasionally have caught glimpses of it in the lectures of the professors. Unhappily, after a couple of years, all this enchanted world was closed to him through financial difficulties, and he was forced to return home.

romanticism, and advanced attitude in science.

His Adoption of Teaching, and the Crystallization of His Law of 'Unity.'—For the next four years, Froebel was wandering and groping for a niche in life. Eventually, in 1805, while beginning the study of architecture in Frankfort, he met Anton Grüner, head of a Pestalozzian model school, who persuaded him of his fitness for teaching and gave him a position in the institution. Here he undertook a systematic study of Pestalozzianism under the guidance of Grüner, and began to develop his own principles and methods. Through the use of modeling in paper, pasteboard, and wood with some private pupils, he came to see the value of motor expression as a means of education. After three years in Frankfort he withdrew to study and practice at Yverdon. The two years he

Through Grüner he stumbled upon his life work of teaching.

After three years of teaching, he studied with Pestalozzi at Yverdon, and learned much about physiography, nature study, play of children, training by mothers, and music.

spent there proved most profitable. He gained much from the training in physiography and nature study that he gave the pupils during long walks in the country; he found an opportunity to study the play of children in its effect upon intellectual as well as physical development; he first came to attach importance to that earliest training of a child by its mother; and his knowledge of music, which was to play so important a part in his methods, was greatly enlarged. As a further result of his stay in Yverdon, Froebel began to see more than ever the need of a broader training, if he were going to unify education, and as soon as possible he gave up his work in Frankfort, and renewed his university studies. He went first to Göttingen in 1811, but was the next year attracted to Berlin by the reputation of Professor Weiss in mineralogy. While with Weiss, he became fully "convinced of the demonstrable connection in all cosmic development," and declared that "thereafter my rocks and crystals served me as a mirror wherein I might discern mankind, and man's development and history." Thus he crystallized that mystic law of 'unity' with which he had long been struggling.

He next studied at the University of Berlin and crystallized his mystic law of 'unity.'

The School at Keilhau and the *Education of Man*.—Except for a year of service in the Prussian army, where he met his enthusiastic young friends and lifelong assistants, Langethal and Middendorf, Froebel remained at Berlin for four studious years. But he never lost sight of his original purpose of educational reform. While at the university he continued his study of child nature by teaching in the Pestalozzian school of Plamann,[1] and, in 1816, he undertook the education of five young nephews,

In 1816, with Langethal and Middendorf, he started his 'Universal German Institute' at Keilhau.

[1] See footnote 1 on p. 146.

with the hope of working out his pedagogical theories. In this venture he was soon joined by Middendorf and Langethal, and with them he founded 'The Universal German Institute of Education' at the Thüringian village of Keilhau. The education there aimed to develop the pupils harmoniously in all their powers through the exercise of their own activity in subjects whose relations with one another and with life had been carefully thought out. Self-expression, free development, and social participation were the ruling principles of the school. Much of the training was obtained through play, and, except that the pupils were older, the germ of the kindergarten was already present. There was much practical work in the open air, in the garden about the schoolhouse, and in the building itself. The children built dams and mills, fortresses and castles, and searched the woods for animals, birds, insects, and flowers. They learned to work out practical problems in form and number, and had the world of imagination opened to them through romances, ballads, and war-songs.

There he trained his pupils to self-expression through play, construction, nature study, and romances and ballads;

To popularize the institute, Froebel published in 1826 a complete account of the theory practiced at Keilhau in his famous *Education of Man*. While this work is compressed, repetitious, and vague, and its doctrines had afterward to be corrected by experience, it contains the most systematic statement of his educational philosophy that Froebel ever made. It describes Froebel's interpretation of the universe and the consequent meaning of human life, makes an exposition of his chief principles of education, and applies them to the various stages of life and to the chief school subjects. But the times were not ripe for the radical educational methods

and, to popularize his principles, in 1826 published his *Education of Man*.

practiced in the community at Keilhau. The institute was suspected of socialistic tendencies, and the government inspector of schools was ordered to investigate. This official, however, reported that he "found here a closely united family of some sixty members held together in mutual confidence and every member seeking the good of the whole. . . . That this union must have the most salutary influence on instruction and training and on the pupils themselves, is self-evident. . . . No slumbering power remains unawakened; each finds the stimulus it needs in so large a family. . . . The aim of the institution is by no means knowledge and science merely, but free self-active development of the mind from within."

For various reasons Froebel transferred his work to Switzerland; while there, he began to devise playthings, games, songs, and movements, as a means of training; and in 1837 he started his 'Kindergarten' at Blankenburg, and six years later published his *Mother Play and Nursery Songs*.

Development of the Kindergarten and Froebel's Later Works.—Nevertheless, gossip and detraction did not cease, and, for various reasons, the school soon found itself in serious straits. Froebel then strove to secure some place where he might not only rehabilitate himself, but even extend his work and give it a firmer basis. He went to Switzerland, and for five years (1832–1837) he continued his educational experiments in various locations there. Eventually, in 1835, while conducting a model school at Burgdorf, it became obvious to him that "all school education was yet without a proper initial foundation, and that, until the education of the nursery was reformed, nothing solid and worthy could be attained." The *School of Infancy* of Comenius [1] had been called to his attention and "the necessity of training gifted and capable mothers" had been growing upon him. The ed-

[1] For Comenius and *The School of Infancy*, see Graves, *History of Education during the Transition*, pp. 275f.; *Great Educators*, pp. 33f.

ucational importance of play now appealed to him more strongly than ever. He began to study and devise playthings, games, songs, and bodily movements that would be of value in the development of small children, although at first he did not organize his materials into a system. Then, two years later, when his wife's failing health compelled him to return to Germany, he actually established a school for children between the ages of three and seven. This institution was located at Blankenburg, two miles from Keilhau, in one of the most romantic spots in the Thüringian Forest, and was before long appropriately christened 'Kindergarten.'[1] Here he put into use the material he had invented in Switzerland, added new devices, and developed his system. The main features of this were the 'play songs' for mother and child; the series of six 'gifts,' consisting of the sphere, cube, and other geometrical forms; and the 'occupations,' which applied to different constructions the principles the child had learned through the 'gifts.' During his seven years in Blankenburg, he constantly expanded his principles and added new material, and the accounts of these additions have been collected in the works known generally as *Pedagogics of the Kindergarten* and *Education by Development.* By 1843 he had also enlarged his collection of songs into that attractive and popular book known as *Mother Play and Nursery Songs*. This work was intended to illustrate concretely the principles and methods suggested in the *Education of Man.*

[1] That is to say, a 'garden' in which 'children' are the unfolding plants. Froebel at first called the institution by the cumbersome and uneuphonious name of *Kleinkinderbeschäftigungsanstalt* or *Anstalt für Kleinkinderpflege*, and the term *Kindergarten* came to him like an inspiration one day while walking in the forest.

His want of financial ability forced him to close the school, and, after five years of lecturing, he settled down at Liebenstein.

The kindergarten attracted considerable attention, and many teachers came to Blankenburg to study the system, but Froebel's want of financial ability compelled him to close the institution after an existence of only seven years. The next five years he spent largely in travelling about Germany and lecturing upon his system, with much success, especially before groups of mothers and women teachers. In 1849 he settled down near the famous mineral springs at Liebenstein in Saxe-Meiningen, and married his favorite kindergartner.[1] During this period Froebel obtained the friendship and support of the Baroness Berthe von Marenholtz-Bülow, who brought a large number of people of distinction in the political and educational world to see his work in operation, and secured a magnificent seat for his institution upon the neighboring estate of Marienthal. She also wrote most interesting *Reminiscences* of Froebel's activities during the last thirteen years of his life, and after his death she spread his principles throughout most of Europe. Froebel's closing days now bade fair to be most happy and successful, but in 1851, through a confusion of his principles with the socialistic doctrines of his nephew Karl, a decree was promulgated in Prussia by the minister of education, closing all kindergartens there. Froebel never recovered from this unjust humiliation, and died within a year.

Through Baroness von Bülow, he made many influential friends, but in 1852 Prussia issued a decree against kindergartens, and Froebel died under the strain.

His underlying principles go back to Pestalozzi and Rousseau, but his conception and

Froebel's Fundamental Principle of 'Unity' and Its Applications.—Such, in brief, is the historical development of Froebel's positions, as they were expanded and corrected by application to practical teaching, and came to their culmination in the kindergarten. While his

[1] His first wife had died in 1839.

underlying principles go back to the developmental aspect of Pestalozzi's doctrines and even to Rousseau's naturalism, his conception of them, his imagery, and statement, seem to be a joint product of the religious influences of his boyhood and possibly his early communion with nature,[1] combined with the idealistic philosophy, the romantic movement, and the scientific spirit of the day. These latter tendencies seem to have been assimilated by Froebel not only through his residence in Jena and Berlin, but through the influence of Langethal, Middendorf, and his first wife. His conclusions as to educational theory and practice would have been possible as inferences from a very different point of view, but as he developed them logically and consistently with his metaphysical position, it may be of value to consider briefly the groundwork of the Froebelian philosophy. This would seem the more important because at least one class of his present-day followers have deemed his philosophy absolutely essential to a proper understanding of his practices.

statement of them are the product of boyhood experiences, the idealism, the romanticism and the scientific thought of the times.

From idealism Froebel probably took that interpretation of the universe which holds to the unity of nature with the soul of man. The 'Absolute,' or God, he regarded as the self-conscious spirit from which originated both man and nature, and he consequently adopted an organic and unitary view of life.[2] This was probably emphasized

[1] It seems likely that Froebel has exaggerated the impression made on him by these boyhood experiences. Probably the chief influences in shaping his philosophy were those with which he came in contact at the University of Jena.

[2] Froebel is unconsciously following Schelling, when he talks of nature, symbolism, or æsthetics; and Fichte, when he deals with will, duty, personality, and morality. Most striking is his resemblance to Schelling,

through the scientific thought of the times, in which appear a feeling of unity and inner relation and a conception of ordered evolution.[1] Similarly, the weird religious experiences of his youth may have drawn him to the mysticism and symbolism of the current romanticism. Hence, while his writings are scientific in form, they appear vague and sentimental, and are filled with an extreme symbolism. His fundamental view of organic unity appears in his general conception of the universe, and the *Education of Man* opens with the statement:—

He holds to organic 'unity' in the universe,

> "In all things there lives and reigns an eternal law. . . . This law has been and is enounced with equal clearness and distinctness in nature (the external), in the spirit (the internal), and in life, which unites the two. This all-controlling law is necessarily based on an all-pervading, energetic, living, self-conscious, and hence eternal Unity. . . . This Unity is God. All things have come from the Divine Unity, from God, and have their origin in the Divine Unity, in God alone. All things live and have their being in and through the Divine Unity, in and through God. The divine effluence that lives in each thing is the essence of each thing.[2]

and from it derives a number of subsidiary educational ideals,—

This fundamental mystic conception Froebel constantly reiterates in various forms, and from it derives a number of educational ideals. But as these subsidiary

especially as he seems to have borrowed some of his phraseology from the pupil of Schelling, his friend Krause.

[1] See pp. 220f. One of the science lecturers at Jena seems to have had some idea of the "interrelations of all animals" and to have foreshadowed Darwinism in his conception of man as "but a more developed type which all the lower forms are striving to realize." Judging from the strong similarity of Froebel's works in thought and diction to those of Oken, it may well be that the school of *Naturphilosophie* was more influential than either idealism or romanticism in shaping his point of view. An unpublished paper by W. H. Kilpatrick of Columbia University makes this relation very likely.

[2] *Education of Man* (Hailmann edition), pp. 1 and 2.

conceptions do not play a prominent part in the actual practice of his system, it is sufficient to give them in outline only. As corollaries of the *unity* of man and nature, Froebel holds to *continuity* in creation and progressive development from the lower to the higher grades of being both in the history of the race and in the life of the individual. On the one hand, he holds, "God develops the most minute and imperfect elements, through ever-rising stages, according to a law eternally founded in itself"; on the other, "it is highly pernicious to consider the stages of human development—infant, child, boy or girl, man or woman—as really distinct, and not, as life shows them, as continuous in themselves in unbroken transitions." In carrying out the former of these interpretations of 'continuity,' Froebel approaches the Herbartian theory of 'culture epochs' by holding that "each successive generation and each successive human being, inasmuch as he would understand the past and present, must pass through all preceding phases of human development and culture." And the latter conception he elaborates into the declaration that "the vigorous complete development of each successive stage depends on the vigorous, complete, and characteristic development of each and all preceding stages of life," and maintains that "the child, the boy, the man indeed should know no other endeavor but to be at every stage of development wholly what this stage calls for." In this he would seem to revert from the general Pestalozzian principle of 'development' to the more fixed and set Rousselian theory of 'delayed maturing.'[1] Froebel likewise insists not only upon a 'unity' in age periods,

continuity

culture epochs,

delayed maturing,

[1] See pp. 22f.

but at all periods upon a unity in intellectual, physical, and moral life, and in the relations of the mental phases of knowing, feeling, and willing.

connectedness,

Moreover, he extends his principle of 'unity' to the subject-matter of the school, and maintains that there should be a *connectedness* in the course of study. "Human education," he declares, "requires the knowledge and appreciation of religion, nature, and language in their intimate living reciprocity and mutual interaction. Without the unity of the three, the school and we ourselves are lost in the fallacies of bottomless, self-provoking diversity." He holds that this interrelation of studies should exist because of their mutual dependence upon the divine effluence. Nature study, for example, gives acquaintance with the handiwork and manifestation of God, mathematics makes clear the reign of law in the universe, and language must be connected with religious instruction, in order that words may be joined with real ideas in life. Furthermore, there should be a 'connectedness' between the home and school life, and the means of education should combine domestic and scholastic occupations. Hence, while these pedagogical conclusions are drawn from his mystic philosophy, they do not differ in spirit from the 'correlation' and 'concentration' based upon the Herbartian psychology.

and correlation and concentration.

His general method is that of 'self-activity,'

'Self-activity' and 'Creativeness.'—But the most fruitful consequence of this law of 'unity' is Froebel's inference as to the proper procedure in education. He holds:

> "In every human being, as a member of humanity and as a child of God, there lies and lives humanity as a whole; but in each one it is realized and expressed in a wholly particular, peculiar, per-

sonal, and unique manner, and it should be exhibited in each individual human being in this wholly peculiar, unique manner." [1]

Hence he maintains that there is in every person at birth a coördinated, unified plan of his mature character, and that, if it is not marred or interfered with, it will develop naturally of itself. While he is not entirely consistent, and at times implies that this natural development must be guided and even shaped, in the main he reiterates Rousseau's doctrine that 'nature is right,' and clearly stands for a full and free expression of the instincts and impulses. Moreover, since the natural or unmarred impulses are in accord with this unique implicit character, and may be interfered with or thwarted by an unwise education, he insists that "education in instruction and training should necessarily be *passive*, *following; not prescriptive*, *categorical*, *interfering*," [2] and thus presents Rousseau's idea of 'negative education' with but slight disguise.

But in his conclusion as to the proper method for accomplishing this 'development,' Froebel naturally holds that it "should be brought about not in the way of dead imitation or mere copying, but in the way of living, spontaneous self-activity," [3] for "the eternal divine principle as such demands and requires free self-activity and self-determination on the part of man, the being created for freedom in the image of God." [4] And this principle of *self-activity* as the method of education is most distinctively Froebelian and has proved most important and influential. By it Froebel implies more than mere activity. It is not simply activity in response

[1] *Op cit.*, p. 18.
[2] *Op. cit.*, p. 7.
[3] *Op. cit.*, p. 18.
[4] *Op. cit.*, p. 11.

to suggestion or instruction from parents or teachers that he seeks, but activity of the child in carrying out his own impulses and decisions. Individuality must be developed by such activity, and selfhood given its rightful place as the guide to the child's powers when exercised in learning. It is not sufficient that the learner shall do all for himself, but the activity must enlist the entire self in all its phases of being.

with which is connected his principle of 'creativeness' or motor expression.

Froebel, therefore, advocates not only motor activity, but self-expression as the chief aim of educational method. Hence with this idea of development through 'self-activity' is connected his principle of *creativeness*, by which new forms and combinations are made and expression is given to new images and ideas. Here also he at first gives his theory a mystic garb and states it in religious language. He declares that "since God created man in his own image, man should create and bring forth like God; this is the high meaning, the deep significance, the great purpose of work and industry, of productive and creative activity."[1] But when he comes to deal with constructive handwork in the school, like Rousseau he bases his position upon psychological grounds and says:—

"To learn a thing in life and through doing is much more developing, cultivating, and strengthening, than to learn it merely through the verbal communication of ideas. Similarly, plastic material representation in life and through doing, united with thought and speech, is by far more developing and cultivating than the merely verbal representation of ideas."[2]

He also stresses the social aspects of

The Social Aspect of Education.—His emphasis upon this psychological principle of motor expression

[1] *Op. cit.*, p. 31.

[2] *Op. cit.*, p. 279.

under the head of 'self-activity' and 'creativeness' is the chief characteristic of Froebel's method. Rousseau had recommended motor activity as a means of learning, but he had insisted upon an isolated and unsocial education for Emile. Froebel, however, stresses the social aspects of education quite as clearly as he does the principle of self-expression, and seems to hold that the one is essential to the other. The increasing self-realization, or individualization through 'self-activity,' must come through a process of socialization. The life of the individual is necessarily bound up with participation in institutional life. Each one of the various human institutions in which the mentality of the race has manifested itself—the home, the school, the church, the state, and society at large—becomes a medium for the activity of the individual, and at the same time a means of social control. The social instinct is primal, and the individual can be truly educated only in the company of other human beings.

education, and holds that self-realization comes through social participation.

Hence, Froebel held that in education 'self-activity' should be used to enable the child to enter into the life about him and to find the connection between himself and the activities of others. As far as he enters into the surrounding life, he is to receive the development needed for the present, and thereby also to be prepared for the future. Through imitation of coöperative activities in play, he obtains not only physical, but intellectual and moral training. Hence Froebel rhetorically asks:

"Justice, moderation, self-control, truthfulness, loyalty, brotherly love, and again, strict impartiality—who, when he approaches a group of boys engaged in such games, could fail to catch the fragrance of these delicious blossomings of the heart and mind, and of a firm will; not to mention the beautiful, though perhaps less fragrant, blossoms of courage, perseverance, resolution, prudence, together with the severe elimination of indolent indulgence?" [1]

Such a moral and intellectual atmosphere Froebel sought to cultivate at Keilhau by coöperation in domestic labor,—'lifting, pulling, carrying, digging, splitting,' [2] and through coöperative construction out of blocks of a chapel, castle, and other features of a village;[3] and such an educative participation was conceded to exist by the inspector of schools sent there with hostile intent.[4] Similarly, Baroness von Bülow tells us, the kindergarten was intended to "represent a *miniature state* for children, in which the young citizen can learn to move freely, but with consideration for his little fellows," [5] and thus obtain mental and moral preparation for life.

These basal principles of motor expression and social participation Froebel undertook to realize in a school without books and set tasks, and thereby made a third great contribution to educational practice.

The Kindergarten, and Its Mother-Play, Gifts, and Occupations.—Thus throughout all Froebel's educational works and experiments, his basal principles of motor expression and social participation are constantly implied and illustrated. But Froebel also made a third contribution to educational practice in advocating as a means of realizing these principles *a school without books or set intellectual tasks*, and permeated with play, freedom, and joy. Even in the *Education of Man* he declares that the systematic use of 'self-activity' and 'creativeness' has been neglected in the education of the day. He consequently advocates development through drawing, domestic activities, gardening, building of dams, houses, fortresses, paper-cutting, paste-

[1] *Op. cit.*, pp. 113f.

[2] *Op. cit.*, pp. 101f.

[3] *Op. cit.*, pp. 110ff.

[4] See p. 224.

[5] *Reminiscences*, p. 13.

board work, modeling, and other forms of creation. It was not, however, until the period of Froebel's kindergarten at Blankenburg that these means of expression and socialization obtained their definite school organization. In the kindergarten, 'self-activity' and 'creativeness,' together with social coöperation, found complete application and concrete expression, and Froebel devoted the rest of his life to developing and describing the course of this new educational institution. The training has always consisted of three coördinate forms of expression: (1) song, (2) movement and gesture, and (3) construction; and mingled with these and growing out of each is the use of language by the child. But these means, while separate, often coöperate with and interpret one another, and the process is connected as an organic whole. For example, when the story is told or read, it is expressed in song, dramatized in movement and gesture, and illustrated by a construction from blocks, paper, clay, or other material by modeling or drawing. By thus embodying the ideas in objective form, imagination and thought are stimulated, the eye and hand trained, the muscles coördinated, and the motives and sentiments elevated and strengthened.

The training of the kindergarten has chiefly consisted of

The *Mother Play and Nursery Songs* were believed by Froebel to contain the best illustration of his system. Of them he says, "I have here laid down the fundamental ideas of my educational principles." This work consists of an organized series of carefully selected songs, games, and pictures, and is intended to make clear and direct the educational instinct of the mother. The songs should enable her to see that the child's education begins at birth, and should awaken her to the responsibility of

songs and the accompanying games and gestures,

motherhood. They should likewise exercise the infant's senses, limbs, and muscles, and, through the loving union between mother and child, draw both into intelligent and agreeable relations with the common objects of life about them. For the culture of the maternal consciousness, Froebel prefixed to the 'play songs' seven 'mother's songs,' in which he depicts the mother's feelings in viewing her newborn infant, and her hopes and fears as she witnesses the unfolding physical and mental life of the child. The fifty 'play songs' are each connected with some simple nursery game, like 'pat-a-cake,' 'hide-and-seek,' or the imitation of some trade, and are intended to correspond to a special physical, mental, or moral need of the child. The selection and order of the songs were determined with reference to the child's development, which ranges from almost reflex and instinctive movements up to an ability to represent his perceptions with drawings, accompanied by considerable growth of the moral sense. Each song contains three parts: (1) a motto for the guidance of the mother; (2) a verse with the accompanying music, to sing to the child; and (3) a picture illustrating the verse. A more complete commentary is afforded by the 'closing thoughts' and the 'explanations' furnished by Froebel at the end of the work.[1]

The most original and striking of the kindergarten

[1] For a description of the songs, see especially Wiggin and Smith's *Kindergarten Principles and Practice*, pp. 42–61 and 92–108; or White's *Educational Ideas of Froebel*, Chap. IX. Frances and Emily Lord have rendered the *Mutter-Spiel und Kose-lieder* into English under the title of *Mother's Songs, Games, and Stories*, while Susan E. Blow has translated *The Songs and Music* and *The Mottoes and Commentaries* in separate volumes.

materials are the so-called 'gifts' and 'occupations.' The distinction between these two types of media is rather arbitrary, as they are both intended to stimulate motor expression and are closely connected in use. The 'occupations' represent activities, while the 'gifts' furnish ideas for these activities. The 'gifts' combine and rearrange certain definite material, but do not change the form, while the 'occupations' reshape, modify, and transform their material. The products obtained from the one are transient, but from the other are more permanent. The emphasis in kindergarten practice has come to be transferred from the 'gifts' to the 'occupations,' which have been largely increased in range and number. Froebel strove to carry out his principle of 'development' in the order and gradation of the 'gifts.' They are so arranged as to lead from the properties or activities of one to those of the next, and, while introducing new impressions, repeat the old. Every new 'gift' is used alternately with the old, and the use of the new makes the play with the old freer and more intelligent. The first 'gift' consists of a box of six woolen balls of different colors. They are to be rolled about in play, and thus develop ideas of color, material, form, motion, direction, and muscular sensibility. A sphere, cube, and cylinder of hard wood compose the second 'gift.' Here, therefore, are found a known factor in the sphere and an unknown one in the cube. A comparison is made of the stability of the cube with the movability of the sphere, and the two are harmonized in the cylinder, which possesses the characteristics and powers of each. The third 'gift' is a large wooden cube divided into eight equal cubes, thus teaching the relations of the

and of the 'gifts' and 'occupations

parts to the whole and to one another, and making possible original constructions, such as armchairs, benches, thrones, doorways, monuments, or steps. The three following 'gifts' divide the cube in various ways so as to produce solid bodies of different types and sizes, and excite an interest in number, relation, and form. From them the children are encouraged to construct geometrical figures and 'forms of beauty' or artistic designs. The exercise the gifts afforded was not unlike the inventional drawing of Pestalozzi, except that actual material was used instead of outlining with a pencil. The most surprising ingenuity in invention was often displayed by the pupils in Froebel's kindergarten. In addition to the six regular 'gifts,' he also introduced additional play with 'tablets,' 'sticks,' and 'rings,' sometimes known as 'gifts seven to nine.' This material introduces surfaces, lines, and points in contrast with the preceding solids, and brings out the relations of area, outline, and circumference to volume. It offers innumerable opportunities for the invention of symmetrical patterns and artistic design.[1]

The 'occupations,' which apply to practice what has been assimilated through the 'gifts,' comprise a long list of constructions with paper, sand, clay, wood, and other materials. These require greater manual dexterity and include considerable original design. They should not be undertaken until after the 'gifts,' as one must be conscious of ideas before attempting to express them.

[1] Pictures of the 'gifts' and a more complete account of their use can be found in Froebel's *Pedagogics of the Kindergarten* (translated by Jarvis), Chaps. IV–XIII; White's *Educational Ideas of Froebel*, Chap. VIII; Wiggin and Smith's *Froebel's Gifts;* and especially Kraus-Bölte's *Kindergarten Guide*, First Volume.

Corresponding with the 'gifts' that deal with solids, may be grouped 'occupations' in clay modeling, cardboard cutting, paper folding, and wood carving; and with those of surfaces may be associated mat and paper weaving, stick shaping, sewing, bead threading, paper pricking, and drawing.[1]

Froebel's superficial faults are obvious,—

The Value of Froebel's Principles.—For one pursuing destructive criticism, it would not be difficult to find flaws in both the theory and practice of Froebel. The more superficial defects of his practice are singularly obtrusive, as, for example, in the material of the *Mother Play*. In this work the pictures are rough and poorly drawn, the music is crude, and the verses are lacking in rhythm, poetic spirit, and diction. They are difficult to memorize, and their arrangement and sequence seem at times to lack consistency. But the illustrations and songs served well the interests and needs of those for whom they were produced, and Froebel himself was not insistent that they should be used after more satisfactory compositions were found. He wished only to afford examples of how the mother might aid in the development of her child, and no other collection of children's songs has ever been devised to compare with his in educational value. Other criticism of his material has been made on the ground that it was especially adapted to German ideals, German children, and the relatively simple village life of his experience, and that it needs considerable modification to suit other countries and the industrial organization of society to-day. Also the ar-

the pictures, music, and verses of his *Play Songs* are crude;

but he gave them only as examples.

His material is too much tied to the locality and the times, and much of his practice violates modern psychol-

[1] An excellent account of the 'occupations' is given in Wiggin and Smith's *Froebel's Occupations*, and even greater details in Kraus-Bölte's *Kindergarten Guide*, Second Volume.

ogy, but his more liberal disciples have held to the spirit and not the letter of his methods.

gument of 'formal discipline' for care and accuracy in the use of the gifts, and the insistence upon the employment of every part of each gift upon all occasions in the exact order mentioned by Froebel, have been shown to violate the principles of modern psychology. This would not be conceded by the literal followers of the master or those inclined to make a cult or mystery of Froebelianism. But his more liberal disciples realize that it is the spirit of his underlying principles, and not the letter of his practice, that should be followed, and have constantly struggled to keep the kindergarten matter and methods in harmony with the times and the environment.

But the greatest weakness of Froebelianism is the explanation of the practice on the basis of mysticism and symbolism, rather than by means of the laws of child development.

The greatest hindrance to the acceptance of Froebelianism, however, has not arisen from a skepticism concerning the value of the material used in his practice so much as from the modern antipathy to his bizarre philosophy. Froebel was quite ignorant of the laws of child development now known to modern science, and, in explaining his educational practice, substituted principles of mysticism and symbolism that grew out of the weird religious experience of his youth and the intellectual movements of the times. Hence he often resorts to most fantastic and strained interpretations. Since all things live and have their being in and through God and the divine principle in each is the essence of its life, everything is liable to be considered by Froebel as symbolic in its very nature and as made by God to reveal and express himself. Thus with Froebel the sphere becomes the symbol of diversity in unity,[1] the faces and edges of crystals all have mystic meanings,[2] and the numbers three and

and, in consequence, many artificial, fantastic, and vague doctrines are offered.

[1] *Education of Man*, § 69.

[2] *Op. cit.*, §§ 70–72

five reveal an inner significance.[1] At times this symbolism descends into a literal and verbal pun, where it seems to a modern that Froebel can hardly be in earnest, or is struggling for a suggestive system of mnemonics. Such is his explanation of the 'nursling' as a great appropriating 'eye,' and the 'boy' as one who strives to 'announce' himself.[2] His theory of knowledge is likewise peculiar. He implies that general conceptions are implicit in the child, and each of these can be awakened by 'adumbration,' that is, by presenting something that will symbolically represent that particular 'innate idea.' Thus in treating the gifts and games, he maintains that from a ball the pupil gathers an abstract notion of a 'self-dependent whole and unity,' while to the same child a cube represents a 'developing manifold body.'[3] Similarly, his cosmology leads him to curious conclusions. Since God is the self-conscious spirit that originated both man and nature, Froebel held that everything is interconnected, and each part of the universe may throw light on every other part. Hence he takes seriously every variety of poetic analogy between physical phenomena and mental or social. He constantly holds that a knowledge of external nature,—such as the formation of crystals, will enable one to comprehend the laws of the mind and of society.

Unfortunately, this mystic symbolism, vague and extreme as it is, is regarded by the strict constructionists

[1] This is seen in his description of plants and flowers, while in his treatment of the family he especially vents an eccentric disquisition on the number five.

[2] *Säugling* is interpreted as one who (S) *augt*, and *Kind* as the stage where he (ver) *kündigt*. See *op. cit.*, pp. 24 and 50.

[3] *Pedagogics of the Kindergarten*, pp. 32 and 105.

Unfortunately, this mystic symbolism is regarded by strict constructionists as the most essential feature, and this often tends to foster insincerity and sentimentalism in the pupil.

among the kindergartners as the most essential feature in Froebelianism, and they expect the innocents in their charge to reveal the symbolic effect of the material upon their minds. There is no real evidence for supposing that such associations between common objects and abstract conceptions exist for children. But such an imaginary symbolic meaning may be forced upon an object by the teacher. Hence pupils in conservative kindergartens, without appreciating the underlying principles, soon learn to adopt the phrases and attitudes that will satisfy the teacher. This often tends to foster insincerity and sentimentalism rather than to inculcate abstract truth through symbols. Had Froebel possessed the enlarged knowledge of biology, physiology, and psychology that is available for one living in the twentieth century, it is unlikely that he would have insisted upon the symbolic foundations for his pedagogy. His real principles in education are heavily handicapped by these interpretations, and while quite consistent with his type of philosophy, might as easily have been inferred from very different positions in modern psychology.

But Froebel has, upon the whole, had a most happy effect upon education. He has corroborated or developed many of the best features of Rousseau, Pestalozzi, and Herbart;

But whatever may be said of his philosophy, inconsistencies, or other shortcomings, Froebel has had a most happy effect upon education as a whole. In some respects he utilized features from other reformers. We have seen that he adopted many of Pestalozzi's objective methods in geography, natural history, arithmetic, language, drawing, writing and reading, and constructive geometry; he reiterated Rousseau's views upon the infallibility of nature, negative education, and theory of maturing; and advocated the physical training and excursions and walks as a means of study that are stressed by both these reformers. In his hint at correlation and culture epochs, and especially in his use of stories, legends, fables, and fairy-tales, he paralleled his contemporary, Herbart, in his influence upon the curriculum. But in his emphasis upon motor expression, and upon the social aspects of education, together with his advocacy of a school without books or set tasks, Froebel was unique, and made a most distinctive contribution to educational practice. Pestalozzi had in his earlier career developed motor activity as a means of education through industrial training, but the 'observation,' which he introduced at the same time, was rather passive and but little connected with constructive expression. And while his use of drawing, music, and modeling provided a means of expression, it remained for Froebel to organize these and other subjects into the school procedure and to make motor expression essential instead of incidental. In his emphasis upon this factor of education, he might, however, seem to be reverting to Rousseau, except that, quite in opposition to that reformer, Froebel also held that the training should not be given to isolated individuals, but should operate through social participation. These two underlying and associated principles, worked out as they were through activities and informal schooling, have become most distinctive of the Froebelian method, and have been most fruitful in their influence upon subsequent education.

and in his emphasis upon motor expression, social aspects of education, and an informal school, he made distinctive contributions to educational practice.

Whenever the real significance of his principles has been comprehended, they have been recognized as the most essential laws in the educational process, and are valued as the means of all effective teaching. Froebel himself never worked out his theories in connection with

His principles comprehend the most essential laws of education at all stages.

the schooling beyond the kindergarten, although there is reason to believe that he intended to do so when he had time. But, in harmony with Froebel, all stages of education are coming to realize the value of discovering and developing individuality by means of initiative, execution, and coöperation, and spontaneous activities, like play, construction, and occupational work have become more and more the means to this end. For example, the 'busy work,' 'whittling,' 'clay-modeling,' and 'sloyd,' which have during the past generation found a place in the grades of American schools, together with the more advanced types of 'manual training,' which have been introduced into the high schools and sometimes become the staple of a special type of secondary institution, have to a large degree sprung from the influence of Froebel.

Largely from his influence have sprung 'busy work,' 'whittling,' 'clay-modeling,' 'sloyd,' and 'manual training.'

Uno Cygnaeus (1810–1888), who started the manual training movement, owed his inspiration to Froebel and his own desire to extend the kindergarten occupations through the grades. As a result of his efforts Finland in 1866 became the first country in the world to adopt manual training as an integral part of the course in the elementary and training schools. In 1874, through the visit of *Otto Salomon* (1849–1907) to Cygnaeus, Sweden transformed its sloyd from a system of teaching elementary trades and industrial training to the more educative method of manual training. This use of constructive and occupational work for educational purposes rather than for industrial efficiency soon spread throughout Europe, and, together with other forms of manual training, was first suggested to the United States by the Centennial Exposition of 1876 at Philadelphia. Various types of modern educational theory and practice, especially those associated with experiments made in the United States, also reveal large elements of Froebelian influence. Among these might be included the work of Colonel Parker and of Professor John Dewey. Parker's adaptation of part of Herbartianism, especially concentration, has already been noted, but the Froebelian emphasis upon motor expression, the social aspect of education, and informal schooling are evident throughout his work in the elementary school, and are even extended so as to include speech and the language-arts. Similarly, Dewey's occupational work and industrial activities, which were used through the entire course of his 'experimental school' in Chicago,[1] although not copied directly from Froebel, closely approached the modified practice of the kindergarten. Moreover, in all these modern systems and materials where the factor of motor expression is prominent, emphasis is also laid upon informality of training and the social aspect of education. Thus the influence of all three of the Froebelian contributions is everywhere patent.

The educational work of Colonel Parker and Professor Dewey reveal large elements of Froebelian influence.

The Spread of Froebelianism through Europe.— Froebelianism and the kindergarten, then, contained principles that were destined to disseminate themselves by virtue of their educational value. But the spread of the kindergarten itself began directly after the death of Froebel through the reformer's devoted followers. Froebel's widow, Middendorf, and the Baroness von Bülow especially became the heirs of his spiritual possessions, and proceeded at once to make the heritage productive. Middendorf did not long survive the master, and Frau Froebel's part in the wide evangelization was somewhat

Froebel's principles were spread by Baroness von Bülow throughout Europe,

[1] See pp. 379ff.

limited by her education. It remained for the intellectual and cultured noblewoman, by means of her social position and knowledge of modern languages, to become the great apostle of Froebel throughout Europe. Shortly after his death, having failed to obtain a revocation of the edict in Prussia from either the ministry or the king, the baroness turned to foreign lands. She visited France, Belgium, Holland, Italy, Russia, and nearly every other section of Europe, and in 1867 was invited to speak before the 'Congress of Philosophers' at Frankfort. This distinguished gathering had been called to inquire into contemporary educational movements, and after her elucidation of Froebelianism, a standing committee of the Congress, known as the 'Froebel Union,' was formed to study the system.

and the kindergarten has been everywhere eagerly embraced, except in Germany.

As a result of the labors of the baroness, the propaganda was everywhere eagerly embraced. Kindergartens, training schools, and journals devoted to the movement rapidly sprang up on all sides. While the kindergarten was not generally adopted by the governments, it was widely established by voluntary means throughout western Europe, and has since met with a noteworthy growth. Instruction in Froebelian principles is now generally required in most normal and teacher training institutions of Europe. Sometimes, as in France and England, it has been combined with the infant school movement,[1] and has lost some of its most vital characteristics, but even in these cases the cross-fertilization has afforded abundant educational fruitage. Only in Germany, the native land of the kindergarten, has serious hostility to the idea remained. The deaden-

[1] See pp. 63 and 69.

ing effects of the decree in Prussia hung over the German states for a decade; and even since the removal of the ban, kindergartens have, with few exceptions, never been recognized as genuine schools or part of the regular state system. Even to-day the German kindergarten is regarded as little more than a day nursery or convenient place to deposit small children and have them amused.[1]

The kindergarten has had its widest influence in the United States.

The Kindergarten in the United States.—The development and influence of the kindergarten have been more marked in the United States than in any other country, and its history there demands consideration in some detail. The first attempts at kindergartens in America were made shortly after the middle of the nineteenth century. Educated Germans, who had emigrated to America because of the unsettled conditions at home resulting from the revolutionary days of 1848, established private schools, which usually included kindergartens, for their children.

It was introduced in Boston by Elizabeth P. Peabody,

In 1860 Elizabeth P. Peabody and others became interested in accounts of Froebel's system made by Mrs. Carl Schurz, and, without a proper knowledge of the details, undertook to open a kindergarten in Boston. Notwithstanding the immediate success of this institution and the evident enjoyment of the children, Miss Peabody felt that she had not succeeded in getting the real principles and spirit of Froebel, and in 1867 she went to study with his widow, who had been settled in Hamburg for several years. Upon her return the following year Miss Peabody

[1] When Professor Payne of the London College of Preceptors visited the kindergartens in six German cities in 1874, he found that, while the theory was just, natural, and all-sided, the teachers were inefficient, and the rooms were often small, unsanitary, and ill-lighted. (See Payne, *Lectures on the History of Education*, pp. 203–271.) Even now, forty years later, the same general conditions seem to obtain.

corrected the errors in her work and established a periodical to explain and spread Froebelianism. The remainder of her life was spent in interesting parents, philanthropists, and school boards in the movement, and a service was done for the kindergarten in America almost equal to that of Baroness von Bülow in Europe. In 1868 through Miss Peabody the first training school for kindergartners in the United States was established at Boston. A similar institution was opened in New York by 1872 in charge of Maria Bölte.[1] Fräulein Bölte had studied with Frau Froebel, and had been induced to settle in New York. Through her pupils and those of other German kindergartners, the cause was rapidly promoted. The same year saw the beginning of Susan E. Blow's great work in St. Louis, where her free training school for kindergartners was opened. Two years later S. H. Hill of Florence, Massachusetts, started a munificent provision for free kindergartens in his vicinity, and four years after that Mrs. Quincy A. Shaw began establishing them at various locations in the neighborhood of Boston, until she was supporting at least thirty such institutions. Many other philanthropic persons became much interested, and over one hundred voluntary associations were soon organized to found and maintain kindergartens. Through the work of Emma Marwedel, who was invited to California in 1876 by the 'Froebel Union,' successful training classes were established at Los Angeles, Oakland, and Berkeley. Voluntary kindergartens were also rapidly opened, and there was organized in 1878 the 'Golden Gate Association' at San Francisco,

in New York by Maria Bölte, and in St. Louis by Susan E. Blow.

Support was given the work by S. H. Hill, Mrs. Quincy A. Shaw and others;

Emma Marwedel developed it in California;

[1] She afterward became widely known as Mrs. Maria Kraus-Bölte, and is still (1913) living in New York City.

which at its height supported forty-one free institutions and an excellent training school. In Milwaukee, Cincinnati, Detroit, Pittsburg, Baltimore, Philadelphia, Cleveland, Washington, Chicago, Louisville, and other centers, between 1870 and 1890 subscriptions were raised by the churches and other philanthropic agencies, and the work everywhere grew apace. By the close of the century there were about five hundred such voluntary associations.

and voluntary associations sprang up in five hundred centers before the end of the century.

But philanthropy and private foundations, after all, are restrictive, and it was not until the kindergartens began to be adopted by the school systems that the movement became truly national in the United States. Boston in the early seventies added a few kindergartens to her public schools, but after several years of trial gave them up on account of the expense. The first permanent establishment under a city board was made in 1873 at St. Louis through the efforts of Miss Blow and Dr. William T. Harris, then city superintendent of schools. Twelve kindergartens were organized at first, but others were opened as rapidly as competent directors could be prepared at Miss Blow's training school. Within a decade there were more than fifty public kindergartens and nearly eight thousand pupils in St. Louis. San Francisco authorized the incorporation of kindergartens in the public schools in 1880; and between that date and the end of the century New York, Boston, Philadelphia, Buffalo, Pittsburg, Rochester, Providence, Milwaukee, Minneapolis, and most other progressive cities and even many smaller municipalities made the work an integral part of their system. In some states the adoption of kindergartens was delayed by the necessity of securing special legislation to admit children to school under the age of five or six. Statutes,

It soon became a part of the public school system in St. Louis, San Francisco, Boston, and other cities.

however, were eventually passed in most states where they were needed, and by 1900 there were some two hundred cities that included this stage of education in their schools. That indicated a total of about fifteen hundred public kindergartens, with nearly twice as many teachers and considerably over one hundred thousand pupils. About twenty of the cities employed a special supervisor to inspect the work. Excellent training schools for kindergartners are now maintained by half a hundred public and quasi-public normal institutions. A large number of extensive treatises, manuals, and periodicals devoted to the subject of kindergarten work are published, and have a wide circulation in every state of the Union.

Few tendencies in educational practice to-day cannot be traced back to Herbart and Froebel, or to their master, Pestalozzi, and all three have their roots in Rousseau.

The Influence of Herbart and Froebel.—It is now obvious how large a part in the development of modern educational practice has been played by Herbart and Froebel. There are few tendencies in the curricula and methods of the schools to-day that cannot be traced back to them, or to Pestalozzi, their master. But the reforms of all three find their roots in Rousseau. By his insistence upon a 'natural' education, he started the modern social, psychological, and scientific movements in education, and opened the road for the present-day improvements in organization, method, and content. This 'naturalism' was continued by Pestalozzi's 'development' and 'sense perception,' and these aspects were further elaborated by Froebel and Herbart respectively. Through his own 'observation' methods, Pestalozzi greatly improved the teaching of arithmetic, language work, geography, elementary science, drawing, writing, reading, and music, and, by means of Fellenberg's work, developed industrial and philanthropic training. As a result of

Herbart's moral and religious aim, marked advances in the teaching of history and literature have taken place, and, through his carefully wrought educational doctrines, order and system have everywhere been introduced into instruction. From Froebel's mystic interpretation of 'natural development,' we have obtained the kindergarten training for a period of life hitherto largely neglected, and the informal occupations, manual training, and other studies of motor expression, together with psychological and social principles that underlie every stage of education.

The reforms of Pestalozzi, Froebel, and Herbart all fall within the nineteenth century both in Europe and the United States, and have produced a great impulse in the psychological and sociological movements in modern education.

Pestalozzi's reforms were felt in Europe throughout the first half of the nineteenth century, but did not have any wide effect upon the United States until after the 'Oswego movement'[1] in the sixties. The influence of Froebel appeared in Europe shortly after the middle of the century, and began to rise to its height in America about 1880. The Herbartian theory and practice became popular in Germany between 1865 and 1885, while the growth of Herbartianism in the United States began about five years after the latter date. Hence the development of modern educational practice, due to these three great reformers, falls distinctly within the period of the nineteenth century. Owing to them the past century witnessed a mighty impulse in both the psychological and sociological movements in education.

[1] See pp. 152f.

SUPPLEMENTARY READING

I. Sources

A. Herbart

ECKOFF, W. J. *Herbart's A B C of Sense Perception and Minor Pedagogical Works.*

FELKIN, H. M. and E. *Herbart's Letters and Lectures on Education.*

FELKIN, H. M. and E. *Herbart's Science of Education.*

LANGE, A. F., and DEGARMO, C. *Herbart's Outlines of Educational Doctrine.*

LANGE, K. *Apperception.* (Translated by Herbart Club.)

MULLINER, B. C. *Herbart's Application of Psychology to the Science of Education.*

SMITH, M. K. *Herbart's Text-Book in Psychology.*

VAN LIEW, C. C., and I. J. *Rein's Outlines of Pedagogics.*

B. Froebel

FROEBEL, F. W. A. *Autobiography* (translated by Michaelis and Moore); *Education by Development* (translated by Jarvis); *Education of Man* (translated by Hailmann); *Letters* (edited by Heinemann); *Letters on the Kindergarten* (translated by Poesche, and edited by Michaelis and Moore); *Mother Songs, Games, and Stories* (translated by F. and E. Lord); *Mottoes and Commentaries of Mother Play* (translated by Eliot and Blow); *Pedagogics of the Kindergarten* (translated by Jarvis); *Songs and Music of Mother Play* (translated by Blow).

LANGE, W. *Froebel's Gesammelte Pädagogische Schriften* (three volumes) and *Reminiscences of Froebel* (*American Journal of Education*, Vol. XXX, pp. 833–845).

MARENHOLTZ-BÜLOW, BERTHE M. von. *Reminiscences of Friedrich Froebel.*

SEIDEL, F. *Froebel's Mutter-Spiel und Kose-Lieder.*

II. Authorities

A. Herbart

Adams, J. *The Herbartian Psychology Applied to Education.* Chap. III.

Darroch, A. *Herbart and the Herbartian Theory of Education.* Lect. V.

DeGarmo, C. *Essentials of Method.*

DeGarmo, C. *German Contributions to the Coördination of Studies* (*Educational Review,* Vol. IV, pp. 422–437); and *A Working Basis for the Correlation of Studies* (*Educational Review*, Vol. V, pp. 451–466).

DeGarmo, C. *Herbart and the Herbartians.*

Felkin, H. M., and E. *An Introduction to Herbart's Science and Practice of Education.*

Gilbert, C. B. *Practicable Correlations of Studies* (*Educational Review,* Vol. XI, pp. 313–322).

Graves, F. P. *Great Educators of Three Centuries.* Chap. X.

Harris, W. T. *Herbart and Pestalozzi Compared* (*Educational Review,* Vol. V, pp. 417–423); *Herbart's Doctrine of Interest* (*Educational Review,* Vol. X, pp. 71–81).

Harris, W. T. *The Psychological Foundations of Education.* Chap. XXXVI.

Herbart Society. *Year Book.* Nos. I and II.

Jackman, W. S. *The Correlation of Science and History* (*Educational Review,* Vol. IX, pp. 464–471).

Lukens, H. T. *The Correlation of Studies* (*Educational Review,* Vol. X, pp. 364–383).

McMurry, C. A. *The Elements of General Method.*

McMurry, F. M. *Concentration* (*Educational Review,* Vol. IX, pp. 27–37).

Parker, F. W. *Talks on Pedagogics. An Outline of the Theory of Concentration.*

Parker, S. C. *History of Modern Elementary Education.* Chap. XVII.

Rein, W. *Pestalozzi and Herbart* (*The Forum,* Vol. XXI, pp. 346–360).

SMITH, M. K. *Herbart's Life* (*New England Journal of Education*, Vol. XXIX, pp. 139ff.).

TOMPKINS, A. *Herbart's Philosophy and His Educational Theory* (*Educational Review*, Vol. XVI, pp. 233–243).

UFER, C. *Introduction to the Pedagogy of Herbart.* (Translated by J. C. Zinser).

VANDEWALKER, NINA C. *The Culture Epoch Theory* (*Educational Review*, Vol. XV, pp. 374–391).

VAN LIEW, C. C. *Life of Herbart and Development of his Pedagogical Doctrine.*

B. Froebel

BARNARD, H. (Editor). *Kindergarten and Child Culture.*

BLOW, SUSAN E. *Educational Issues in the Kindergarten; Kindergarten Education* (*Monographs on Education in the United States*, edited by N. M. Butler, No. I); *Letters to a Mother;* and *Symbolic Education.*

BOWEN, H. C. *Froebel and Education by Self-activity.*

BUTLER, N. M. *Some Criticisms of the Kindergarten* (*Educational Review*, Vol. XVIII, pp. 285–291).

EUCKEN, R. *The Philosophy of Froebel* (*The Forum*, Vol. XXX, pp. 172ff.).

GOLDAMMER, H. *The Kindergarten* (Translated by Wright).

GRAVES, F. P. *Great Educators of Three Centuries.* Chap. XI.

HAILMANN, W. N. *Kindergarten Culture.*

HANSCHMANN, A. B. *The Kindergarten System* (Translated by Franks).

HARRISON, ELIZABETH A. *A Study of Child Nature.*

HOPKINS, LOUISA P. *The Spirit of the New Education.*

KRAUS-BÖLTE, MARIA, and KRAUS, J. *The Kindergarten Guide.* Two volumes.

MARENHOLTZ-BÜLOW, BERTHE M. von. *The Child and Child Nature.*

MEIKLEJOHN, J. M. D. *The New Education.*

MONROE, P. *Textbook in the History of Education.* Chap. XI.

MUNROE, J. P. *The Educational Ideal.* Chap. VIII.

PARKER, S. C. *History of Modern Elementary Education.* Chap. XVIII.

PAYNE, J. *Froebel and the Kindergarten.*

PEABODY, ELIZABETH P. *Education in the Home, the Kindergarten, and the Primary School; Lectures in the Training School for Kindergartners.*

POLLOCK, LOUISE. *National Kindergarten Manual.*

POULSSON, EMILIE. *Love and Law in Child Training.*

SCHAEFFER, MARY F. *A Cycle of Work in the Kindergarten.*

SHIRREFF, EMILY. *A Short Sketch of the Life of Friedrich Froebel* and *The Kindergarten System.*

SNIDER, D. J. *Froebel's Mother Play Songs; The Life of Froebel;* and *The Psychology of Froebel's Play Gifts.*

THORNDIKE, E. L. *The Psychology of the Kindergarten* (*Teachers College Record*, Vol. IV, pp. 377–408).

VANDEWALKER, NINA C. *Kindergarten in American Education.*

WEAVER, EMILY A. *Paper and Scissors in the Schoolroom.*

WIGGIN, KATE D. *Children's Rights.*

WIGGIN, KATE D. (Editor). *The Kindergarten.*

WIGGIN, KATE D. and SMITH, NORA A. *Froebel's Gifts; Froebel's Occupations; Kindergarten Principles and Practice;* and *The Republic of Childhood.*

CHAPTER VIII

LATER DEVELOPMENT OF PUBLIC EDUCATION IN THE UNITED STATES

The 'revival' in New England was part of a general awakening, but the effects of the movement there have been most striking.

Common Schools in New England since the Revival.— We may now return to our account of the progress in American public education. The development of common schools that took place in 1835–1860 was not confined to New England. The new ideals of democracy were coming to be felt in American education, and during this period a rapid advance was taking place in the evolution of that unique product, the American common school. The 'revival' in New England has been most emphasized by historians, but the movement was general and did not have its sole source there. The work of Horace Mann and his predecessors and associates was but part of a much wider tendency. A little study reveals the fact that the influence of the awakening was felt in the education of practically every state, and that New England is simply typical of the country at large. It is true, however, that, owing to the decadence which had taken place in the schools of Massachusetts and Connecticut since colonial days, the effects of the awakening have been most profound and striking there. In Massachusetts Horace Mann has been succeeded in the central administration by seven scholarly and experienced educators, who have believed as firmly as he that all stages of education below the college should be open at public expense without let or hindrance to the richest and poorest child alike, and that the smallest town should possess as good opportunities as the largest. Since the revival the state has likewise seen a steady growth of sentiment for universal education and improved schooling, and never again has such an upheaval of the educational strata been necessary. The income of the state school fund and additional appropriations have been steadily increased, their apportionment among the towns has been rendered more equitable from time to time, and an effort has constantly been made to distribute them in such a way as to encourage local effort and coöperation. The school term has been lengthened to ten months and the average attendance of a pupil to seven years. The amount of truancy and irregularity has become almost negligible through strictly enforced attendance laws. The improvements in school buildings, sanitation, and equipment begun by Mann have steadily advanced. The district system died hard. Mann's official successors all strove tactfully to abolish it, but not until 1882 was it altogether forced out of existence. Most of the academies, which proved such a hindrance to the development of public secondary education, gradually died or were merged in the public system as high schools. By means of state aid, it has been possible since 1903 for the smallest towns to afford a high school training for their children at public expense. Supervision has also become universal during the past quarter century. Springfield first introduced a superintendent of schools in 1841, Gloucester in 1850, Boston in 1851, and the other cities much later, but since 1888, through increasing state aid and the combination of smaller towns into a

In Massachusetts universal education, school support, buildings, equipment, high schools, supervision, normal schools, the training of teachers, and the organization of the state system have been constantly increasing and improving; and the district system has been forced out of existence.

district superintendency, expert supervision has become possible everywhere, and during the last decade it has been compulsory. The normal schools, which have now increased to ten, have brought about a striking improvement in teaching. It is practically impossible at present for an untrained teacher to secure a position in the primary, intermediate, or grammar schools of Massachusetts, and, through a system of examinations and investigations, teachers of exceptional ability have, since 1896, been granted an extra weekly allowance by the state. Since the middle of the century, the state board has been permitted to appoint a number of agents, to assist in inspecting and improving the schools, especially in the smaller towns and rural districts.

A similar development has taken place in Connecticut, Rhode Island, and the other New England states.

The course of development since the awakening has been very similar in the other New England states. Barnard was succeeded in the central administration both in Rhode Island and Connecticut by a series of skilled and earnest educators, and, while their reports lacked his literary touch, they were of a rather more practical character. Until 1856, under John D. Philbrick, Barnard's immediate successor, Connecticut made no attempt to return from the parish to the town organization. Even this, as well as all subsequent legislation on the subject, was 'permissive,' and not until the twentieth century was the 'school society,' or district system, given up in half of the towns. In Rhode Island, even after Barnard's reforms, almost one-third of the districts did not own their school buildings, owing to the survival of the method in use when the schools were private, but this condition has gradually been remedied. Likewise the number of towns levying sufficient local taxes to secure a share in the state apportionment rapidly grew, and the state appropriation itself doubled and quadrupled within a generation. The odds against the rapid development of public education in the three other New England states were much greater than in Massachusetts, Rhode Island, and Connecticut. In Vermont, New Hampshire, and Maine the amount of wealth was small, the soil infertile, the population sparse, and large cities few in number. But while effective education could be reached only by slow and cautious steps, it was at last attained. These states have gradually followed the example of the older commonwealths, and centralized their educational administration through the abolition of the district system and the creation at various times of a state superintendent, a state commissioner, or a state board and secretary. This reorganization and renewed educational spirit has resulted in increased state school funds and appropriations, more systematic statistics and reports from the schools, and great advances in universalizing all stages of education at public expense, regularity of attendance, length of school term, material equipment, course and methods, text-books, supervision, and training of teachers.

Influence of the Awakening upon the Middle States.— Thus the New England states, responding to the call of Horace Mann, Henry Barnard, and their forerunners, contemporaries, and successors, rose to the enlarged ideals of the time, and therein furnish a typical representation of the democratic process by which the American state moves toward educational reform. But this awakened sentiment for education and progress in the common schools was not peculiar to New England, although the

The enthusiasm for public education was likewise felt in nearly all the other states.

effects have been most patent and spectacular there. Nearly all of the other states seem to have exhibited a similar enthusiasm during the period and to have felt the influence of the awakening afterward. In close conjunction with the awakening in New England, the movement appeared in New York, especially the western part, and was more or less evident in Pennsylvania, New Jersey, and Delaware. But because of its cosmopolitanism and the need of fusing so many different political, religious, and industrial traditions, the older parts of New York, where the school system had until the awakening been rather in advance of other states, did not progress as rapidly in the development of public education as Massachusetts and Connecticut, with their more homogeneous population. It had, however, by the time of the Civil War, succeeded in working over its heterogeneous people into a unified civilization and in causing their children to be educated together for a common citizenship. The most distinct advances during this period of final organization were in the administration and supervision of the system, the establishment of state normal schools, in the place of subsidized academies, for training teachers, and in the methods of state support of education. In 1842 county supervision had been provided, but, after a contest of three years, this provision was abolished, and was not restored until 1856, when it took the form of district superintendence. In this latter year school commissioners were established for the supervision of cities and villages. Two years before (1854), the state superintendency had once more been separated from the secretaryship of state, with which it had been combined for thirty-five years. The

New York had unified its people and made great advances in administration and supervision, normal training, and school funds;

governor, secretary of state, and others for several years urged the establishment of state normal schools, and at length, in 1844, the first was opened at Albany. This pioneer institution was eventually followed by ten others. In 1856, after considerable agitation, a three-quarters of a mill tax was placed upon the property valuation of the state, and during the next dozen years many improvements were made in the disbursing and accounting of public funds. At length, in 1867, the long fight that had been made for entirely free education was successful. Until then nearly fifty thousand children had been deprived of all education, because their parents were too proud to secure payment of their tuition fees by confessing themselves paupers. It was during this era of progress, too, that New York City was, in 1842, allowed to place the direction of its schools in the hands of a board of education, elected by the people, instead of giving over the city's share of the state funds to a quasi-public society, controlled by a close corporation. For eleven years, however, the Public School Society refused to give up its work, but by 1853 it decided to disband and merge its buildings and funds with those of the city.[1]

and finally (1867) made education entirely free, and allowed New York City (1842) to establish a board of education, into which the Public School Society was merged (1853).

Pennsylvania was slower than New York in showing the effects of the educational awakening, but the leaven was at work. While a number of progressive governors and other statesmen continually recommended the development of public education, and the 'Pennsylvania Society for the Promotion of Common Schools' had been organized, the towering leader in this movement was Thomas H. Burrowes. As secretary of state and *ex officio*

While slower than New York, Pennsylvania, through Thomas H. Burrowes and other statesmen, began to discontinue appropriations to private in-

[1] See pp. 97f.

stitutions (1843) and to abolish the 'permissive' feature of the first public school law (1848), and finally (1854) established a complete state system of education. This was virtually a separate department, and soon (1857) came under the care of an independent superintendent.

superintendent of schools (1836–1838), as a private citizen, public speaker, and educational journalist (1838–1860), and as state superintendent (1860–1862), he constantly urged a complete system of public education, the establishment of normal schools, a separate state department of education, and the organization of state and county supervision. In the interest of common schools, he visited, interviewed, and circularized every portion of the state, organized meetings, and wrote articles and treatises. By 1843 school directors of counties and boroughs were empowered to examine and certify teachers and to appoint a salaried inspector of schools, and the appropriations to colleges, academies, and seminaries were cut in two, preparatory to discontinuing them altogether. Five years later the 'permissive' feature of the law of 1834 was abolished,[1] and the two hundred districts that had thus far refused to establish public schools were forced to do so under its provisions. In 1854 a revised school law was passed, which, after twenty years, now made the state system of education complete. It established in the secretary of state's office a deputy superintendent of schools, who had virtually a separate department; provided for county superintendents; and improved the teachers' examinations, graded schools, introduced uniform text-books, and defined the limits of a school district as coterminous with the township. The next six years constituted a period of great activity in educational reform, and in 1857 the state educational department was made absolutely independent under the care of a superintendent, and a system of normal schools was provided. Twelve of these institutions were to be estab-

A system of normal schools was also provided (1857).

[1] See p. 102.

lished at first by private enterprise and without state subsidy. By 1877 they were in operation in ten counties and were maintained largely by the state, and a number of others have at various times since been added.

New Jersey eventually applied its state funds to public schools only and allowed towns to levy local taxes (1838), and, after a state superintendency was established (1848), the appropriations were greatly increased, a state normal school was established, and county supervision was introduced.

Educational progress in New Jersey also took some time to get under way, but when the reforms once started, they continued until an excellent system of common schools had been inaugurated. In 1838 the limitation of state funds to the education of the poor was removed, and the apportionment of the income from them was thereafter applied only to public schools. The townships were allowed to levy local taxes to the amount of twice what they received from the state, but for about a decade not more than one-half to two-thirds of them adopted a tax, and the state money was spent so wastefully that nearly four-fifths of the cost of public schools had to be paid by tuition fees. After 1848, when a state superintendency was established, the development was more rapid. Within a dozen years, the appropriations were greatly increased, the expenditures in the townships rose to more than twelvefold, one-quarter of the schools became absolutely free, a state normal school was established at Trenton, and county supervision was introduced. Thus before the Civil War New Jersey had been brought out of the depressing educational conditions of the past.

Delaware did not establish a state system until after the war, and even then the supervision was left incomplete.

Delaware, on the other hand, failed to live up to the possibilities under her early 'permissive' laws.[1] Even the organization of the friends of common school education, under the presidency of Judge Willard Hall, showed itself very conservative, and would not advocate the introduction of a state superintendent or the establish-

[1] See p. 103.

ment of state normal schools. As in most of the Southern states, Delaware did not establish a completely organized state system until after the war. Even then, while a state board and state superintendency were established in 1875, there were no county superintendents, and when county supervision was introduced in 1888, the state superintendency was abolished.

Ohio, Indiana, and Illinois were enabled to overcome the opponents of public education, and shortly after the middle of the century fully realized local taxation and free common schools, and established a state commissionership or superintendency.

Public Education in the West.—The budding of a common school system, which had just begun to appear in the new commonwealths of the Northwest before 1840, rapidly unfolded into full blossom through the nurture of this educational springtime. The common school advocates in Ohio, Indiana, and Illinois were thereby greatly aided in their struggle to overcome the opposition of settlers from the states not committed to public education.[1] Their efforts to unify the cosmopolitan peoples of the state in the interest of common schools were greatly stimulated by this awakening, and were favored to some extent by further accessions in the way of emigrants from the home of the public school movement. During the decade just preceding the middle of the century, there was a decided elevation of public sentiment going on. Under the leadership of Samuel Lewis and Samuel Galloway in Ohio, Caleb Mills in Indiana, and Ninian W. Edwards in Illinois, the friends of public education had marshalled themselves for battle. Reports and memorials were constantly presented to the legislatures of these states, and public addresses in behalf of common schools were frequent in most large communities. A group of devoted schoolmen appeared, who were as successful in lobbying for good

[1] See pp. 113ff.

legislation as they were with institutes and public lectures. While reactions occasionally happened, like that in Ohio between 1840 and 1845, when the state superintendency was temporarily abolished, public education gradually came to be regarded as something more than merely free education for the poor, and public school funds were no longer granted as a subsidy to private institutions. After a quarter century of 'permissive' laws, local taxation and free common schools were fully realized in all three states early in the fifties. In 1853 Ohio once more obtained a separate state department of education under the care of an elected 'commissioner';[1] the year before, Indiana eliminated all option concerning taxation on the part of the counties, and organized universal education; and in the year following, a system of public education with a state superintendent was established by Illinois. The contest, of course, was not ended, as reactionary elements, with selfish, local, and sectarian interests, still remained, but their contentions have never again been more than partially successful. New features of the common schools, such as efficient teachers for the rural districts, county supervision, state normal training, and free higher education in state universities, have gradually rendered the state systems more consistent and complete.

From the beginning of statehood Michigan provided for a school fund

In Michigan, on the other hand, where there was not such a mixture of population, and a complete sympathy with the common school idea appeared, there was almost unhampered progress from the beginning of

[1] This method was not changed until the constitutional convention of 1912, when it was arranged that a 'state superintendent' should be appointed by the governor.

and a local tax; and soon d veloped 'union' and high schools to fit for the university, which became free, and founded a state normal school.

statehood. Under the first constitution (1837), there was provision made for a permanent school fund and for a local tax in every district. There was also provided a system of 'branches' of the university, whereby a liberal grant was made for an academy in any county that would furnish suitable buildings and a sum equal to the appropriation from the state. This dissipation of the university funds, however, was gradually stopped, and between 1852 and 1860 'union' and high schools were rapidly developed to supply the means of fitting for the university. This latter institution became virtually free in 1842, and in 1850 a state normal school was founded.

Similar rapidity of educational development has occurred in the other states as they have been admitted, and in the West the triumph of the common school idea has been most complete and consistent.

In all the other territory acquired or purchased by the United States in its westward expansion, the educational history has been very similar to that in the first states of the Northwest. Progress in common school sentiment has been made *pari passu* with the settlement of the country. Each state, upon admission, has received its sixteenth section of school land and two townships for a university, and in the states admitted since 1848 the endowment of schools has been increased to two sections, while Texas, which had been an independent republic (1836–1845), stipulated before becoming a state that it should retain sole possession of its public lands, and has set aside for education nearly two and one-half millions of acres. Hence in the first constitution permanent school and university funds have generally been provided, and a regular organization of the schools of the state, with a central authority of some sort, has simultaneously appeared with the entry of new states. In few cases have sectarian interests been able to delay or injure the growth of common schools in any of the later commonwealths, and the interpretation of public education as schools for the children of paupers has never seriously influenced the West. The triumph of the common school idea has been made complete, but it has been rendered more consistent in the West and has there developed original elements of the greatest value.

Organization of State Systems in the South.—Thus through the awakening of common schools that occurred throughout the union from 1835 to 1860 was the old-time country and city district school of the North lifted up to the present system of graded free elementary, secondary, and normal schools, together with city and state universities. But these results were not at first as fully realized in the South, because of the approach and precipitation of the dreadful internecine conflict that weighed down and finally prostrated the resources of that section of the United States. During the earlier years of the awakening, and in some states up to the very verge of the Civil War, however, great progress in public education was noticeable. The attendance in the common schools, established in several states by 'permissive' legislation, had been rapidly growing for a score of years, and there was an increasing body of prominent men desirous of enlarging popular education. During the early forties there were many efforts and suggestions for a system of public schools, and several conventions were held in the interest of such institutions. North Carolina, moreover, established a public school system in 1839, and state, county, and local administrative organization was well provided for and support obtained through the 'literary fund' and local taxation. Tennessee (1838–1843) and Kentucky (1838) made similar

While the awakening was strongly felt in the South and there were at first many efforts to establish systems of public schools, as the war approached, educational progress was forced to give way to the preservation of state and home, and after the war educational facilities were a wreck.

efforts toward state organizations, which, while less successful, were maintained for some time. As late as 1858 Georgia took a distinct step forward in this direction, while Charleston (1856) and other leading cities of the South greatly strengthened their public school systems. The Southern states generally seem to have been profoundly stirred by the vigorous movement that was going on. Such leaders as Barnard and Mann were greatly esteemed in the South, and their advice was not infrequently sought in various commonwealths. Even in their secession conventions some states, like Georgia, adopted resolutions or constitutional amendments looking to the education of the people, and North Carolina in 1863, with the union army actually at its doors, undertook to grade the schools and provide for the training of teachers. But, in general, as the impending conflict drew near, attention to educational progress was forced to give way to the preservation of state and home, and after the war, which crushed and ravaged nearly every portion of the South, educational facilities had for the most part been totally wrecked.

But the war caused the South to realize more fully than ever the need of universal education, and by 1870 many of the Southern states, despite their poverty and other obstacles, had begun a system of public education.

Nevertheless, in the end the war served as a stimulus to common schools. It brought about a complete overturn of the old social and industrial order, and the South realized more fully than ever that it could arise from its desperate material and educational plight only through the institution of universal education. As early as 1865, school systems were organized in the border states,—Maryland, Kentucky, Missouri, and West Virginia, and even during the harsh and unhappy days of 'reconstruction' (1867–1876),[1] efforts were made in other states to

[1] The presidential plan of reconstruction (1865–1867), which sought to

build up systems of free public education.[1] The organization of education became more thorough and mandatory than before the war. All children, white and black, were to attend school between six and twenty-one, and the term was to last from four to six months each year. Property and poll taxation were established for the support of the schools. A state superintendent and state board of education, and county commissioners and a county board and trustees in each district, were provided for. Text-book commissions were often established, and free books were granted to poor children. The foundation for a real system was thus laid. This was a tremendous undertaking, and it shows the greatest courage and executive ability upon the part of the South to have brought it to pass. Property had been diminished in valuation to the extent of nearly two billion dollars, and there were two million children to be educated. Moreover, under the reconstruction régime, the tax on property was often not collected, and the appropriations for education remained on paper.[2] Indifference and inexperience were aggravated by the fear that 'mixed' schools would be forced upon the white population by a reconstruction legislature or a Congress with

enlist the coöperation of the native white citizens, was too quickly supplanted by the congressional plan to have much effect upon education.

[1] *E. g.* Tennessee in 1867, North and South Carolina in 1868, and Virginia and Georgia in 1870.

[2] E. W. Knight has shown in his *Influence of Reconstruction on Education in the South* (New York, 1913) that undue credit has been given the reconstruction régime for interest in popular education. "The legislatures were indeed most liberal in making appropriations for schools; but the appropriations seem not to have been paid fully or even in large part."

millennial zeal in behalf of universal brotherhood. These and many other obstacles for fully a decade constituted an enormous stumbling-block. Several factors, however, aided and encouraged the South in its efforts. Of these the most important was the foundation in 1867 of the Peabody Educational Fund of $2,000,000, well characterized as "a gift to the suffering South for the good of the Union." George Peabody, the donor, while a native of Massachusetts, had lived for a time in the South, and realized that the nation could not prosper while such an untoward educational situation existed anywhere. Under a board of trustees, composed of the most distinguished men of the nation, and through the direct management of the wisest and most sympathetic agents, this fund performed a magnificent service. By an appeal to the higher sentiment of the communities and states, it awakened and stimulated educational effort by granting the necessary assistance. When it proved insufficient for the great task, the trustees pleaded with Congress for an additional subsidy, and made the whole country aware of the crying needs of education in the South. Mr. Peabody hoped that his example might be followed by others, and such has been the case, for more than ten million dollars have been contributed for similar purposes from several sources. Aid has thus been granted to various grades of public education, institutions to train teachers for the new schools have been established, and both white and colored children are being given opportunities for a thorough public school education.

In this they were aided by the Peabody Educational Fund, and large sums have since been contributed for similar purposes.

Despite the tremendous rally during the seventies, however, the struggle for public education in the South was not won for twenty years, but complete systems

While the struggle was not won for twenty years,

of common schools have now at length been generally established. Even the first results of this universal education were gratifying, especially in the poorer districts, and advanced features have rapidly been added. With the cessation of the reconstruction influence and the subsidence of the dread of mixed schools, attendance and appropriations have greatly increased, girls have come to be given equal opportunities with the boys, the education of colored children has been adequately supported, and provision has been made for training and stimulating teachers of both races. Separate state institutions for higher education, cultural and vocational, have been established to furnish a broad education for both whites and negroes. Since 1890 there has been no evidence of any widespread hostility to public education, and the expenditures and intensive improvement of the schools have been constantly progressing. Thus in the Southern states there has been a continual, though somewhat fluctuating, growth of a sentiment for common schools from the time of its initiation by the broad-visioned Jefferson to the universal sentiment of to-day. It evolved through long years of varied success and failure, and broke its chrysalis after the wreck of the Civil War, and gradually attained to its present proportions. Its achievements during the past two decades seem almost unparalleled in history.

the sentiment and opportunity for public education have since 1890 been complete.

With its final development in the South during the last decade of the nineteenth century, the distinctly American public school system may be said to have been fully elaborated. The educational ideals and traditions imported from Europe have gradually been modified and adapted to the needs of America. Schools have become pub-

And with the development in the South, the American public school system has been fully elaborated,

lic and free in the modern sense. The control of education has passed from private parties and even quasi-public societies to the state. The schools have likewise come to be supported by the state, and are open to all children alike without the imposition of any financial obligation. This latter step has been taken very slowly, and it was not accomplished in most states until after the Civil War. In secondary education, the academies, which supplanted the 'grammar' schools, first became 'free academies' and made no charge for tuition from local patrons, though remaining close corporations, and then were in time replaced by the true American secondary institution,—the high school. Colleges became largely nonsectarian, even when not nominally so, and state universities were organized in all except a few of the oldest commonwealths. Thus has the idea of common schools and the right to use the public wealth to educate the entire body of children into sound American citizenship been made complete. Although the system is still capable of much improvement, it is expressive of American genius and development. It is simply the American idea of government and society applied to education. It is the educational will of the people expressed through the majority, and the resultant of the highest thinking and aspirations of a great nation made up of the most powerful and progressive elements of all civilized peoples. This development marks an advanced phase of the modern sociological tendency in education. While it may at times appear unscientific, illogical, and disordered, no short cut is possible for this characteristic evolution of American civilization. The process of educating public opinion and of directing public administration is slow and tortuous. Nor is the system to be

and marks an advanced phase of the modern sociological tendency in education.

wedded to any fixed organization or practice, but it should be allowed to move with the expanding vision of the people. Each state may, therefore, constantly adapt to its own use whatever seems of value in other commonwealths or countries, and under the American plan reap the benefit of the broadest educational experience everywhere.

SUPPLEMENTARY READING

I. Sources

Revised constitutions, statutes, and legislative documents, and the reports of Superintendents, Commissioners, and Boards of Education, of the various states, 1835 to the present; and the Annual Reports of the United States Commissioner of Education, 1867 to the present.

II. Authorities

Blackmar, F. W. *History of Federal and State Aid to Higher Education in the United States.*

Boone, R. G. *Education in the United States.* Parts III and IV.

Boone, R. G. *History of Education in Indiana.*

Bourne, W. O. *History of the Public School Society of the City of New York.* Chapters XII–XV.

Brown, E. E. *The Making of Our Middle Schools.* Chapters XIV–XX.

Butler, N. M. (Editor). *Education in the United States.* I.

Cubberley, E. P. *Changing Conceptions of Education.*

Curry, O. H. *Education at the South.*

Dexter, E. G. *History of Education in the United States.* Chapters VIII–XII.

Hinsdale, B. A. *Horace Mann and the Common School Revival.* Chap. XIII.

Knight, E. W. *The Influence of Reconstruction on Education in the South.*

Martin, G. H. *Evolution of the Massachusetts Public School System.* Lectures V and VI.

MAYO, A. D. *Report of the United States Commissioner of Education.* 1893–94, XVII; 1898–99, VIII; 1899–1900, VII; 1900–01, X; 1903, VIII and IX; 1904, XVI.

MERRIWETHER, C. *History of Higher Education in South Carolina.*

PALMER, A. E. *The New York Public School.*

PRATT, D. J. *Annals of Public Education in the State of New York.*

RANDALL, S. S. *History of the Common School System of the State of New York.* Third and Fourth Periods.

SMITH, C. L. *History of Education in North Carolina.*

SMITH, W. L. *Historical Sketch of Education in Michigan.*

STEINER, B. C. *History of Education in Connecticut.*

STEINER, B. C. *History of Education in Maryland.*

STOCKWELL, T. B. *History of Public Education in Rhode Island.*

THWING, C. F. *Education in the United States since the Civil War.*

WICKERSHAM, J. P. *History of Education in Pennsylvania.* Chaps. XVII–XXVIII.

CHAPTER IX

THE DEVELOPMENT OF MODERN SCHOOL SYSTEMS

During the past century and a half the leading powers of Europe have developed state systems of education somewhat different from each other and that of the United States, which may afford mutual suggestions, when understood in their historical perspective.

National Systems of Education in Europe and Canada.—In previous chapters (IV, VI, VIII,) we have witnessed the gradual evolution in America of state systems of universal education out of the unorganized and rather aristocratic arrangement of schools that had first been transplanted from Europe in the seventeenth century. But development of a centralized organization of public schools has not been confined to the United States. During the past century and a half, the leading powers of Europe, especially Germany, France, and England, and the more recently federated Dominion of Canada, have likewise organized state systems of education similar in some respects to those of the American union. All of these countries have now established universal elementary education free to all, although as yet in few instances are secondary schools also gratuitous. France alone has completely secularized its system, but the public schools of the other nations, while still including religious instruction, have been emancipated from ecclesiastical control, and are responsible to the civil authorities. In all of them school attendance is compulsory. As we have already noticed,[1] accounts of this development of national systems of education by the European states have proved a great source of illumination and inspiration for America.

[1] Pp. 168 and 178ff.

Yet the educational system in none of these countries is identical with that in the United States, but has been adapted in each case to the genius and social organization of the people concerned. Its characteristics must, therefore, be considerably modified, in order to be utilized or to prove suggestive to other nations, and can be understood only in the light of the educational history of the particular country to which it belongs. For an intelligent appreciation of these modern school systems, we must, therefore, trace the gradual development to their present form in response to the changing ideals of successive periods, although it will take us considerably back of the period we are now considering.

In Germany the universities date back to the fourteenth and fifteenth centuries, but have been modified in character during the subsequent educational movements;

Early History of German Educational Institutions. — The earliest of the European school systems to be established upon anything like the present basis appear in the various states of Germany during the eighteenth century. Some centuries before, however, most of the elements in these educational organizations had arisen and had since passed through various stages of their history. The universities in many instances date back to the general spread of these institutions in Germany during the fourteenth and fifteenth centuries.[1] In the fifteenth and sixteenth centuries they began to feel the influence of humanism and to introduce chairs of classic literature.[2] During the Reformation many of them withdrew from the control of church and pope, and came under the state and the Protestant princes; and, as an outgrowth of the theological agitation, several new universities, Protestant and Catholic, were founded.[3] By the end of the eight-

[1] See Graves, *History of Education during the Transition*, pp. 81f.

[2] *Op. cit.*, p. 145.

[3] *Op. cit.*, pp. 202 and 236.

eenth century, as a result of the progress of 'realism,' most of the Protestant universities had come to create professorships in the natural sciences. Meanwhile *Gymnasien*, Jesuit colleges, and other classical secondary schools of Germany had grown up during the sixteenth century out of the humanistic and religious training of the Northern Renaissance.[1] But their course was somewhat modified through the development of realistic studies,—mathematics and science, in the seventeenth century, and these classical schools were complemented, and, during the nineteenth century, rivaled by the *Realschulen*, or 'real-schools,' which, in their earliest form, began to spread about the middle of the eighteenth century.[2] The German elementary schools, which came to be known as *Volksschulen*, or 'people's schools,' on the other hand, find their roots in the Reformation. Luther and his associates continually urged the education of the common people, and a rudimentary system of elementary schools began to be established by the princes in various German states during the sixteenth and seventeenth centuries.[3] During the latter century there was a decided tendency throughout the people's schools to add to the realistic content of the course, especially elementary instruction in science.[4] Thus it is evident that the various stages in the education of Germany sprang up separately, and the system has chronologically grown from the top down. First came the higher training of the universities, then the secondary education of the classical institutions, and last of all the people's schools. Up to the later years of the eighteenth century all of these educational elements

the gymnasia grew up in the sixteenth century; the real-schools arose in the seventeenth; and the people's schools had their roots in the Reformation.

Thus the various stages of education have grown from the top down.

Until the eighteenth century, all

[1] *Op. cit.*, pp. 154ff. and 210ff.

[2] *Op. cit.*, pp. 290ff.

[3] *Op. cit.*, pp. 183ff. and 197ff.

[4] *Op. cit.*, p. 289.

institutions remained under ecclesiastical control, but they have since been gradually taken over by the state.

remained almost entirely under ecclesiastical control, but during this period the schools and universities were gradually taken over by the state from the church, and centralized national systems were gradually organized. Legislation for compulsory attendance at the elementary schools began to be passed, and by the beginning of the nineteenth century the schools had become political rather than ecclesiastical institutions. The state assumed the real management of education, although the clergy were still allowed to exercise a few educational prerogatives.

This movement is well illustrated in the Prussian educational system, whose development may well be taken as typical of that in all the other states.

The Beginning of Central Control in Prussia.—Among these German states the first one of importance to organize and centralize universal education and make it compulsory was Prussia. While each of the others is characterized by an educational history and peculiarities of its own, they have all been considerably guided by this largest and most influential of the states of Germany. It may, therefore, well be considered as typical of all, and the discussion of German school systems will here be limited to the Prussian. The rise of Prussia, educationally as well as politically, seems to have been due to a strong line of monarchs, despotic in power, but benevolent and thoroughly awake to the best interests of their people. The continuity of the Hohenzollern dynasty with the almost unbroken maintenance of sound policies has gradually brought about the elevation of its dominion from a small electorate (1415) to a great kingdom (1688) and the headship of the German empire (1871). Early in the sixteenth century Prussia began the development of central control in education, but for two centuries this was generally carried on through the

The educational rise of Prussia has been due to a despotic but benevolent and enlightened line of monarchs.

The development of central control in education be-

medium of the church. A 'consistory' of clerical and lay officers was first appointed to inspect and superintend both church and school affairs (1532 and 1573), then a special board for the supervision of educational institutions was formed (1604), and finally schools were declared to be not simply church organizations, but to belong to the state (1687), although the teacher was still regarded as a sort of pastor's assistant. Various other steps were also taken toward strengthening the system. A reformation and reorganization of schools was inaugurated (1540), parents were ordered to keep their children regularly in school (1648), and it was decreed that schools should as far as possible be established in the villages as well as the cities (1687).

gan in the sixteenth century, but for two centuries it was carried on through the medium of the church.

The Reforms of Frederick William I.—These reforms, however, were not fully realized at the time, although they pointed out the direction of educational progress. The greatest developments occurred in the eighteenth century during the reigns of Frederick William I (1713–1740) and Frederick the Great (1740–1786). The advanced steps that were then taken in education formed but part of the general plan of these monarchs for the improvement of national life and character, the elevation of the peasantry, and the overthrow of ecclesiastical despotism. They sought by means of centralized and universal education to develop Prussia into a strong, prosperous, and unified state. While narrow, parsimonious, and hostile to science, Frederick William I accomplished much for both the material and educational welfare of the kingdom. He built up a powerful army, in which merit alone counted for promotion, and he created a strong centralized administration through an

In the eighteenth century decided steps in advance were taken by Frederick William I, who established a large number of elementary schools, did much to make attendance compulsory (1717 and 1736), and founded two teachers' seminaries;

efficient organization of the civil service. He was liberal toward elementary schools, establishing some eighteen hundred of them with money saved from the expenses of the royal household, and he endeavored to make attendance compulsory. In 1717 he decreed that, wherever schools existed, children should be required to attend during the winter, and in the summer whenever they could be spared by their parents, which must be at least once a week. He founded the first teachers' seminary at Stettin in 1735 from his own private means, and the next year he caused another to be established at Magdeburg. The same year (1736) he also had a definite law passed, making education compulsory for children from six to twelve years of age.

Educational Achievements of Frederick the Great.—By such acts Frederick William I demonstrated his belief that the state should not relegate elementary training to the church and locality, but should itself see that adequate provision was made, and he thus started an educational tendency that was to be further developed during the reign of his more able son. Frederick the Great was humane, tolerant in religion, and sympathetic with the scientific spirit of the rationalists. He made great material improvements in his domains, humanized his government and laws, permitted freedom of speech and of the press, and greatly promoted research. In no way did he show his enlightenment more clearly than in his care for the education of his subjects. He encouraged academic freedom at the universities and reëstablished the 'Academy of Sciences'[1] in Berlin. He also founded and formulated a course for the 'Acad-

and by his son, Frederick the Great, who encouraged academic freedom, founded an academy of sciences, centralized and improved secondary education, and achieved much for universality

[1] *Akademie der Wissenschaften.*

emy of Nobles,'[1] to train young aristocrats to become army officers and diplomats. Likewise he greatly improved secondary education by placing all the provincial 'consistories,' except that in the Catholic duchy of Silesia, under the jurisdiction of the one at the capital (1750). Through this central control, a few excellent *Gymnasien* with uniform courses were developed out of a large number of weak classical schools. His achievements in behalf of universal education were even more noteworthy. During the earlier years of his reign he issued several decrees concerning the support of schools established in villages, and in 1750 he ordered that all vacancies in schools on the crown lands and administrative villages be filled by graduates from the real-school and seminary founded by Hecker at Berlin three years before. But the greatest step toward a national system did not take place until 1763, when he issued his *General School Regulations for the Country*.[2] This decree required children to attend school from five until thirteen or fourteen, and until they "know not only what is necessary of Christianity, fluent reading, and writing, but can give answer in everything which they learn from the school books prescribed and approved by our consistory." If any pupils should arrive at this state of proficiency before thirteen or fourteen, they could even then leave school only through the official certification of the teacher, minister, and inspector. Provision was also made for the attendance of children who had to herd cattle or were too poor to pay the school fees. Sunday continuation schools were to be established for young people beyond the school age. Teachers must have

and efficiency in elementary education through the *General School Regulations* (1763).

[1] *Académie des Nobles.*

[2] *Generallandschulreglement.*

attended Hecker's seminary and had to be examined and licensed by the inspector. Arrangements were also made for stated visits to the school and conferences with the teacher by the local pastor and for annual inspection and report by the superintendent and inspector of each administrative district. This decree was supplemented in 1765 with similar *Regulations for the Catholic Schools in Silesia*, drawn up by Abbot Felbiger.

Frederick's improvements, while bitterly resented by conservatives, became the foundation for even more effective laws, especially through Zedlitz, who not only accomplished several reforms during the reign of Frederick, but after his death brought about the foundation of an *Oberschulcollegium*, or central board of education (1787).

Frederick, however, was somewhat in advance of general sentiment. The carrying out of the decree was stubbornly opposed by many teachers, who could not meet the new requirements; by farmers, who objected to the loss of their children's time; and by the nobles, who feared the discontent and uprising of the peasants, in case they were educated. The execution of the regulation was still in the power of the clergy, and for some time it proved but little more than a pious wish.[1] But the monarch strove hard to have it enforced, and it became the foundation for the more effective laws that have since become embodied in the Prussian school system. After 1771 the educational work of Frederick was substantially aided by the appointment of Baron von Zedlitz as head of the Department of Lutheran Church and School Affairs. This great minister had been much impressed by Basedow's principles and experiments and by Rochow's application of the 'naturalistic' training in reforming rural education.[2] He was eager to assist in elevating the condition of the peasants, and, through his efforts, before the close of Frederick's reign the course

[1] Much of the good was undone also by the permission in 1779 to employ veteran soldiers as teachers without examination.

[2] See pp. 25ff. and 32.

of the village schools was greatly strengthened and enriched, and a regular normal school was opened at Halberstadt (1778). Zedlitz likewise took a decided interest in the movement of 'new humanism,' which, under the leadership of Gesner, Heyne, and Ernesti, had for a generation been stressing a study of the literature, thought, and content of the classics rather than the linguistic and formal grind that was in vogue. While he lacked the hearty support of the conservative school authorities in the reforms he was commissioned to make in the *Gymnasien* (1779), he succeeded in reviving the humanistic ideal in secondary education.

Zedlitz and the Inauguration of an Oberschulcollegium.—The management of the schools, however, still remained in the hands of the clergy. It was not until the year after Frederick's death that his policy of nationalizing education culminated in the organization of an *Oberschulcollegium* or central board of administration for all affairs in Prussia (1787). This new method of control was largely the work of Zedlitz, who had been influenced by Basedow's suggestion of a central board of education in his *Address on Schools and Studies* (1768).[1] He held for some time that an organization of this sort, made up of experts, would be much more efficient than church consistories under the king's minister, and he persuaded the new sovereign, Frederick William II (*r.* 1786–1797), to transfer the schools from ecclesiastical to state control. Unfortunately this king was a reactionary. He did not really wish to establish a national system of education, and held that the main business of the schools was to teach religion. While Zedlitz was made chairman, the

But the new king, Frederick William II, made up the membership of this board from the clergy and refused to extend its jurisdiction.

[1] See p. 26.

membership of the *Oberschulcollegium* was mostly filled from the clergy, and the king refused to extend its jurisdiction to the higher schools. It was thus impossible to complete a uniform system, and the schools remained under the control of the church and were only indirectly responsible to the state.

The General Code of 1794 and Further Development of a National System.—Despite the reactionary policy of Frederick William II, a further step toward a national school system was taken during his reign. In 1794 there was published a *General Code*, or fundamental civil law of Prussia, and in the chapter upon education[1] was formulated the centralization that had been developing throughout the century. The law declared in unequivocal terms:

Nevertheless, a *General Code* was published in this reign (1794), which declared all schools and universities to be state institutions,

> "All schools and universities are state institutions, charged with the instruction of youth in useful information and scientific knowledge. Such institutions may be founded only with the knowledge and consent of the state."

It further held that "all public schools and educational institutions are under the supervision of the state, and are at all times subject to its examination and inspection." Moreover, teachers were not to be chosen without the consent of the state, and where their appointment was not vested in particular persons, it was to belong to the state. Teachers of all secondary schools were to be regarded as state officials. No child was to be excluded from the schools because of his religion, nor compelled to stay for religious instruction when it differed from the belief in which he had been brought up.

[1] *Allgemeine Landrecht*, Pt. II, tit. 12.

This liberal and comprehensive code marked the culmination of the attempts to establish a national nonsectarian system of education. It naturally met with opposition from the clergy and the ignorant masses, but the system persisted and has continued to develop. For a time, under the well-intentioned, but weak Frederick William III (*r.*1797–1840), however, the conservatism and corruption in government continued and the schools were neglected. The complete humiliation of Prussia in the battle of Jena (1806) and the treaty of Tilsit (1807), however, opened the eyes of that good-natured monarch to the need of universal education for the nation. It was then that he gave voice to that policy whose implied prophecy was so speedily fulfilled during the reign of his son, William I:

and marked the culmination of a nonsectarian system.

The humiliation of Prussia in the treaty of Tilsit (1807)

"Although we have lost territory, power, and prestige, still we must strive to regain what we have lost by acquiring intellectual and moral power; and therefore it is my earnest desire and will to habilitate the nation by devoting most earnest attention to the education of the masses of my people."

In his efforts for a national system of education the king was stimulated and aided by his heroic queen Louise, and by the patriotic songs of Arndt for the common people and the appeals of Fichte to the leaders in thought and action.[1] The reconstruction of the civil administration was accompanied by a more centralized organization of the Prussian school system. The *Oberschulcollegium* was abolished, to get rid of the clerical domination that had crept in, and a Bureau of Education was created as a section of the Department of the Interior (1807). Within a decade (1808–1817), under the management of the

stimulated the good-natured Frederick William III to further efforts for universal education, and the clerical domination of the Oberschulcollegium was replaced by a Bureau of Education,

[1] See p. 146.

and a corresponding advance was evident in secondary education.

scholarly philosopher, Von Humboldt, and his successor, Von Schuckman, national education was made a reality. Schools were held to exist for the state, to train religious and patriotic citizens, and much progress took place in the education of the masses. Great improvements were made in method and content, and a new spirit was introduced into the training of elementary teachers. A corresponding advance was evident in secondary education. In order to teach in the gymnasiums, a strict examination was instituted, and the work was given professional standing by withdrawing the privilege from ministerial candidates while waiting for a church position (1810). The 'leaving examination' for those graduating from the gymnasiums, which had been attempted by Zedlitz nearly a quarter of a century before (1788), was likewise revived, and all classical schools were forced to come to a uniform standard of attainment (1812). A commissioner was appointed to revise the course of study, and a comprehensive *Lehrplan* was shortly published (1816), which pleased the new humanists by its emphasis upon Greek, and the realists and formal disciplinarians by the increased amount of mathematics. These reforms could not be effective at once, especially as competent teachers were lacking, but pedagogical seminaries, to train secondary instructors, were eventually instituted at the universities (1825), a 'year of trial' was demanded of all teachers (1826), and new requirements, including the main subjects taught in the secondary schools, together with philosophy, pedagogy, and theology, were introduced into the examination of gymnasial teachers (1831). A gymnasium leaving certificate also came to be required of candidates for the civil service, and for eligibility to examination for admission to the learned professions (1834).

The External Organization of the Prussian System.— Meanwhile, the Bureau of Education was erected into a separate department (1817).[1] Next the state was divided into educational provinces, and a *Schulcollegium*, or administrative board, with considerable independence, but subject to the minister, was established over each province (1825). This organization of the state system was further elaborated by the Prussian constitution of 1850 and by many educational acts[2] and ministerial decrees that have since become effective. The provinces are now divided into 'governments,' each of which has a 'school commission' over it, and every government is divided into 'districts,' whose chief officer is a 'school inspector.' Under the district inspector are local inspectors, and each separate school also has a local board, to take charge of repairs, supplies, and other external matters. The supreme management of the schools has thus been gradually coming into the hands of the state for nearly two centuries. The decrees of 1717 and 1763, the establishment of the *Oberschulcollegium* in 1787, the General Code promulgated in 1794, the foundation of a Bureau of Education in 1807 and of a separate department in 1817, and the organization of educational provinces in 1825, are the milestones that mark the way to state control. But, while the influence of the church

Later, the Bureau of Education became an independent department (1817); a *Schulcollegium* was established over each province (1825), and a further organization of the state system was elaborated by several subsequent acts.

[1] *Ministerium für den Cultus und für Unterricht,* but this title was soon expanded to *Ministerium der geistlichen, Unterrichts—, und Medizinal—Angelegenheiten.* In 1911 the division of public health was separated from this ministry, but public worship still forms one of its three departments.

[2] Especially the elementary school law of 1906.

Despite this establishment of state control, the influence of the church is still somewhat felt in education.

has been constantly diminishing, it is still felt to some extent. Many of the board members are ministers or priests and the inspectors come mostly from the clergy. Moreover, religious instruction forms part of the course in every school, although it is given at such an hour that any pupil may withdraw if the teaching is contrary to the faith in which he has been reared. The secondary schools are largely interdenominational, but in elementary education there are separate schools for Catholics and Protestants, alike supported by the state.

In Germany the secondary work of the gymnasia and the real-schools parallels the course in the people's schools rather than supplements it; and the secondary institutions are attended by the children of the upper classes and the elementary by those of the lower.

The Volksschulen and the Mittelschulen.—Prussia, like most of the principal states of Europe, as a result of their educational history,[1] has its elementary and secondary schools quite separate and distinct. The universities continue the work of the gymnasiums and real-schools, but these two latter institutions parallel the work of the people's schools rather than supplement it. The course of the secondary school ordinarily occupies the pupil from nine to eighteen years of age, while that of the elementary school carries him from six to fourteen, and after the first three years it is practically impossible to transfer from the elementary to the secondary system. A pupil cannot enter a gymnasium or real-school after completing the people's school, and the only further training he can obtain is that of a commercial, industrial, or 'continuation school,'[2] which is not part of the system

[1] See p. 315.

[2] These *Fortbildungsschulen* are sometimes held in the evening and even in a few instances on Sunday, but they are mostly conducted during the week in the daytime. They are not intended to review work previously done, but to treat some subjects already covered from the point of view of application to future vocational needs, and also to consider new subjects that serve the same purpose.

proper. The people's schools are gratuitous and are attended mostly by the children of the lower classes, while the gymnasiums charge a substantial tuition fee and are patronized by the professional classes and aristocracy. Hence the line between elementary and secondary education in Prussia is longitudinal and not latitudinal, as it is in the United States; the distinction is one of wealth and social status rather than of educational grade and advancement. There are also some *Mittelschulen* ('middle schools') for the middle classes of people, who cannot send their children to the secondary schools, and yet can afford some exclusiveness. They have one more class than the people's schools, include a foreign language during the last three years, and require teachers with a better training.

There are also some 'middle schools' for the middle classes.

The Gymnasien and Other Secondary Schools.— The main types of secondary schools in Prussia are the *Gymnasien*, with the classic languages as the main feature of their course, and the *Realschulen*, characterized by larger amounts of the modern languages, mathematics, and the natural sciences. For more than a century after the first real-school was opened in Berlin by Hecker (1747), this type of institution had only six years in its course, and was considered inferior to the gymnasium. The practical needs of the people were not regarded in secondary education, but only the ideal training of the ideal citizen. By the ministerial decree of 1859, however, two classes of real-schools were recognized. Those of the first class had a course of nine years, and included Latin, but not Greek. They were given full standing as secondary schools, and graduates were granted admission to the universities, except for the study of the-

In 1859 two classes of real-schools were recognized, and out of these arose in 1882 the real-gymnasia and the higher real-schools.

ology, medicine, or law. The course of the second class of these institutions contained no Latin, and they were dependent upon the good-will of the communities in which the real-schools were located. They were recognized as secondary schools only when their course was up to the official standard. In 1882 the compromise character of the course of the first class of institutions led to their being designated as *Realgymnasien*, while the second class in some instances had their work extended to nine years and became known as *Oberrealschulen*. Their graduates were allowed the privilege of studying at the universities in mathematics and the natural sciences. In rural and other districts, however, where a complete course cannot be maintained, there are often secondary institutions that do not carry the student more than six years, and these are known, according to the curriculum, as *Progymnasien*, *Realprogymnasien*, and *Realschulen*. The first two classes are far less common than institutions with the longer course of the same character, but the *Realschulen* are nearly twice as numerous as the *Oberrealschulen*.

A six-year course is sometimes offered by a 'progymnasium' or a 'real-progymnasium,' as well as by the real-schools.

In order that the determination of a boy's career may be deferred, new secondary institutions known as 'reform-schools' have been rapidly developing.

Since these three types of secondary institutions are so distinct from each other, it is evident that a parent is forced to decide the future career of his boy at nine years, long before his special ability can be known. If he once enters a real-school, he can never transfer to a gymnasium, because the Latin begins in the latter course at once, nor can he enter the gymnasium from the real-gymnasium after twelve, since he has had no Greek. To overcome this objection, during the past quarter of a century efforts have been made to delay the irrevocable decision by grouping all three courses as one institution and making them identical as long as possible. In secondary schools of this new sort, French is usually the only foreign language taught for the first three years. Then the course divides, and one section takes up Latin and the other English. After two years more a further bifurcation takes place in the Latin section, and one group begins with the Greek, while the other studies English. These institutions are known as *Reformschulen* and the plan was first introduced at Frankfort in 1892.[1] The 'reform schools' are now growing rapidly, and there is evident an increasing tendency to postpone the choice of courses as long as possible. The three years of training preliminary to admission to a secondary school of any type may be obtained through the people's or the middle schools. But there has also grown up, as an attachment of the secondary schools, a *Vorschule* ('preparatory school'), to perform this function for pupils of the more exclusive classes.

The three years of preparation for any secondary school may be obtained in the people's schools or in a regular 'preparatory school'

The Universities.—Like the other stages of education, the universities are now emancipated from ecclesiastical control, and may be regarded as part of the national system of education. The university is now coördinate and under the same authority with the church, for both are legally state institutions. Universities can, therefore, be established only by the state or with the approval of the state. In general, however, they are not controlled by legislation, but through charters and special decrees of the minister of education. As their income from endowments and fees is very small, they are for the most

The universities are now considered state institutions and part of the national system, although they are controlled by charters and decrees rather than by legislation.

[1] Several years before this, a combination of the *Realgymnasium* and the *Realschule* was made by Dr. Schlee at Altona, but this plan was tentative and by special permission, and has spread to only a few schools.

part supported by the state. They are managed internally by the rector and senate. The rector is annually chosen from their own number by the full professors, with the approval of the minister, and the senate is a committee from the various faculties. The professors are regarded as civil servants with definite privileges, and they are appointed by the minister, although the suggestions of the faculty concerned are usually respected. The civic status of the universities is further shown in their being recognized by representation in the Diet or upper house of the legislature.

While a national system began in France almost a century later than in Germany, the earlier history of the secondary and higher institutions was not radically different.

Educational Institutions in France before the Revolution.—The development of a centralized system of education in France began almost a century later than in Germany. During the eighteenth and the early nineteenth century the different monarchic powers were not at all favorable to training the masses, and popular education was badly neglected. It required several revolutions in government and the establishment of a permanent republic, to break the old traditions completely, and to make it evident that universal suffrage should be accompanied by universal education. The earlier educational history of France, however, was not radically different from that of Germany and the rest of western Europe. Thanks to the Renaissance and the efforts of such men as Budæus, Corderius, and Ramus, the anæmic scholasticism and narrow theological dogmatism in the higher institutions were replaced in the fifteenth and sixteenth centuries by humanism and the study of the classic authors. A chair of Greek was established at the University of Paris (1458), and the College of France (1530) was founded by Francis I as a protest and a means of permitting freedom in thought.[1] The Jesuit colleges, with their humanistic courses, began to open (1540), and before the close of the century Henry IV undertook a reform of the university. Further broadening of higher and secondary education took place in the seventeenth century through the organization of the Oratorian and Port Royalist courses and the introduction of realism.[2] Toward the close of this century also Rollin wrought his reformation of the university.[3] After the middle of the eighteenth century the revolutionary spirit began to manifest itself. The *Emile* presented its successful protest against the artificial education of the times (1762); the Jesuits were suppressed in France (1764); and, at the request of the Parliament of Paris, a general plan for a reorganization and centralization of education was presented by Rolland (1768).

Educational Development since the French Revolution.—Up to this time little attention had been given to elementary education, except through a small number of parochial schools and the institutions established by the Institute of Christian Brethren in the seventeenth century.[4] But this plan of Rolland, while not adopted, suggested that relatively less should be expended for secondary education, and recommended universal education and an adequate number of training schools for teachers. The Constitutional Convention in 1793 was more destructive in its reforms, and abolished all the old educational organization, including the University of Paris

Toward the close of the eighteenth century a number of plans for popular education were proposed.

[1] See Graves, *History of Education during the Transition*, pp. 141ff.

[2] *Op. cit.*, pp. 222ff. and 243ff.

[3] *Op. cit.*, p. 228.

[4] *Op. cit.*, pp. 230ff.

and the 'colleges' or secondary schools. Then followed the confusion of the revolutionary legislation. A large number of short-lived proposals and enactments were passed and repealed, but during this period of protest there were formulated great principles of educational administration and practice that were destined later to be embodied in more practical form and to rehabilitate French education upon a grander and more national scale. Each of the three revolutionary assemblies had its own scheme of popular education, put forward by Talleyrand, Condorcet, and Daunou respectively, but the first two plans never got beyond the paper stage, and the last (1795) was too loosely drawn to be carried out. It did, however, introduce the influential conception of 'central schools,' which were the only type of secondary education during the Revolution. The year before (1794) a system of department normal schools, with a great central normal at Paris, was also proposed but never really consummated.[1]

In Napoleon's time the lycées and communal colleges were recognized as the means of secondary education, and, together with the faculties of higher education, were united in the 'University of France.'

After the Revolution, during the consulate of Napoleon (1802–1804), the 'central schools' were replaced by the modern lycées, and the communal 'colleges' were recognized as secondary schools. When he had become emperor, Napoleon went further with his educational reorganization, and ordered all the lycées, secondary colleges, and faculties of higher education to be united in a single corporation, dependent upon the state and known as the 'University of France' (1808). This decree of centralization divided the country into twenty-seven administrative districts, called 'academies,' each of which was

[1] The school at Paris, however, was founded and continued through the spring months of 1795.

to establish university faculties of letters and science near the principal lycées. For want of adequate support, these faculties were to borrow part of their instructional corps from the local lycées, and their chief function was to be the conferring of the degrees of bachelor, master (*license*), and doctor. This organization, however, did not include elementary education, and little attempt was made to provide for schools of this grade before the reign of Louis Philippe. Upon the advice of his great minister of education, Guizot, that monarch organized primary education, requiring a school for each commune, or at least for a group of two or three communes, and starting higher primary schools in the department capitals and in communes of over six thousand inhabitants (1833). He also instituted inspectors of primary schools, and established department normal schools under the more effective control of the state authorities. The plan for higher primary schools was never fully realized, and the institutions of this sort that had been established disappeared during the second empire. The reactionary law of Falloux (1850) did not even mention these schools, but encouraged the development of denominational schools, and permitted teachers with scant qualifications to teach without further authorization than a bishop's 'letter of obedience.'

This organization did not include elementary education, and it remained for Louis Philippe, through Guizot, to require a primary school in each commune, to start higher primary schools in the larger centers, and to establish department normal schools, but much of this progress was lost under the reactionary law of 1850.

The Primary School System.—Guizot, however, had given a permanent impulse to popular education, and during the third republic foundations for a national system of education have rapidly been laid. Schools have been brought into the smallest villages, new and convenient buildings have been erected, and elementary education has been made free to all (1881) and compulsory be-

However, a permanent impulse to popular education had been given, and during the third republic elementary education has

been made free to all, compulsory, and secular; two higher normal schools to train teachers for the lower have been opened; and the higher primary schools have been reëstablished and 'supplementary courses' have been started.

tween the ages of six and thirteen (1882). To provide trained teachers, each department has been required to provide a normal school;[1] and two higher normals, one for men and one for women, to train teachers for the departmental normal schools, have been opened by the state (1882).[2] Secularization of the school system has also gradually taken place. First, the courses of study were secularized by the substitution of civic and moral instruction for religious (1881); next, the instructional force was secularized by providing that members of the clergy should no longer be employed in the public schools (1886), and by recognizing public school teachers as state officers (1889); and finally, the schools themselves were completely secularized by compelling the teaching orders[3] to report to the state authorities (1902), and by afterward closing the free schools directed by them (1904). The higher primary schools have been reëstablished and extended (1898), and 'supplementary courses' offered for pupils remaining at the lower primary schools after graduation. The studies in the supplementary courses are technical, as well as general, and some of the higher primary schools have been established for vocational training rather than literary. In addition, there are continuation 'schools of manual apprenticeship' in the various communes, subsidized by the state for indus-

Likewise, schools of 'manual apprenticeship' have been

[1] There should, under the present law, be one for boys and one for girls in each department, but for the sake of economy two adjacent departments have lately been allowed to unite in the support of normal schools, and there are (1912) in all eighty-seven normals for boys and eighty-six for girls instead of ninety for each sex.

[2] These are located at Saint Cloud and Fontenay-aux-Roses respectively, and must be distinguished from the higher normal schools at Paris and Sèvres, which prepare teachers for the secondary schools.

[3] Mostly the Christian Brethren.

trial and agricultural education, and five large schools for training in special crafts have been organized in Paris. Institutions for children between two and six years of age became part of the primary system in the days of Guizot (1833), and half a century later the present name, *écoles maternelles*,[1] was adopted (1881), although there have since been marked reforms made in the curriculum. There are also 'infant classes' for pupils from five to seven years of age. These theoretically form a separate stage of training between the maternal and the lower primary schools, but are, as a matter of fact, usually attached to one or the other. Thus within a generation universal elementary education has been established in France and brought completely under state control.

established in the communes, and five schools for special craft training in Paris, while 'infant classes' connect the maternal and primary schools.

The Lycées and Communal Colleges.—As in Prussia, the secondary school system of France does not connect with the primary, but is quite separate and distinct. The training has, since the time of Napoleon, been furnished chiefly by the lycées and communal colleges. During the Restoration (1814–1830) and the reign of Louis Philippe (1830–1848) the lycées were known as 'royal colleges,' but, with the advent of the second republic (1848–1851), the old name was restored and the curricula were completely reorganized. By this revision some elasticity was introduced into the last three years of the lycée by a bifurcation into a literary and a scientific course, and during the third republic further elections and much modern material have been incorporated. The latest revision (1902) has resulted in the establishment of four courses,—the Latin-Greek, the Latin-modern language, the Latin-science, and the science-modern language. The curric-

During the second republic the lycée was divided into a literary and a scientific course, and during the third republic there has been a differentiation into four courses, which takes place mostly during the second 'cycle' of the curriculum.

[1] See p. 63.

A special short course, to prepare for a military or technical school, is also offered in the leading lycées and in most lycées there are also preparatory classes to train the pupils from six to ten.

ulum is divided into two 'cycles,'—the first of four, and the second of three years, and it is during the second largely that the differentiation takes place.[1] In the leading lycées and colleges special preparation is also afforded for schools like the military institution of St. Cyr or the Polytechnic of Paris, and in some there is a short course of three or four years in modern languages and sciences that in function closely approaches that of the German *Realschulen*. The boys ordinarily begin the first cycle of the lycée or college at ten years of age, and while they may transfer from the primary system at this stage, in most lycées and colleges there are preparatory classes to train the pupil from six to ten. Education in a lycée or college is not gratuitous, but the income from tuition fees is so small as to cover but a small fraction of the cost, and the rest is contributed by the state. The communal colleges differ from the lycées in being local, (whereas the latter are considered national), and they are maintained by the communes, as well as the state. They have not the same standing, and the same attainments are not required of their professors. Until 1880 there were no lycées and communal colleges for girls, and convents and private schools furnished the only means of female education. Even now the course in the public secondary institutions for girls is two years shorter than in those for boys, although some of the more important furnish an extra year for students preparing for the higher normal school at Sèvres, which trains teachers

The communal colleges are more local and less efficient than the lycées.

Since 1880 there have been public secondary institutions for girls, but the course is usually two years shorter than in those for boys.

[1] This is not absolutely the case, as at the end of the second year of the first cycle the Latin pupils have the opportunity of electing Greek; and at the end of the cycle those who have selected Latin, but not Greek, are offered a new choice between modern languages and science.

for girls' secondary schools. The teachers for the boys' secondary schools are trained in a special higher normal school at the capital, which has since 1903 become a part of the University of Paris. The examination for graduation from the lycées and colleges, marked by the bachelor's degree, is conducted in each 'academy' by a committee of professors from the university, assisted by a board of professors from the lycées. This degree opens the door to all professional careers, including entrance to the universities.

Teachers for secondary schools are trained in higher normal schools at Paris and Sèvres. Graduation from the lycées and the colleges opens the way to all careers and to university entrance.

The Universities and Other Institutions of Higher Education.—More than one-half of the universities established in the various 'academies' by Napoleon were suppressed as soon as the monarchy was restored. But about half a dozen were reopened in the reign of Louis Philippe, and were gradually improved by the addition of new chairs. Beginning in 1885, a number of decrees established a general council of faculties in each academy to coördinate the different courses and studies, and in 1896 a law was passed, which established a university in each of the sixteen 'academies,' except one. Only a few of these universities have all the faculties, and they differ greatly in size. Of late years university attendance has grown about one-third, and Paris has fully eighteen thousand students. Above the baccalaureate of lycées and collèges are the *licence*, or master's degree, and the doctorate in the universities. The title of *agrégation*, awarded to a fixed number of licentiates each year through competitive examination, is also of importance to one expecting to teach in a lycée or university. The university degrees are ordinarily conferred in the name of the state and carry certain definite rights

The universities have met with various changes, and in 1896 a university was established in each of the sixteen 'academies,' except one, although only a few have all the faculties, and they differ greatly in size.

They lead to the 'licence' and doctorate and to the title of 'agrégation,' and since 1897 to the 'doctorate of the university.'

with them, but of late years a new type of degree, 'doctorate of the university,' is granted upon easier terms to foreigners more desirous of the degree than of its state privileges. In Paris, besides the university, there is the College of France, which still endeavors to foster freedom of thought,[1] and a dozen other institutions of university grade, connected with some special line, have been established.

In Paris there are a number of higher institutions besides the university.

Education is most thoroughly centralized in France through the minister of education and four directors in the central office, a rector in charge of each academy, the prefect and council in each department, the cantonal delegates, and

Administration of the French System of Education.— The centralization of education is more complete in France than in the United States or even Germany. The control of the schools is not vested in a number of individual states, but is assumed by the national government itself. The supreme head of the system is the minister of education. He is immediately assisted by three directors, one for each of the three departments,— primary, secondary, and higher education, and by a director of accounts, who has charge of all expenditures. All three departments contain several bureaus, each of which has special functions. A rector is in charge of each of the 'academies,' except Paris, where the minister nominally holds the office and a vice rector performs the duties. The rector has authority over all three fields of education in his department, but does not appoint the teachers. This office is performed by the prefect, or civil head of each department, upon the recommendation of the academy inspector. There is also a departmental council, which is presided over by the prefect, and consists of general counsellors, teachers, and inspectors. It appoints the delegates of each canton, who take charge of the school premises and equipment,

[1] See p. 292.

and determine the number and location of the primary schools, the number of teachers, and the penalties to be exacted of them, in case of misconduct. Further organization is effected through the maintenance of a complete corps of general, academy, and primary inspectors. Thus the French educational administration is the most thoroughly centralized of all modern nations.

a corps of inspectors.

English Education before the Nineteenth Century.— In England the nationalization and universalizing of education were delayed even longer than in France. This country was never controlled by enlightened despots, who could, as in Germany, anticipate and force the growth of public educational sentiment, nor was it overwhelmed by the sweep of a great revolution, destroying, as in France, all opposition to popular progress. The development of national education in England has gradually grown out of the conflict of a number of elements represented in its society. It has been the product of a series of compromises among many different factors,—the church, state, economic conditions, private enterprise, and philanthropy. While such a process of educational evolution seems exceedingly slow, and the resulting system is based upon practical sense rather than upon any well-considered theory or plan, it has not been subject to serious retrogression or abrupt change. Throughout the nineteenth century there was some attempt to weld together the various conflicting forces into a national system, but until late in this period the feeling prevailed that the state was not responsible for education. This function was regarded as belonging to the church and family, and the growing sentiment for universal education was retarded in its enactment into

National education in England has slowly evolved through a series of compromises between various elements in society.

law by the attitude of the House of Lords, which, for the most part, strove to keep the poor in ignorance and to maintain the authority of the established church.

Until the eighteenth century the Anglican church retained the monopoly of education,

The mediæval monopoly of the church remained even after the Anglican Reformation, for the schoolmasters were then licensed and controlled by the bishops of the Church of England, just as they had formerly been by the Roman episcopate.[1] The sway of formal humanism in secondary and higher education also became complete.[2] This domination in administration and content was first challenged in the seventeenth century, when the struggles of the Dissenters began,[3] and the period of realism developed with Bacon, Mulcaster, Milton, Hartlib, and Locke.[4] In the eighteenth century established authorities were even further questioned. Although court and parliamentary decisions still generally held that the bishops had power over elementary, as well as secondary education, this became a period of preparation for the activities in nationalizing education that appeared during the nineteenth century. Except for the meager training furnished through the Society for the Promotion of Christian Knowledge, the Sunday schools, and other philanthropic institutions,[5] the Church of England made little effort in behalf of elementary education during the eighteenth century. But these organizations, together with the 'monitorial' instruction of the British and Foreign, and the National societies,[6] greatly advanced the cause of universal education. And toward

and the eighteenth century accomplished little for elementary education, except to prepare for the nationalizing of the nineteenth.

Through various types of philanthropic instruction, universal education was greatly advanced.

[1] See Graves, *History of Education during the Transition*, p. 201.

[2] *Op. cit.*, p. 176.

[3] *Op. cit.*, pp. 196f., 291f., and 298f.

[4] *Op. cit.*, pp. 250ff., and 263ff.

[5] See pp. 37ff.

[6] See pp. 55 and 58.

the last of the eighteenth century there began to appear a new point of view, especially among philosophers, jurists, reformers, and economists, like Bentham, Blackstone, Robert Owen, and Adam Smith, who advocated universal education, compulsory attendance, and a national system of schools.

Movements in the Nineteenth Century Leading to the Act of 1870.—The theory of these great thinkers was somewhat in advance of the times, but, early in the nineteenth century, social changes in the way of liberty in thought and speech and of industrial improvement began to favor better educational opportunities. The Factory Act of 1802 restricted child labor and provided for the obligatory training of apprentices, and, although it was often evaded by masters and mistresses, it became an important precedent. Five years later came Mr. Whitbread's bill to permit the civic officials of any township or parish to establish schools for the poor wherever none existed. It passed in the lower house, but was defeated by the lords on the ground that it took education 'out of the superintendence and control of the clergy.' The contest, however, was reopened in 1815 by Henry Brougham. While that reformer lost his bill in 1820, he had previously secured a commission of inquiry on popular education (1816) and one on endowed schools (1818), and a large mass of information was thus collected that greatly contributed to the final success of universal education. In 1832, the passage of a reform bill, which largely increased the suffrage, aroused parliament to the need of educating the masses, and the next year the first parliamentary grant, £20,000, was made for elementary education. This sum was to be used solely to

Early in the nineteenth century various social changes improved educational opportunities, and a large amount of information that furthered universal education was secured through Brougham.

The extension of the suffrage aroused Parliament in 1833 to grant £20,000 for elementary education

through the National and British and Foreign societies.

aid in building schoolhouses for which subscriptions had been privately obtained, and so could be passed as a vote of 'supply,' without referring it to the House of Lords. It was apportioned through the National and the British and Foreign societies, which remained the channels of distribution for the state subsidies until 1870,[1] and, becoming in this way a vested interest, greatly hindered the development of a national system of education. Nevertheless, agitation in behalf of the cause was continually carried on, especially through public school organizations in the new manufacturing towns. The most influential of these were the 'Lancashire Public School Association,' established at Manchester in 1847, which was soon broadened to a 'National Public School Association,' and 'The League,' which was started at Birmingham in 1869, and rapidly spread through the country. Governmental activities constantly increased. In 1839 the annual grant was increased to £30,000 and allowed to be used for elementary education without restriction, and the same year the queen, despite the protest of the lords, appointed a separate committee of her Privy Council to administer the educational grants. This greatly curbed the ecclesiastical power and inaugurated state supervision of elementary education, as the new committee insisted that, in order to share in the funds, a school must be open to government inspection. State control was further organized in 1856 by the appointment of a Vice President of the Council to act as chairman of this educational committee and be responsible for the use of the funds to the House of Commons. The only other step of importance prior to

The cause was further advanced through the foundation of the Lancashire Public School Association (1847) and of The League (1869).

In 1839 the annual grant was raised to £30,000, and a special committee of the Privy Council was appointed to administer it, and in 1856 a Vice President of the Council was chosen to act as chairman of this educational committee.

[1] See pp. 58f.

1870 was the appointment in 1858 of a royal commission to inquire into the state of popular education. As the result of its findings, the bill of Robert Lowe was passed in 1861 to establish 'payment by results,' that is, to base the grant to any school upon the results shown by the pupils in the governmental examinations. This method was intended to increase efficiency, but, used as the sole means of testing, it soon proved narrowing and unfair, and had to be supplemented by the general opinion formed of the school by the inspectors.

In 1861, upon the recommendation of a commission upon popular education, a bill to establish 'payment by results' was passed.

'Board Schools' and their Development since 1870.— When the franchise was further extended in 1868, Mr. Lowe exhorted his fellow liberals: "Let us educate our new masters." This necessity of preparing millions of the common people for new responsibilities and authority in public affairs led in 1870 to the passage of the epoch-making bill of William E. Forster. Under this act 'board schools,' or institutions in charge of a board chosen by the people of the community, were to be established wherever a deficiency in the existing accommodations required it.[1] The 'voluntary,' or denominational schools, most of which belonged to the Church of England, were to share in the government grants upon equal terms with the new institutions, but the latter had also the benefit of local 'rates.' Elementary instruction in all schools had to be open to government inspection, and the amount of the grant was partly determined by the report of the inspectors. The board

A further extension of the suffrage led to the epochal bill of 1870, establishing 'board schools' supported by government grants and local 'rates,' and permitting the 'voluntary schools' to share in the government grants.

[1] The act resulted in the establishment of some fifteen hundred new 'voluntary schools,' as before any 'board schools' could be established, six months were allowed for the deficiencies to be supplied by private means.

schools were forbidden to allow "any religious catechism or religious formulary, which is distinctive of any particular denomination"; and religious instruction in either type of school had to be placed at the beginning or end of the school session, so that, under the 'conscience clause' of the act, any scholar might conveniently withdraw at that time.

This *magna charta* of national education was supplemented by compulsory attendance and minimum age laws, and the creation of a Board of Education, and a 'consultative committee.'

This act of 1870 was, of course, the *magna charta* of national education, and has become the basis of much school legislation since that time. The compromise in the bill that allowed the voluntary schools, with their sectarian instruction, to continue receiving government support, has, however, prevented a logical and consistent system from being established. The struggle to complete the nationalization of the schools has lasted until the present, and meanwhile the dual system of elementary schools has continued to be developed in a variety of enactments. Compulsory attendance laws were passed (1876, 1880), and the minimum age of exemption was set first at eleven years of age, and then raised to twelve (1893, 1899). An extra grant, to take the place of tuition fees (1891), soon made it possible for most schools to become absolutely free. A still more advanced step toward a national system of schools was taken by the creation of a central 'Board of Education' (1899). This body assumed the functions of the Committee of Privy Council on Education, which had been providing for the elementary schools and for science and art instruction; of the Charity Commissioners, who were reorganizing the educational trusts and endowments; and of the Board of Agriculture. The act also provided for a 'consultative committee,' to represent the views of the universities and other bodies interested in education, and advise the board on any question referred to it. In addition to its control of the elementary institutions, the board was authorized "to inspect any school supplying secondary education and desiring to be inspected."

The Education Act of 1902.—The next important movement toward centralization took place in 1902. The board schools had in their generation of existence met with a phenomenal growth, and the voluntary schools could no longer compare with them. The former had come to include about seventy per cent of the pupils, and were doing a splendid work, especially for the concentrated population in great industrial communities. They were spending about half as much again upon each pupil as were the voluntary schools, since the subscriptions, endowments, and tuition fees of the latter could not keep pace with the local rates, and the board schools were able to engage a much better staff of teachers. This extension of civil influence in education was bitterly opposed by the established church, and when the conservatives came into power through the assistance of the clergy (1895), they were pledged to secure better maintenance for the voluntary schools. Such a provision they at first attempted to obtain through a special government grant (1897), but this proved inadequate, and they then passed the act of 1902, whereby the denominational schools were permitted to share in the local rates. The administration of both board and voluntary schools was now centralized in the county councils, except in the case of cities and large boroughs, which were given independent control through their own councils. But the immediate supervision of instruction,

The development of the board schools was phenomenal; and, when the conservatives came into power, as a result of their pledge to the clergy, they passed the Act of 1902, which enabled the denominational schools to share in the local rates.

By this act the administration of both types of schools was centralized in the county or city councils, but the immediate supervision was placed in the hands of a board of managers, and, in the case of the voluntary schools, despite their receipt of local rates, only two of the six managers were appointed by the council.

religious as well as secular, in the individual schools was placed in the hands of a board of managers; and, despite their receipt of local taxes, the voluntary schools were required to have but two of their managers appointed by the council, and the other four were still selected by the denomination. Serious opposition to the enforcement of the new law arose among nonconformists and others, and extreme coercive measures were taken by the government. The new act, however, while unfair to those outside the Church of England, tended to sweep away the dual system of public and church schools, since both were coming to rest upon a basis of public control and support. Since 1902 all elementary schools have been considered as part of one comprehensive system, and the board schools have been distinguished as 'provided schools' and the voluntary as 'nonprovided.' Under the legislation of 1902 steps were also taken to coördinate secondary with elementary education, and bring it somewhat within the public system. The board schools had early in their existence begun to develop upward into secondary education and before long had come to compete with the older grammar and public schools. In 1900, however, the grants of the science and art department were withdrawn from the support of secondary education in board schools, the 'Cockerton judgment' forbade the use of local rates for other instruction than elementary, and fifteen years of age was fixed by the Board of Education as the upper limit for pupils in the board schools. Thus secondary training was excluded from public administration, but, in keeping with the agreement to deal "not with secondary education or with primary education in their isolation, but with both in one measure," the Act of 1902 imposed upon councils the duty to support instruction in subjects beyond the elementary work. The Board of Education was also empowered to pass judgment upon the work of the great public schools and other endowed secondary institutions, and to allow grants to all schools meeting the conditions of the Board, as determined by the reports of the government inspectors.

The Act of 1902, however, required the councils to support instruction beyond the elementary work, and empowered the Board of Education to pass judgment upon the endowed secondary schools.

Even since the liberals returned to power, they have continued the conservatives' policy of granting local rates to all elementary schools, of bringing secondary education under public support and control, and of making the county and city councils the unit of school administration, with the national Board of Education as a unifying force in the entire field. While the education bill of 1906, which was kept from passage by the House of Lords, did not recognize church schools as such, and insisted upon bringing them under the complete control of the public authorities, it made no attempt to return to the former dual system of schools and the isolation of secondary from elementary education. It still held also to religious, and, under safeguards, even to sectarian instruction in the elementary schools, and, with the recent readjustment of the power of the House of Lords (1911), it may yet be passed in a revised form. A voluntary committee for a 'resettlement in English elementary education,' through the mediation of the President of the Board of Education and the Archbishop of Canterbury, has been at work for half a dozen years formulating a *modus vivendi* acceptable to both sides. Their plan concedes the principle of public control and support for all elementary schools and religious freedom for teach-

The liberals have continued the policy of uniting both types of schools in a single system and of encouraging public control of secondary education, but as yet they have been unable to alter the sectarian control of instruction in the voluntary schools.

ers and pupils, but provides local option for the continuance of denominational schools. Thus, while England is not prepared to adopt a secular system, like that of France and the United States, and has not yet articulated all its secondary education with elementary, it is upon the high road to a complete centralization of school administration in the national government.

During the latter half of the nineteenth century the classical and ecclesiastical monopoly has been broken in Cambridge and Oxford, and new universities adjusted to modern demands have arisen in manufacturing centers.

During the nineteenth century the classical and ecclesiastical monopoly in higher education was also broken. A recognition of the scientific and industrial ideals began to appear in the curriculum of Cambridge (1851) and Oxford (1853), and the theological requirements for a degree were dropped (1856). By the last quarter of the century actual workshops and laboratories had been introduced, and students were freed from all doctrinal tests at both universities. Moreover, new universities, better adjusted to modern demands and more closely related to the school systems and the civil government, began to arise in manufacturing centers. Since 1889 such institutions as the Universities of Birmingham, Manchester, Leeds, Liverpool, and Bristol have sprung up as the product of private benefactions, municipal enterprise, and parliamentary subsidy, and the University of London, started as an examining body in 1836, was made a teaching institution in 1900.

Types of Education in the Dominion of Canada.—The state systems of schools which have grown up in the Canadian provinces approach those of the United States much more closely than do those of the European nations. Yet they are sufficiently distinctive and important to deserve description and to offer suggestions to the older countries. Canada developed schools in very early days. In the beginning education was cared for in the four provinces separately, and when the Dominion of Canada was finally formed (1867), the federal government left to each province the administration of public education within its borders. The same autonomy was extended to the provinces that have since been admitted to the federation. Two types of educational control,—state and ecclesiastical, have been developing from the first. The former method is best illustrated by the system of public schools, with grants of public funds, that has been organized in Ontario; and the latter by the public supervision of parochial schools that has been established in Quebec. Ontario was settled mostly by English and Scotch emigrants, many of whom had, as 'union loyalists,' come from the United States after the Declaration of Independence, and practically all the colonists had brought with them the concept of public control of education. The French settlers of Quebec, on the other hand, naturally followed their traditions of parish schools.

In the Canadian provinces there have from the first been developed two types of educational control,—the state, represented by Ontario, and the ecclesiastical, developed by Quebec.

The Public School System of Ontario.—The system of schools in Ontario began before the middle of the nineteenth century. As early as 1841 the provincial parliament provided for the establishment of township 'common schools' and for district 'grammar schools' after the English type of secondary education. Two years later the college at York, now relocated and known as the 'University of Toronto,' opened its doors. Then, in 1846, through Egerton Ryerson, the Common Schools Act for Ontario was passed. This was formulated after a careful study of the systems of Massachusetts, New York, and the European states, and it included many

The common school system of Ontario was started by Ryerson in 1846, and during the thirty years he was in office much was accomplished for universal education and centralization.

excellent elements from various systems and a number of valuable original features. Through tenure of office during thirty years, Dr. Ryerson was able to develop and fix this system, and the Ontario law of 1871, after the Dominion had been formed, included free tuition, compulsory attendance, county inspection, uniform examinations, and all the other features for which he had contended.

Since then the growth of centralization has been even more marked through the development of a ministry of education with the largest powers.

Since 1876 an even greater centralization of the provincial system has been effected through substituting for the chief superintendent a 'minister of education' with much larger powers, and bringing all stages of public education,—the elementary, secondary, and higher schools, into much closer relationship. The minister has many assistants and advisors, including since 1906 an Advisory Council of Education, which is made up of representatives from the universities and public schools, the inspectional corps, and local trustees. He initiates and directs all school legislation, decides complaints and disputes, sets examinations for the high, elementary, model, and normal schools, prescribes the courses of study, chooses the text-books, and appoints the inspectors. His is an office of great power and dignity. The system is also administered by subordinate authorities elected in the localities, whose duties are clearly defined by law. The province is for educational purposes divided into counties, which are in turn divided into townships, and subdivided into sections and incorporated cities, towns, and villages. The central and local administrations are wisely balanced, and while the one determines scholastic standards through its professional requirements, the other establishes schools, ap-

The system is also administered by subordinate authorities elected in the counties, townships, and sections; and the central and local administrations are wisely balanced.

points teachers, and regulates expenditures under the general control of the minister. The system of elementary schools, high schools, collegiate institutes, and universities, is fully unified, and the work of each stage fits into the others even more exactly than in the 'ladder' system of the United States. The training of teachers is cared for through the departments of Education in the universities, the eight provincial normal schools, and a model school in each county. The teachers for secondary institutions are prepared at the universities, the normal schools grant a life certificate to teach in the elementary schools, while the model schools afford fourteen weeks of training for country teachers. The buildings, equipment, courses, and instruction of the high, elementary, and model schools are each reported upon by inspectors of assured scholarship and experience. Since 1863 permission has been granted to establish 'separate schools' for any peculiar creed or race, whereever there are five families requesting it. This opportunity to have schools of their own faith has not been embraced by any save the Roman Catholics. Any one paying toward the support of a 'separate school' is exempt from taxation for the regular public schools. Special provincial inspectors report upon these schools, but in the same way as for the public schools. An effort has frequently been made to get rid of this provision by instituting purely secular schools throughout the province, but it has never been successful, and even in the public schools nonsectarian religious exercises are still conducted.

The system is even more unified than in the United States; the training of teachers is cared for by institutions of different grades; and there is a complete system of inspectors.

'Separate schools' for any race or creed may be established, when needed.

Systems of Education in Other Provinces of Canada.— The Ontario system may be considered typical of the

The Ontario system is typical of all provinces, except Quebec,

educational administration in the various provinces of Canada, except Quebec. While each province has a history and peculiarities of its own, many of the features in them all have been taken from the Ontario model. Every one has sought uniformity of school provision and educational standards through government control, although none of them grant their central official as much power as Ontario. In Nova Scotia, Manitoba, and British Columbia the 'executive council' constitutes the educational authority of the province, and the chief officer, known as 'superintendent,' is appointed by the lieutenant governor. New Brunswick vests the authority in a Board of Education, composed of the lieutenant governor, the members of the executive council, the president of the provincial university, and the superintendent, who is secretary and chief executive. Alberta and Saskatchewan permit 'separate schools,' and they existed in Manitoba until 1890, when, after a bitter contest, they were abolished.

But the ecclesiastical type of control in Quebec is very different from that of the other provinces. The educational system originated there in the schools of the parishes and of the teaching orders, like the Jesuits and Christian Brethren, and in 1845 the parish was by law made the unit of school administration. But seven years later government inspectors were established, and in 1859 a central organization was completed with a Council of Public Instruction. This authority is composed of two divisions, a Roman Catholic and a Protestant, which sit separately and administer the schools of their respective creeds. Each division makes regulations for the instruction and texts of its own schools, and appoints in-

which has a central Council of Public Instruction, with two divisions,—a Catholic and a Protestant, each of which makes regulations for the schools of its own faith.

spectors of its own faith. The provincial superintendent of schools, appointed by the lieutenant governor, is *ex officio* chairman of both divisions, but he can vote only with the division to which he belongs by religion. The proceeds from the general public school fund, a special tax, or any educational legacies are divided in proportion to the Catholic and Protestant inhabitants, but the regular school rate of one-fifth cent on a dollar may be assigned to whichever of the two school systems the taxpayer wishes. The local unit in education is the municipality, which may be divided into districts, and the trustees in each district have full control of the schools there, subject to the requirements of the Council.

The proceeds of the public fund, special taxation, and legacies are divided *pro rata* between the two faiths, but the school rate may be assigned to whichever of the two systems the taxpayer wishes.

Comparison of Modern School Systems.—Thus, during the eighteenth and nineteenth centuries, systems of education have been centralized in the civil governments of the leading European nations and of Canada. With the exception of the Canadian provinces, however, no one of these states has yet altogether welded its primary and secondary systems.[1] Moreover, while France alone has been completely centralized and rendered purely secular, all the others have been liberated from ecclesiastical control and are under civic organization and management. This development represents a very different situation from the conditions in the administration of schools that furnished America with its first educational traditions, but the evolution of state control in the United States took place quite independently of that in Europe. In fact, until the early part of the nineteenth century, so little was known in America concerning European education that adaptations to the systems

Although, outside the United States, Canada alone has welded its primary and secondary systems, and only France has centralized and secularized its schools, all these states have been liberated from ecclesiastical control and are under civic management. While the United States

[1] See pp. 277, 297, and 302.

has met with a similar evolution, it has occurred independently.

of the various states were practically impossible. Since then, however, any improvements in method, content, and administration that have taken place in German, French, or English schools have speedily been heralded by American educators, and have often proved suggestive. Much, too, may be learned in the United States from the thorough and systematic, though somewhat less elastic, educational organization of Canada, especially Ontario; and in all cases a comparison of the modern system of education in one great nation with that of another should prove broadening and mutually beneficial.

SUPPLEMENTARY READING

A. Germany

ARNOLD, M. *Higher Schools and Universities in Germany.*

BARNARD, H. *American Journal of Education* (Volume IV, pp. 245–258; VIII, 369–460; IX, 569–578; XX, 335–434; and XXII, 743–902).

BOLTON, F. E. *The Secondary School System of Germany.*

BROWN, J. F. *The Training of Teachers for Secondary Schools in Germany and the United States.*

CLAUSNITZER, L. *Geschichte des preussischen Unterrichtsgesetzes*

DITTES, F. *Geschichte der Erziehung und des Unterrichts.*

HUGHES, R. E. *The Making of Citizens.* Chaps. IV and X.

KANDEL, I. L. *The Training of Elementary School Teachers in Germany* (*Teachers College Contributions to Education*, No. 31).

KLEMM, L. R. *Public Education in Germany and the United States.*

LEXIS, W. *Unterrichtswesen im deutschen Reich.*

MÜNCH, W., SCHIELE, F. M., and ZIERTMANN, P. *Education in Germany* (*Monroe's Cyclopædia of Education*, Vol. III).

NOHLE, E. *History of the German School System* (*Report of the U. S. Commissioner of Education*, 1897-98. Vol. I, pp. 26–44).

PARSONS, J. R., JR. *Prussian Schools through American Eyes.*

PAULSEN, F. *German Education* (translated by Lorenz). Books III and IV.

PAULSEN, F. *The German Universities* (translated by Thilly and Elwang).

PETERSILIE, A. *Das öffentliche Unterrichtswesen im deutschen Reiche.*

RAUMER, K. VON. *Geschichte der Pädagogik.*

RUSSELL, J. E. *German Higher Schools.*

SADLER, M. E. *The Unrest in Secondary Education in Germany and Elsewhere* (*Great Britain, Board of Education, Special Reports*, IX, 1).

SEELEY, L. *Common School Systems of Germany.*

WINCH, W. H. *Notes on German Schools.*

B. FRANCE

ARNOLD, M. *Special Report on Certain Rights connected with Elementary Education in Germany, Switzerland, and France.*

BEARD, MARY S. *Écoles maternelles of Paris* (*Great Britain, Board of Education, Special Reports on Educational Subjects.* Vol. VIII, No. 8).

COMPAYRÉ, G. *Contemporary Educational Thought in France* (*Educational Review*, Vol. II, pp. 171–177; X, 313–324; XVI, 132–146; XXVII, 19–35).

COMPAYRÉ, G. *Education in France* (*Monroe's Cyclopædia of Education*, Vol. II).

FARRINGTON, F. E. *French Secondary Schools.*

FARRINGTON, F. E. *The Public Primary System of France* (*Teachers College Contributions to Education*, No. 7).

FRIEDEL, V. H. *Problems of Secondary Education in France* (*School Review*, Vol. XV, pp. 169–183).

GRÉARD, O. *Education et instruction. Enseignement primaire.*

GRÉARD, O. *Législation de l'instruction primaire en France depuis 1789.*

HUGHES, R. E. *The Making of Citizens.* Chaps. V and IX.

KIRKMAN, F. B. *The Position of Teachers in the State Secondary*

Schools for Boys in France (*Great Britain, Board of Education, Special Reports*, II, 24).

KLEMM, L. R. *European Schools.* Pp. 317–391.

PARSONS, J. R., JR. *French Schools through American Eyes.*

SALMON, LUCY M. *Training of Teachers in France* (*Educational Review*, Vol. XX, pp. 383–404).

SIMON, J. *La reforme de l'enseignement secondaire.*

SMITH, ANNA T. *Report of the United States Commissioner of Education.* 1890–91, Vol. I, pp. 95–108; 1893–94, I, 187–201; 1894–95, I, 289–305; 1895–96, I, 635–639; 1896–97, I, 29–56; 1897–98, I, 704–749; 1898–99, I, 1095–1138; 1899–1900, II, 1712–1721; 1900–1901, I, 1082–1103; 1901, I, 1103–1109; 1902, I, 668–698; 1905, I, 76–80; 1906, I, 19–32; 1907, I, 143–159; 1908, I, 230–238.

C. ENGLAND

ADAMS, F. *History of the Elementary School Contest in England.*

ARNOLD, M. *Reports on Elementary Schools*, 1852–1882.

BALFOUR, G. *The Educational Systems of Great Britain and Ireland.*

BINNS, H. B. *A Century of Education*, 1808–1908.

BOARD OF EDUCATION. *Annual Reports.*

COMMITTEE OF COUNCIL ON EDUCATION. *Annual Reports.*

GREENOUGH, J. C. *The Evolution of the Elementary Schools of Great Britain.*

GREGORY, R. *Elementary Education.*

HOLMAN, H. *English National Education.*

HUGHES, R. E. *The Making of Citizens.* Chaps. III and XII.

KAY-SHUTTLEWORTH, J. *Four Periods in Public Education.*

MONTMORENCY, J. E. G. DE. *National Education and National Life.*

MONTMORENCY, J. E. G. DE. *Progress of Education in England.*

MONTMORENCY, J. E. G. DE. *State Intervention in English Education.*

MORLEY, J. *The Struggle for National Education.*

NATIONAL EDUCATION UNION. *Verbatim Report of the Debate in Parliament during the Progress of the Education Bill, 1870.*

SALMON, D. *The Education of the Poor in the Eighteenth Century.*

SANDIFORD, P. *The Training of Teachers in England and Wales* (*Teachers College Contributions to Education*, No. 32).

SHARPLESS, I. *English Education in Elementary and Secondary Schools.*

SMITH, ANNA T. *Education in England* (*Monroe's Cyclopædia of Education*, Vol. II).

SMITH, ANNA T. *The Education Bill of 1906 for England and Wales* (*U. S. Bureau of Education Bulletin.* 1906, No. I).

D. CANADA

BOARD OF EDUCATION, GREAT BRITAIN. *Special Reports on Educational Subjects.* Vol. IV, A.

CHAVEAU, M. *L'instruction publique au Canada.*

COLEMAN, H. T. J. *Public Education in Upper Canada.*

DOMINION EDUCATIONAL ASSOCIATION. *Proceedings.*

EWART, J. S. *The Manitoba School Question.*

HODGINS, J. G. *Documentary History of Education in Ontario.*

MILLAR, J. *Educational System of the Province of Ontario.*

MORANT, R. L. *History of the Manitoba School System.* (*Great Britain, Board of Education, Special Reports*, I, 23).

ROSS, G. W. *The School System of Ontario.*

RYERSON, E. *Report on a System of Public Elementary Instruction for Upper Canada.*

SMITH, ANNA T. *Education in Canada* (*Monroe's Cyclopædia of Education*, Vol. I).

CHAPTER X

THE MODERN SCIENTIFIC MOVEMENT

The Development of the Natural Sciences in Modern Times.—The germ of the modern tendency to introduce the natural sciences into the content of education was apparent as early as Rousseau. The *Emile*, on its constructive side, may be held to advocate the scientific, as well as the sociological and psychological movements in modern times. Some description has been given in previous chapters of the consequent efforts to improve the ideals, organization, and methods of education in accordance with our modern knowledge of society and the mental development of the individual, and we may now turn to a more specific consideration of the gradual expansion of the course of study and of the modern scientific movement. Such a tendency has constituted one phase of the remarkable growth of natural science during the past two centuries. This rapid movement can best be understood by recalling the development of society and education at the times. Science started to develop back in the time of Roger Bacon, but even during the Renaissance it was bitterly opposed, because of the tendency to conflict with religious dogma, although this age did not object to the revival of the classics. Accordingly, the latter became strongly intrenched in educational tradition, and became the most obstinate opponent of the sciences. Its numerous representatives

The expansion of the sciences in the course of study is simply one phase of the growth of natural sciences during the past two centuries.

struggled hard to keep the sciences out of education. But toward the close of the seventeenth century, with the growth of reason and the removal of the theological ban, the scientific movement, which had been held back so long, began to make a rapid advance.

How extensive this development was, can scarcely be appreciated without a brief enumeration of the marvellous discoveries and inventions that have been called into being since the eighteenth century began. For more than a millennium the Greek developments in astronomy had been accepted as final, but in the course of the seventeenth century these dicta were completely upset by the revelations of Copernicus, Tycho Brahé, Kepler, and Galileo.[1] The work of these investigators paved the way for the formulation of universal gravitation and the laws of motion by Isaac Newton, which united the universe into a single comprehensive system and completed the foundations for modern mechanics. About the same time the other great development in science among the Greeks,—anatomy and physiology, was completely revolutionized through Harvey's discovery of the double circulation of the blood and the microscopic demonstration by Malpighi of the existence of capillaries connecting the veins and the arteries. From these days on the desire for scientific investigation steadily grew until, during the nineteenth century, its ideals, methods, and results became patent in every department of human knowledge. The strongholds of ignorance, superstition, and prejudice were rapidly stormed and taken through new discoveries or new marshallings of facts already discovered. But it will be quite impos-

The Greek developments in astronomy and medicine were upset during the seventeenth century by such investigators as Copernicus, Newton, and Harvey,

and from this time on there has been a rapid development in all lines of science,—

[1] See Graves, *History of Education during the Transition*, pp. 262f.

sible here to do more than mention a few of the more important scientific achievements and outline the broad sweep of progress in the nineteenth century. In astronomy the Newtonian theory was confirmed by the investigations of Lagrange and Laplace (1785) and by the discovery of Neptune through purely mathematical reasoning from the effects of its gravitation (1845). After the middle of the century, when chemistry had been more fully developed, innumerable celestial discoveries were made through the spectroscope and astral photography. Owing to more complicated phenomena and the opposition of theologians to disturbing the Biblical chronology, the progress in geology was slower. Yet during the century were established Hutton's 'Plutonic' theory of the origin of continents and islands, Lyell's 'uniformitarian' doctrine that past changes in the earth were like the present in degree and kind, and Agassiz's hypothesis of a universal ice-age. Paleontology also arose during the century, and Cuvier, Lyell, and other prominent investigators proved, by means of the fossils, that the earth had known successive rotations of population and countless æons of time. Despite Lyell's inconsistent advocacy of 'special creation,' these discoveries strengthened the conception of evolution in biology. Early in the century Lamarck formulated his transmutation of species through 'accumulated and inherited use.' But this was displaced by the influential theory of 'natural selection,' made public by Darwin and Wallace half a century later, although the Lamarckian 'inheritance of acquired characteristics,' tacitly held also by Darwin, remained in dispute between the Neolamarckians and the followers of Weissmann. Much was contributed

astronomy, geology, paleontology, biology,

to the theory of inheritance by Galton and Mendel, while Pasteur and Tyndall thoroughly disposed of 'spontaneous generation.' Physiology and other more special phases of biology met with a similar advance. Bichat showed the existence of the two sets of processes,—volitional and non-volitional, in every vertebrate, and reduced all animal structures to a few types of tissue. Lister settled the question as to the form of the red corpuscles in the blood. Through the development of microscopy, numerous important discoveries were made in minute anatomy, which gave rise to histology as an independent science. Embryology also became established as a separate science, and proved of great importance in developing the 'cell theory.' This concept was first formulated by Schwann (1839), and, in the modified form given it by Virchow and others (1860), became the central generalization of physiology. About the same time, the researches of Liebig and others brought physiology within the province of chemistry, and, taken in connection with the cell theory, the greatest light was shed upon the action of the saliva, the stomach, and the gastric juice in digestion, and upon the functioning of the lungs and liver. Contemporaneous with all these discoveries in geology and biology was an epochal development of the physical sciences. Early in the century Dalton's rain-gauge and the study of evaporation led to the theory of 'atoms,' on which is based the structure of modern chemistry, and in 1811 Avogadro proposed that the compound atom be denominated 'molecule.' During the first decade also Young formulated the wave theory of light, which postulates the existence of 'ether' through all space. This theory

physiology, anatomy, histology, embryology, chemistry, and physics.

made matter and energy the fundamental concepts for modern physics, and has been invaluable in the study of radiant energy and the constitution of matter.[1] As an indirect result of it, the doctrine of the 'conservation of energy' was demonstrated by Joule and Mayer, the supplementary theory of the 'dissipation of energy' was formulated by Lord Kelvin, and atomic and molecular conceptions were greatly advanced. The 'periodic law' of the recurrence of similar properties, when the chemical 'elements' were arranged in order of their atomic weights, was formulated by Newlands (1864), and three new elements were shortly discovered, to fit into the existing series (1880).

These scientific investigations were for a long time carried on mostly outside the universities, and seem not to have affected practical life, but

The Growth of Inventions and Discoveries in the Nineteenth Century.—It should be noted that the majority of these investigations were for a long time carried on outside the universities, and, owing to the almost proverbial conservatism of educational institutions, the natural sciences scarcely entered the course of study anywhere. In fact, these great discoveries at first seem not to have affected practical life in any direction. Huxley[2] tells us:

> "The progress of science, during the first century after Bacon's death, by no means verified his sanguine prediction of the fruits which it would yield. . . . Weaving and spinning were carried on with the old appliances; nobody could travel faster by sea or by land than at any previous time in the world's history, and King George could send a message from London to York no faster than King John might have done."

[1] It has also led to many new discoveries and inventions, such as wireless telegraphy and the practical applications of X-rays in medicine.

[2] *Method and Results*, Essay II.

"But a little later," he adds, "that growth of knowledge beyond imaginable utilitarian ends, which is the condition precedent of its practical utility, began to produce some effect upon practical life." The nineteenth century will, on this account, always be known for its development of inventions and the arts, as well as of pure science. During this period science rapidly grew and took the form of applications to the problems of labor, production, transportation, communication, hygiene, and sanitation. The invention of the cotton gin (1792), the reaping machine (1834), the vulcanization of rubber (1837), the sewing machine (1846), the cylinder printing press (1847), and the typewriter (1868) greatly reduced the cost o labor, increased the amount of production, and made new industries possible. By the use of anthracite (1812), the introduction of friction matches (1837), and illumination through petroleum (1853) and incandescent electricity (1879), the conveniences and comforts of life were greatly enlarged. The steamboat (1807), improved by the screw propeller (1839) and the steam turbine (1884), and the locomotive (1830) linked all parts of the world together. The telegraph (1837), the submarine cable (1842), the telephone (1876), and wireless telegraphy (1897) made communication between all places almost instantaneous. Warfare became infinitely more destructive and unprofitable through such inventions as the gatling gun (1861) and smokeless powder (1895). The invention of the stethoscope (1819), the production of anæsthesia through the medium of nitrous oxide (1844), sulphuric ether (1846), and chloroform (1847), the perfection of antiseptic surgery (1867), and the discovery of inoculations for hydrophobia

during the nineteenth century the scientific discoveries were complemented with the development of inventions and the arts.

(1885), tetanus (1892), diphtheria (1892), and other diseases contributed largely to the progress of humanity.

Herbert Spencer and *What Knowledge is of Most Worth.*—Because of these practical results, the vital importance of a knowledge of natural phenomena to human welfare and social progress was more and more felt throughout the century. It gradually became evident that the natural sciences were demanded by modern life and constituted elements of the greatest value in modern culture and education. The German reformers, such as Pestalozzi, Herbart, and Froebel, have already been seen to oppose the prevailing education on the ground that the doctrine of formal discipline was unpsychological. But opposition was also offered upon the score of content, rather than method, by many English and American writers, who maintained that an exclusive study of the classics did not provide a suitable preparation for life. As the content of the sciences became more fully systematized, many prominent persons began to insist upon their inclusion in the curriculum. This step was bitterly opposed by conservative institutions and educators. During a greater part of the century a contest was waged between the advocates of the classical monopoly, with their arguments for formal training, and the progressives who urged that the sciences should be introduced and that the main emphasis in education should be upon content. Advocacy of the new subject matter appeared in treatises on education by various scientists. The representative argument for sciences in the course of study was that made by *Herbert Spencer* (1820–1903) in his essay

As the sciences became more systematized, many prominent men began to insist upon their inclusion in the curriculum, and, in reply to the disciplinary argument of the conservative classicists, they urged that emphasis in education should be upon subject matter.

The representative argument is that of Spencer,

on *What Knowledge Is of Most Worth.*[1] Spencer was the descendant of educators, and during all his youth was surrounded by intellectual and literary traditions. He never went to the university, possibly on account of poor health, from which he suffered all his life, but he read deeply at home on natural science and mathematics, performed experiments and made inventions, and showed remarkable ability in working out original problems. A monumental series of works, including his ideas on education, was issued by him. Spencer did not read widely upon educational subjects, and, while he was somewhat affected by the atmosphere of the times, his conceptions were largely his own. He ventured to raise the whole question of the purpose of education, and was completely subversive of the old classical traditions. His clear exposition and his convincing logic have brought a wide currency and great influence to his work. His discussion runs as follows:

"In order of time decoration precedes dress. And in our universities and schools at the present moment the like antithesis holds. As the Orinoco Indian puts on his paint before leaving his hut, not with a view to any direct benefit, but because he would be ashamed to be seen without it; so a boy's drilling in Latin and Greek is insisted on, not because of their intrinsic value, but that he may not be disgraced by being found ignorant of them. The comparative worths of different kinds of knowledge have been as yet scarcely even discussed—much less discussed in a methodic way with definite results. Before there can be a rational curriculum, we must decide which things it most concerns us to know. To this end, a measure of value is the first requisite. How to live?—that is the essential question for us. Not how to live in the mere material sense only, but in the widest sense. To prepare us for complete

[1] *Education.* I.

who holds that the function of education is 'to prepare for complete living,'

living is the function which education has to discharge; and the only rational mode of judging of any educational course is, to judge in what degree it discharges such function. Our first step must obviously be to classify, in the order of their importance, the leading kinds of activity which constitute human life. They may be arranged into: 1. Those activities which directly minister to self-preservation; 2. Those activities which, by securing the necessaries of life, indirectly minister to self-preservation; 3. Those activities which have for their end the rearing and discipline of offspring; 4. Those activities which are involved in the maintenance of proper social and political relations; 5. Those miscellaneous activities which make up the leisure part of life, devoted to the gratification of the tastes and feelings. We do not mean that these divisions are definitely separable. We do not deny that they are intrinsically entangled with each other in such way that there can be no training for any that is not in some measure a training for all. Nor do we question that of each division there are portions more important than certain portions of the preceding divisions. But after making all qualifications, there still remain these broadly marked divisions; and these divisions subordinate one another in the foregoing order. The ideal of education is complete preparation in all these divisions. But failing this ideal, as in our phase of civilization every one must do more or less, the aim should be to maintain a due proportion between the degrees of preparation in each, greatest where the value is greatest, less where the value is less, least where the value is least."

and that the sciences compose the knowledge of most worth for this purpose.

Applying this test, Spencer finds that a knowledge of the sciences is always most useful in life, and therefore of most worth. He considers each one of the five groups of activities and demonstrates the need of the knowledge of some science or sciences to guide it rightly. An acquaintance with physiology is necessary to the maintenance of health, and so for self-preservation; any form of industry or other means of indirect self-preservation will require some understanding of mathematics, physics, chemistry, biology, and sociology; to care for the physical, intellectual, and moral training of their children, parents should know the general principles of physiology, psychology, and ethics; a man is best fitted for citizenship through a knowledge of the science of history in its political, economic, and social aspects; and even the æsthetic or leisure side of life depends upon physiology, mechanics, and psychology as a basis for art, music and poetry, and "science opens up realms of poetry where to the unscientific all is a blank."

Hence he advocates a substitution of the sciences for the traditional classics.

Hence Spencer advocates a complete change from the type of training that had dominated education since the Renaissance and calls for a release from the traditional bondage to the classics. Instead of Greek and Latin for 'culture' and 'discipline,' and an order of society where the few are educated for a life of elegant leisure, he recommends the sciences and a new scheme of life where every one shall enjoy all advantages in the order of their relative value. "The attitude of the universities toward natural science," he protests elsewhere,[1] "has been that of contemptuous non-recognition. Collegiate authorities have long resisted, either actively or passively, the making of physiology, chemistry, geology, etc., subjects of examination." But Spencer uses the term 'science' rather loosely, and seeks to denote the social, political, and moral sciences, as well as the physical and biological, as being 'of most worth.' Hence he cannot with propriety be stigmatized for his 'utilitarianism,' as he has been so frequently. His 'preparation for complete living' includes more than 'how to live in the material sense only,' and in this respect his underlying principle

[1] *Social Statics*, p. 375.

seems comparable to that of Herbart in his 'moral revelation of the world.' With Spencer, education should contain such material as will elevate conduct and make life pleasanter, nobler, and more effective.

Huxley's Advocacy of the Sciences.—Another great popularizer of the scientific elements in education, who also stressed the value of the sciences for 'complete living' and social progress was *Thomas H. Huxley* (1825–1895). Huxley started his career as a naval surgeon, but rapidly developed a reputation through his investigations in natural science during a voyage around the world. He became a professor of natural history, and devoted much time to lecturing and writing on science. His use of English was vigorous and epigrammatic, and he showed great skill in bringing his conclusions into such simple language that the most unscientific persons could understand them. In an address on *A Liberal Education* [1] before a 'workingmen's college,' he most forcefully depicts the value of the sciences and other modern subjects in training for concrete living and ridicules the ineffectiveness of the current classical education. He graphically argues:

Huxley also brilliantly shows the need of a scientific education, and inveighs against the uselessness of the traditional classical training.

"Suppose it were perfectly certain that the life and fortune of every one of us would, one day or other, depend upon his winning or losing a game at chess. Don't you think that we should all consider it a duty to learn at least the names and the moves of the pieces? Yet it is a plain and very elementary truth that the life, the fortune, and the happiness of every one of us, and, more or less, of those who are connected with us, do depend upon our knowing something of the rules of a game infinitely more difficult and complicated than chess. The chess-board is the world, the pieces are the phenomena of the universe, the rules of the game are

[1] *Science and Education*. IV.

what we call the laws of Nature. What I mean by education is learning the rules of this mighty game. In other words, education is the instruction of the intellect in the laws of Nature, under which I include not merely things and their forces, but men and their ways; and the fashioning of the affections and of the will into an earnest and loving desire to move in harmony with those laws. Where is such an education as this to be had? Has any one tried to found such an education? Looking over the length and breadth of these islands, I am afraid that all these questions must receive a negative answer. The whole circle of the sciences, physical, moral, and social, are even more completely ignored in the higher than in the lower schools. Now let us pause to consider this wonderful state of affairs; for the time will come when Englishmen will quote it as the stock example of the most stolid stupidity of their ancestors in the nineteenth century. If there be a nation whose prosperity depends absolutely and wholly upon their mastery over the forces of Nature, upon their intelligent apprehension of, and obedience to the laws of the creation and distribution of wealth, and of the stable equilibrium of the forces of society, it is precisely this nation. And yet this is what these wonderful people tell their sons: 'At the cost of from one to two thousand pounds of our hard-earned money, we devote twelve of the most precious years of your life to school. There you shall not learn one single thing of all those you will most want to know directly you leave school and enter upon the practical business of life.' What does the middle class school put in the place of all these things that are left out? It substitutes what is usually comprised under the compendious title of the 'classics'—that is to say, the languages, the literature, and the history of the ancient Greeks and Romans, and the geography of so much of the world as was known to these two great nations of antiquity. It means that after a dozen years spent at this kind of work, the sufferer shall be incompetent to interpret a passage in an author he has not already got up; that he shall loathe the sight of a Greek and Latin book; and that he shall never open, or think of, a classical writer again, until, wonderful to relate, he insists upon submitting his sons to the same process. For the sake of this net result (and respectability) the British father denies his children all the knowledge they might turn to account in life, not merely for the achievement of vulgar success, but for guidance in the great crises of human existence."

Combe also emphasized the need of sciences in the curriculum.

The Arguments of Combe, Youmans, and Eliot for the Study of Science.—Many other vigorous lecturers and writers entered into this reform of the curriculum. Opposition to the over-emphasis of languages, especially the classics, in the content of education was undertaken even earlier in the century by the distinguished phrenologist, *George Combe* (1788–1858). Phrenology in those days had not yet fallen into disrepute, but the work of Combe and his friends was discredited by their advocacy of what he unfortunately termed 'secular' education, which to most Englishmen of the time seemed synonymous with irreligious training.[1] In his work on *Education*, however, he emphasized instruction in the sciences relating to moral, religious, social, and political life, as well as those bearing upon man's physical and mental constitution, and presented arguments for an improved curriculum which presaged those of Spencer and Huxley. Combe spent two years (1838–1840) in the United States lecturing on science and education, as well as phrenology. He had a great influence upon educational thinkers, including Horace Mann, and did much to promote scientific education.

After the middle of the century a number of men undertook to popularize the sciences in America by tongue and pen. One of the most effective of these was *Edward L. Youmans* (1821–1887), who collected and

[1] 'Secular' education, that is, training in knowledge connected with this world, represented but one side of the matter, as Combe did not exclude religious elements, although he believed they should be non-sectarian in character.

edited a set of lectures urging the claims of the various sciences under the title of *Culture Demanded by Modern Life* (1867). He also founded the *International Science Series* (1871), and the *Popular Science Monthly* (1872). Dr. Youmans spread scientific thought throughout the country, and by means of his republications made Buckle, Darwin, Huxley, Spencer, Tyndall, Haeckel, and others well known in America.

Youmans popularized science and the works of the great scientists.

A service for the sciences, bearing more directly upon the educational world, was that performed by Charles W. Eliot (1835–), President of Harvard. This he accomplished largely by an extension of the elective system and an emphasis upon modern subjects in the curriculum of school and college. Even in his *Inaugural Address* he holds: "In education the individual traits of different minds have not been sufficiently attended to." And fifteen years later, in his description of 'a liberal education,' after showing that "the number of school and college studies admissible with equal weight or rank needs to be much enlarged" and that "a considerable range of choice should be allowed," he argues for the natural sciences as follows:

Eliot extended the elective system in the college, and argued for the choice of the sciences on the ground of their effect upon man's life,

"The arts built upon chemistry, physics, botany, zoölogy, and geology are chief factors in the civilization of our time, and are growing in material and moral influence at a marvelous rate. Since the beginning of this century, they have wrought wonderful changes in the physical relation of man to the earth which he inhabits, in national demarcations, in industrial organization, in governmental functions, and in the modes of domestic life; and they will certainly do as much for the twentieth century as they have done for ours. They are not simply mechanical or material forces; they are also moral forces of great intensity."

Elsewhere he maintains that the elementary school in

and showed that they should be taught even in the elementary school.

its curriculum "should begin early—in the very first grades—the study of nature; and all its teachers should, therefore, be capable of teaching the elements of physical geography, meteorology, botany, and zoölogy, the whole forming in the child's mind one harmonious sketch of its complete environment."

The advocates of the sciences felt that a knowledge of nature was indispensable for human welfare, and that the content rather than the method of study was important in education. They generally opposed the disciplinary conception of education,

The Disciplinary Argument for the Sciences.—In general, the writers and lecturers interested in the scientific movement held that a knowledge of nature was indispensable for human welfare and constituted the 'culture demanded by modern life.' They felt that the content of studies rather than the method was of importance in education. Many of them, like the German reformers also expressed their dissent from the disciplinary conception of education urged by the classicists. Huxley thus parodies the usual linguistic drill:

"It is wonderful how close a parallel to classical training could be made out of that palæontology to which I refer. In the first place I could get up an osteological primer so arid, so pedantic in its terminology, so altogether distasteful to the youthful mind, as to beat the recent famous production of the head-master out of the field in all these excellences. Next, I could exercise my boys upon easy fossils, and bring out all their powers of memory and all their ingenuity in the application of my osteogrammatical rules to the interpretation, or construing, of those fragments. To those who had reached the higher classes I might supply odd bones to be built up into animals, giving great honour and reward to him who succeeded in fabricating monsters most entirely in accordance with the rules. That would answer to verse-making and essay-writing in the dead languages." [1]

Yet the tradition of formal discipline and the belief in faculties or general powers of the mind that might

[1] *Science and Education*, pp. 98f.

be trained by certain favored studies and afterward applied in any direction were too firmly rooted to be entirely upset. Even the greatest of the scientists seem to have been influenced by this notion and to have attempted occasionally a defense of their subjects on the basis of superiority in this direction. After Spencer has made his effective argument for the sciences on the ground that their 'content' is so much more valuable for the activities of life, he shifts his whole point of view, and attempts to anticipate the classicists by occupying their own ground. He admits that "besides its use for guidance in conduct, the acquisition of each order of facts has also its use as mental exercise, and its effects as a preparative for complete living have to be considered under both these heads." But he holds that by "the beautiful economy of Nature those classes of facts which are most useful for regulating conduct are best for strengthening the mental faculties, and the education of most value for guidance must at the same time be the education of most value for discipline." As evidence of this, he undertakes to show that science, like language, trains the memory, and, in addition, exercises the understanding; that it is superior to language in cultivating judgment; that, by fostering independence, perseverance, and sincerity, it furnishes a moral discipline; and even that science, "inasmuch as it generates a profound respect for, and an implicit faith in, those uniform laws which underlie all things" is the best discipline for religious culture. Hence, from the point of view of formal discipline and mental gymnastics, as well as of content and guidance, Spencer declares science, rather than language and literature, to be of most worth in educa-

but the traditional view of faculties and of formalism was so fixed that even the greatest scientists attempted to defend their subjects on this basis.

tion. Thus Spencer shows that he is not altogether emancipated from tradition, and that he has not fully grasped the disciplinary claims of language, which he bases entirely upon memory training. He likewise begs the question in stating that nature is bound, as a matter of economy, to make the training that is best for guidance also the best for discipline. As a matter of fact, nothing is more uneconomical than nature, which always produces a superabundance, since much will necessarily be wasted.

Moreover, numerous other advocates of the sciences, early and late, have similarly undertaken to steal the disciplinary thunder of the classicists. Combe maintains that "it is not so much the mere knowledge of the details of Chemistry, of Natural Philosophy, or of any other science that I value, as the strengthening of the intellect, and the enlargement of the understanding, which follow from these studies." So Youmans declares that "by far the most priceless of all things is mental power; while one of the highest offices of education must be strictly to economize and wisely to expend it. Science made the basis of culture will accomplish this result." In fact, nearly every apologist for the natural sciences at some time or other has advocated these subjects from the standpoint of formal discipline. The arguments of the scientists, however, are often sufficiently rational to harmonize with modern psychology. Huxley, Youmans, Eliot, Karl Pearson,[1] Dryer,[2] and others allude to various mental 'habits,' such as observation, inductive thinking, accuracy, breadth of view, inde-

[1] *Grammar of Science*, p. 9.

[2] *Science in Secondary Schools*, p. 14.

pendence, impartiality, and freedom from superstition, that are fostered by a study of the sciences, although these writers do not appreciate the fact that a 'habit' is by its nature not general, but specific, and that the ideals created by a study of sciences have to be definitely abstracted before they can be transferred.

A similar argument for some sort of mental discipline has been urged in the case of each one of the physical and biological sciences. Galloway claims that chemistry is superior to biology, since it cultivates active, rather than passive observation, and to physics, because "it exercises habits of mind diverse to those induced by mathematics." Tyndall, however, holds that "the study of Physics exercises and sharpens observation: it brings the most exhaustive logic into play: it compares, abstracts, and generalizes, and provides the mental imagery admirably suited to these procedures." "The disciplinary value of zoölogy," writes Bigelow, "is found in that it may contribute to the development of a scientific attitude of mind, by directing various mental processes, such as those involved in scientific observing, classifying facts, reasoning on the basis of demonstrated facts, exercising judgment and discrimination, and learning to appreciate demonstrated knowledge." So botany, according to Henfrey, develops reasoning by analogy, which gives it "a high value as mental discipline, for the cases in which inductions have to be made in common life are most frequently of this kind." Likewise, the peculiar discipline of physiology is held by Paget to rest in its being "occupied with things of admitted incompleteness and uncertainty" and in being "essentially a science of designs and final causes."

While scientific instruction began in the German universities during the eighteenth century, it was not until the middle of the nineteenth that the experimental method of teaching became common there.

Introduction of the Sciences into Educational Institutions; Germany.—Simultaneously with the growth of inventions and the cogent arguments and vigorous campaigns of advanced thinkers during the nineteenth century, training in the sciences was gradually creeping into educational practice. While the sciences began to work their way into institutions of all grades early in the eighteenth century, it was not until about the middle of the nineteenth that the movement was seriously felt in education. Even in Germany the first attempts at studying nature were made outside the universities in the 'academies of science.' But during the first quarter of the eighteenth century Halle, which had been realistic almost from its beginning, had become a center for science instruction, and by the close of the century Göttingen and most of the other Protestant universities had started professorships in the sciences. It was not, however, until the beginning of the second quarter of the nineteenth century that, in Liebig's laboratory at the University of Giessen, students first began to be taught through experiments, and it was after the middle of the century before this investigation work had generally replaced the formal science instruction in German universities. Since then the development of science in the higher education of Germany has been phenomenal.

In German secondary instruction the sciences appeared as early as the seventeenth century

Some science appeared in German secondary instruction by the middle of the seventeenth century through the *Ritterakademien*,[1] and toward the end of the century in the work of Semler at Halle.[2] This realistic instruction of the pietists was brought by Hecker to Berlin, where he

[1] See Graves, *History of Education during the Transition*, p. 290.

[2] *Op. cit.*, pp. 291 and 304.

started his famous *Realschule* in 1747, and before the beginning of the nineteenth century similar institutions had spread throughout Prussia. Early in the nineteenth century, as a result of the influence of the philanthropinists[1] and the urgency of the new humanists,[2] the course of study in the gymnasiums of Prussia was considerably modified, and, as part of the compromise, some science was introduced.[3] The movement later spread into the secondary education of states in South Germany, and, while the total amount of science was not large, it managed to hold its place in the gymnasial curriculum even during the reaction to absolutism between 1815 and 1848. In 1855 recognition was made of two types of real-schools, one retaining Latin in every year of the nine, and the other having its course determined in each case by the local authorities, and in 1882 these became part of the educational system as the *Realgymnasium* in the one case, and the *Realschule* of six years or the *Oberrealschule* of nine in the other.[4] These institutions at present devote approximately twice as much time to the physical and biological sciences as do the gymnasia.

through the *Ritterakademien;* in the eighteenth *Realschulen* appeared; and early in the nineteenth century the gymnasia introduced some science. In 1855 a start was given the *Realgymnasium* and the *Oberrealschule,* which give twice as much time to the sciences.

Technical and trade schools, with scientific and mathematical subjects as a foundation for the vocational work, have also appeared as a species of secondary education in Germany.[5] The first of these were opened in Nüremberg, in 1823, but their rapid increase in numbers, variety, and importance has taken place since the middle of the century, and their development in organization and method has occurred within the past twenty-five years.

Technical and trade schools of secondary grade, with a basis of science and mathematics, have also rapidly increased since the middle of the nineteenth century.

[1] See pp. 30off.

[2] See p. 283.

[3] See p. 289.

[4] See pp. 290f.

[5] See p. 359.

Elementary science was also introduced in the elementary schools of Germany early in the nineteenth century

The scientific movement was also felt in the elementary schools of Germany during the early part of the nineteenth century. Science was considerably popularized by the schools of the philanthropinists,[1] and was widely introduced into elementary education by the spread of Pestalozzianism in Prussia and the other German states.[2] Before the close of the first quarter of the century the study of elementary science,—natural history, physiology, and physics, appeared in various grades; geography and drawing were taught throughout the course; and geometry was included in the upper classes of the *Volksschulen*.

There was little science in the higher or secondary institutions of France before the Revolution, but with the new regime the curricula suggested generally contained sciences, and,

France.—Before the Revolution in France the higher and secondary institutions found little place for instruction in science. There was a chair of experimental physics in the College of Navarre of the University of Paris and at the Universities of Toulouse and Montpellier, and natural history was also taught at the more independent College of France, but, as a whole, education was dominated largely by humanism. However, with the establishment of the Republic a new régime began in education, as in other matters, and science entered more largely into higher and secondary instruction. Talleyrand's scheme of education presented the old ideas in a slightly modified form, but the next year Condorcet's completely subordinated letters to science.[3] The curriculum that he proposed for his *Instituts*, or secondary schools, consisted mainly of science, pure and applied, and his defense of the sciences is not unlike that of Spencer, except that it leans more on the argument of

[1] See pp. 28f.

[2] See pp. 145ff..

[3] See p. 294.

discipline. In 1794 the Republic also founded a normal school, where the famous Laplace and Lagrange gave instruction in science. Science occupied one-third of the course in the 'central schools,'[1] and in 1802 Napoleon had included in the scientific course for the lycée natural history, physics, astronomy, chemistry, and mineralogy. A further advance in quantity and method in secondary instruction was made in 1814, when it was provided by statute that the pupil in the classical course "will one year study animals and vegetables; one year minerals and chemistry; one year experimental physics." On the ground that they were injuring classical studies, Cousin in 1840 had the sciences curtailed, but he was shortly forced to restore them upon an optional basis. A contest between the two types of studies was carried on until 1852, when a bifurcation in the course put the two theoretically upon the same basis.[2] The scientific course, however, has never been able to equal the prestige of the classical, although it has constantly increased in time and difficulty, and now zoölogy, botany, geology, physics, and chemistry extend through all the grades and are taught by laboratory methods.

after a contest, the humanities and the sciences were, by a division of the course, put upon the same footing.

Some instruction in science has come to be given during the past forty years even in the elementary schools of France. In the lower primary schools the work is informal, and consists mostly of object lessons and first scientific notions. These are developed in connection with drawing, manual training, agriculture, and geography of the neighborhood and of France in general. Instruction becomes more formal in the higher primary schools, and includes regular courses in the natural and

The elementary system has also come to give some training in science, especially in agriculture.

[1] See p. 294.

[2] See p. 297.

physical sciences and hygiene, as well as geography, drawing, and manual training. In the normal schools for primary teachers the instruction in all the physical and biological sciences is even more thorough, and it is given especially from the practical point of view. It includes not only the facts and theories of general scientific importance, but it also emphasizes their applications to every day life. For example, the flora and fauna of the neighborhood are studied in their special relation to agriculture.

In England the sciences did not become at all prominent in Oxford and Cambridge until the close of the nineteenth century, but rapid progress was made in a number of municipal universities that sprang up.

England.—In England, through the professorship of Newton at Cambridge, some study of physical science was stimulated at the universities before the close of the seventeenth century, and during the eighteenth several chairs in the natural sciences were established at Cambridge. But it was almost the middle of the nineteenth century before the biological sciences and the laboratory method of instruction were introduced, and not until toward the close of the century did science become prominent at Cambridge and Oxford. And the most marked promotion of the scientific movement in England has occurred within the past fifty years through the foundation of efficient municipal universities in such centers as Birmingham, Manchester, London, and Liverpool.[1] For many years the laboratory instruction was given only in institutions outside the universities. Higher courses in science by the new methods were afforded through the foundation of the Royal School of Mines[2] in 1851, the addition of the Royal School

About the middle of the century institutions affording higher courses in science were

[1] See p. 310.

[2] It passed through three changes of name (1851, 1853, 1859) before the present title was adopted (1863).

of Naval Architecture and Marine Engineering in 1864, and the organization of the Normal School of Science [1] in 1868. All of these were in 1890 combined in a single institution known as the Royal College of Science. In 1907 the City and Guilds (Engineering) College,[2] founded in 1881, was also merged, and the entire corporation became known as the Imperial College of Science and Technology. The associated colleges are mainly supported by grants from the government, the London County Council, and the City and Guilds Institute. They are located at South Kensington, London, and have been furnished a number of excellent buildings in late years. An agency that was instrumental in encouraging this advanced study of the sciences, although formed primarily for the benefit of the elementary and secondary schools, was the Science and Art Department, which was in 1899 taken over as part of the national Board of Education.[3] It had its start through the Board of Trade in an attempt to encourage a knowledge of art and design, but the work was soon extended to the schools and in 1857 the direction of science and art was brought under the charge of the Committee of Council.[4] The following year a regular Science and Art Department was organized to bring under a single management the science, trade, and navigation schools already existing, and to facilitate higher instruction in science. A few years later this

also founded outside the universities.

This movement was furthered by the Science and Art Department, organized in 1857, and taken over as part of the Board of Education in 1899.

[1] These normal training classes were segregated from the work of the School of Mines (1861) and given the name above (1881) before all parts of the work were again consolidated (1890).

[2] It was originally called the City and Guilds Technical College, and was included in the University of London, when that institution was reorganized (1899).

[3] See p. 306.

[4] See p. 304.

organization began to offer examinations and to grant certificates to teach science in the elementary schools.

While the academies offered a rich course in science, they greatly declined before the close of the eighteenth century, and the public schools paid little attention to the sciences.

In English secondary instruction science first appeared through the establishment of 'academies' by nonconformists toward the close of the seventeenth century. The courses of these institutions were rich in realistic subjects, and early in the eighteenth century included considerable work in mathematics, natural philosophy, natural history, anatomy, and other sciences. Although, after the Act of Toleration (1689), the academies were permitted to be regularly incorporated, they had greatly declined before the close of the eighteenth century. At the same time the humanistic 'public' schools and secondary institutions of a private character as yet paid almost no attention to the sciences. In the first half of the nineteenth century an anti-classical campaign began to be waged by George Combe and his friends. They undertook to point out the relative weakness of linguistic studies as an intellectual training, and advocated 'real' training as opposed to that of words. The controversy with the classicists continued with ever increasing force from 1820 to the middle of the century, and the science advocates eventually began to found schools to embody the new ideals. Toward the close of 1848 the first 'secular' school was opened at Edinburgh, and included in its curriculum a study of geography, drawing, mathematics, natural history, chemistry, natural philosophy, physiology, phrenology, and materials used in the arts and manufactures, as well as literary, æsthetic, moral, and religious subjects. Similar institutions were organized at Edinburgh, Glasgow, Leith, London, Manchester, Birmingham, Newcastle,

About the middle of the nineteenth century Combe and others opened 'secular' schools, which did much to stimulate the introduction of the sciences; and,

Belfast, and many other cities of the United Kingdom.

While these schools did not last long, they were very successful for a time, and, together with the writings of Combe, did much to stimulate the reform in secondary education and the introduction of the sciences that shortly followed. The University Commission for Winchester in 1856 held that "good elementary instruction in physical science is essential in the case of many boys and desirable in all cases." Responding to this judgment, Winchester College, the oldest of the great public schools, at once started a brief series of lectures, which was by 1865 expanded into a regular course running through the year. After 1868, as a result of the governmental investigation of the endowed schools, which showed an almost complete absence of science in the curricula, all the leading secondary schools began to establish a 'modern side.' This course generally included physics and natural history, as well as modern languages and history, but it was most reluctantly admitted by the institutions, and, while it has attained to great efficiency, it has never, except in a few schools, been accorded the same standing as the classical course. The Department of Science and Art also afforded much encouragement to secondary instruction in the sciences by subsidizing schools and classes in physics, chemistry, zoölogy, botany, geology, mineralogy, and subjects involving the applications of science. Before its absorption into the Board of Education some ten thousand classes and seventy-five independent schools of secondary grade received assistance from this source.

In 1856, Winchester, the oldest public school, started instruction in science, and, after 1868, the leading public schools began to establish a 'modern side.'

Subsidies for science instruction were afforded to secondary schools by the Department of Science and Art.

The Department also gave aid to the study of science

After the middle of the century subsidies were also granted the elementary schools by the Department of Science and Art; and since 1900 work in science has been made compulsory.

in elementary education. As early as the fifties, grants were made to establish work in elementary science, art, and design, but the educational value was for more than forty years subordinated to practical applications. However, in 1889 a report by a Committee of the British Association wrought a great improvement in the teaching of science. As a result, money was granted the County Councils during the following year, to be distributed for technical instruction, and much aid was furnished for the equipment of laboratories, lecture rooms, and workshops, and an increase in the staff of instructors. Since then laboratory instruction has rapidly gained ground in the elementary schools. Nevertheless, for a decade no subjects except the rudiments were required in the elementary course, and such 'supplementary' subjects as elementary science and geography, if taught, were given a special subsidy. Since 1900 this scientific work has been made compulsory in the elementary curriculum.

In the colleges of the United States there was some science taught in the eighteenth century,

The United States.—In the colleges of the United States the courses show some evidence of science teaching in the eighteenth century and a little even in the seventeenth. Astronomy and 'the nature of plants' appear in the list of studies advertised at Harvard in 1642, and 'natural philosophy' was offered in 1690 by the same institution. During the eighteenth century Yale, Princeton, King's (afterward Columbia), Dartmouth, Union, and Pennsylvania all came to offer work in this latter subject, or in 'natural history,' which might then be used to denote physics, chemistry, geology, and astronomy, as well as botany and zoölogy. As far as physics was concerned, before the Revolution it seems to have been a subordinate branch of mathematical instruction, and owing to the limitations of scientific knowledge at the time, to have consisted simply of lectures on mechanics, hydrostatics, pneumatics, and optics, with possibly brief discussions on heat and sound and a few experiments in electricity. There was even less biology taught. There were, moreover, no laboratories or instruments of precision, and chemistry was apparently not taught at all, except occasionally as an obscure and unimportant branch of physics.

but it was small in amount, and there were no laboratories or instruments of precision.

Since then, owing to the great increase in our knowledge of science, there have been the greatest change and enlargement of instruction. Whole fields of science have been discovered and defined, and others, like geology and astronomy, have been reclaimed from dogmatism, and science studies have slowly come into favor. Instruction in chemistry gradually grew up in the latter part of the eighteenth century through a study of materia medica at the medical schools of Pennsylvania (1768), Harvard (1782), and Dartmouth (1798). The movement was slower in reaching the colleges proper, but spread rapidly after it had once started. A separate chair of chemistry was established at Princeton in 1795, at Columbia in 1800, Yale in 1802, Bowdoin in 1805, South Carolina and Dickinson in 1811, Williams in 1812, and so on, until practically all the colleges had recognized it as an important branch of study. But while experiments were from the first performed as demonstrations by the instructors, it was generally not until almost the middle of the century that students began to be admitted to the laboratories.[1] About the

In the nineteenth century many professorships, laboratory methods, and much equipment were introduced into American colleges;

[1] At Rensselaer Polytechnic Institute from 1825 on the students performed 'demonstrations' before the class. This was in spirit about

same time laboratories in physics began to be equipped with apparatus. Geology was included in the early professorship of chemistry at Yale, and was given a distinct chair upon the advent of James D. Dana about the middle of the century, while by 1825 Amos Eaton taught it as a separate subject through field study at Williams. In astronomy Harvard had a telescope before the beginning of the century, Princeton devoted a room to instruments as early as 1803, Yale improvised an observatory by 1830, and a building was specially equipped by Williams in 1837 and by Western Reserve in 1839. Yet the instruments remained very ordinary and the methods authoritative and prescriptive until the opening of the observatories at Cincinnati (1844), Cambridge (1846), and Michigan (1854), after which the development was most rapid. Biology was even longer studied through mere observation rather than investigation and experiment. Until Louis Agassiz opened his laboratory at Harvard to students just after the middle of the century, the courses were meager, mostly theoretical and classificatory, and were given entirely by lecture, without field or laboratory work. Since Agassiz's time, however, the subject of biology has been divided and subdivided into several sciences and administered by separate departments in the colleges and universities.

The introduction of the sciences and the development of the elective system, which afforded an opportunity for taking them, were greatly promoted in existing American institutions of higher learning after the publication

the same as laboratory work, and within the next decade apparently a number of institutions adopted this 'Rensselaer Plan of Education' in chemistry, botany, geography, history, and geometry.

of Darwin's *Origin of Species* (1859), and the dissemination of that doctrine through Asa Gray, professor of natural history at Harvard, and William B. Rogers, president of the Massachusetts Institute of Technology. The intellectual development ensuing also brought about the foundation of such new institutions as Cornell and Johns Hopkins, which emphasized the teaching of science as an unconscious protest against the exclusively classical training. Special scientific and technological schools likewise began to arise. The Rensselaer Polytechnic Institute (1825) and the Lawrence Scientific School at Harvard (1847) had already been opened, but now similar schools of science, like Sheffield at Yale (1860) and the Massachusetts Institute of Technology (1862), sprang up in all parts of the country. In 1862 the Morrill Act of Congress appropriated lands in every state to promote education in agriculture, mechanic arts, and the natural sciences. These grants, which amounted at first to thirteen million acres, were subsequently extended to new states as they were admitted, and the endowment was increased by the annual grants of money that were made under later acts. From these funds and private benefactions, further schools of science were started or old schools were strengthened in every state, and from 1865 on rapid progress was made in the facilities for pure and applied science in higher education.

new universities, emphasizing science, were founded, and special scientific and technical institutions were organized, and the Morrill law (1862) and later acts of Congress appropriated lands to promote education in agriculture, mechanic arts, and natural sciences

Through the academies, during the latter half of the eighteenth century and the early part of the nineteenth, the sciences were introduced into American secondary education. Sometimes these were extended downward from the colleges, but often they were subjects that had as yet been barely touched by the colleges, such

The sciences were introduced into American secondary education through the academies, and the high

schools in the first half of the nineteenth century continued to emphasize these subjects.

as astronomy, natural philosophy, chemistry, botany, and geography. As a result, the colleges frequently found that their curricula were not meeting the popular needs as those of the academies were, and were forced to enlarge their program of studies. As the early high schools grew up, they continued the attention paid to the sciences by the academies. The first high school to appear, that at Boston in 1821, scheduled geography in the first year; navigation and surveying in the second; and natural philosophy and astronomy in the third. A similar emphasis upon science appeared during the first half of the century in all the secondary institutions, whether known as academies, high schools, union schools, or city colleges. In all cases, however, instruction was given mainly through text-books, and, while experiments were frequently used for demonstration by the teacher, there was no laboratory work for the students. At first the sciences were included in the curriculum on account of their usefulness, but after the middle of the century, the demand was increased on the strength of their scientific value. These studies were by this time becoming more scientific through the discovery of new principles and were being emancipated from the mere classificatory stage. But a tendency to overload the curriculum with sciences, which had been evident in secondary education from the days of the academies, was much increased during the seventies by the demand of the legislatures in several states that candidates for teachers' certificates pass an examination in several sciences. The high schools and academies endeavored to furnish the necessary training to prepare for these examinations, and until toward the end of the century the courses in the sciences

During the seventies, owing to the requirement of sciences for the teachers' certificates, there was a tendency to overload the high school and academy curriculum with them.

were numerous and of rather superficial character. Within the last twenty years, however, the schools have come to limit each student to a relatively few courses taught by thorough laboratory methods.

Science was introduced into the elementary school through Mann's recommendation of physiology and the Pestalozzian object teaching.

Except for geography, which appeared in the curriculum early in the century, the rudiments practically constituted the entire course of the elementary school until the time of Horace Mann. Largely through his efforts, physiology was widely introduced by the middle of the century. About a dozen years later the Pestalozzian object teaching began to come in through the Oswego methods, and tended to become systematized and formalized. Use was made of materials in several of the sciences, and the pupils were required to describe them in scientific terms. Thus there was a transition from object teaching to elementary science, and later on, toward the close of the century, to the more informal presentation of the subject, known as 'nature study.' The nature study movement quickly spread through the country, and has most recently appeared in the guise of agricultural instruction. Many states now require agriculture as a requisite for a teacher's certificate, and many normal schools have come to furnish a training in the subject. The development of institutions to teach this subject will be discussed in the account of recent tendencies given in the next chapter.[1]

Interrelation of the Scientific with the Psychological and Sociological Movements.—It is evident that there has been a marked scientific movement in the educational systems of all countries during the past two hundred years. The sciences began to appear in the curricula of

[1] See pp. 368f.

The scientific movement is closely related to the psychological in its position on formal discipline and in the effect of teaching sciences upon the other subjects.

educational institutions in the seventeenth and eighteenth centuries, but their rapid increase, and the use of laboratories and the scientific method in instruction, dated from the middle of the nineteenth. In some respects this scientific movement has been closely related to the other modern tendencies in education,—the psychological and the sociological. The coincidence of the scientific movement with the psychological on the question of formal discipline has already been considered.[1] The influence of the development of the sciences upon educational method also constitutes part of the psychological movement. The sciences demanded entirely different methods of teaching from the traditional procedure. These innovations were worked out slowly by experimentation, and when they proved to be more in keeping with psychology, they reacted upon the teaching of the older subjects so that educational method in general was placed upon a more scientific basis. Hence the method of the sciences, enforcing both inductive and deductive reasoning, is no longer the exclusive property of the sciences, but has been found to be the true method in history, politics, philology, and other studies. A corresponding improvement in the presentation of the form, content, and arrangement of various subjects has taken place in text-books, and a radically different set of books and authors has been rendered necessary. The scientific movement has thus discovered and popularized the method of teaching that all other branches are beginning to adopt, and has consequently come in direct contact and coöperation with the psychological movement.

The scientific movement has even more points in com-

[1] See pp. 334ff.

The scientific movement coincides with the sociological in stressing content rather than form, in promoting technical and commercial institutions, and in furthering democracy.

mon with the sociological. In its opposition to the disciplinarians and its stress upon the content of education rather than the method, the scientific tendency coincides with the sociological, although the former looks rather to the natural sciences as a means of individual welfare, and the latter to the social and political sciences to equip the individual for life in social institutions and to secure the progress of society. But while the scientist usually states his argument in individual terms, because of his connection in time and sympathy with the individualism of the eighteenth and nineteenth centuries, the same writer usually, as in the case of Rousseau, Combe, Spencer, and Huxley, advocates the social, moral, and political sciences as a means of complete living. Similarly, the sociological movement has especial kinship with the economic and utilitarian aspects of the study of the sciences, for professional, technical, and commercial institutions have been evolved because of sociological as well as scientific demands. Again, the use of the sciences in education as a means of preparing for life and the needs of society overlaps the modern sociological principle of furthering democracy, the best development of all classes, and the abandonment of artificial strata in society. As Hughes says in *The Making of Citizens:*

"Until this tyranny of classicalism has been abolished, and the claims of science recognised, it will be impossible to realise the democratic ideal. Time again will, however, see the ideal realised. The first phase in this realisation will probably be the organisation of a system of schools avowedly independent of the classical spirit and keenly responsive to modern needs. Let us hope that they will not lack the true humanistic spirit. The Berlin Conference of 1890–1891 concluded that two types of secondary school were alone needed—the classical or Gymnasium and the modern or

Realschule. Intermediate types are unnecessary and pedagogically unsound. The adoption of modern sides in both England and France has been condemned in theory and found inefficient in practice. Such a double system, however, cannot be considered as a permanent realising of this ideal. Socially such a separation of the future citizens of the State is unfortunate, and therefore it is with interest and sympathy that all true democrats will watch the efforts of American educators to solve this problem."

SUPPLEMENTARY READING

ARMSTRONG, H. E. (Editor). *The Teaching of Scientific Method.* Chaps. 1 and 18.

BOONE, R. G. *History of Education in the United States.* Pp. 158–169.

BUCKLEY, ARABELLA B. *A Short History of Natural Science.*

CARPENTER, W. L. *Science-Teaching* (In *Elementary Schools* by William Bousfield).

CLARK, F. W. *The Teaching of Chemistry and Physics* (*United States Bureau of Education, Circular of Information*, 1880, No. 6).

COMBE, G. *Education.*

COMPAYRÉ, G. *Herbert Spencer and Scientific Education.*

COULTER, J. M. *The Mission of Science in Education* (*Science*, II, 12, pp. 281–293).

DEXTER, E. G. *History of Education in the United States.* Chaps. VI, XVII, and XIX.

DRYER, C. R. *Science in Secondary Schools.*

ELIOT, C. W. *Educational Reform.*

FARRAR, F. W. *Essays on a Liberal Education.* VI.

FISKE, J. *A Century of Science.* I.

GALLOWAY, R. *Education, Scientific and Technical.*

GRAVES, F. P. *Great Educators of Three Centuries.* Chap. XIV.

HARRIS, W. T. *Herbert Spencer and What to Study* (*Educational Review*, Vol. XXIV, pp. 135–149).

HUXLEY, T. H. *Method and Results.* II.

HUXLEY, T. H. *Science and Education.*

JEVONS, W. S. *The Principles of Science.*

JORDAN, D. S. *Nature Study and Moral Culture* (*Proceedings of the National Education Association*, 1896, pp. 130ff.).
LAURIE, S. S. *Educational Opinion from the Renaissance.* Chap. XVI.
LLOYD, F. E., and BIGELOW, M. A. *The Teaching of Biology.*
MONROE, P. *Textbook in the History of Education.* Chap. XII.
NORTON, W. H. *The Social Service of Science* (*Science*, II, 13, pp. 644ff.).
PEARSON, K. *Grammar of Science.* Chap. I.
QUICK, R. H. *Essays on Educational Reformers.* Chap. XIX.
ROBERTS, R. D. *Education in the Nineteenth Century.* Chap. VII.
SEDGWICK, W. T. *Educational Value of the Method of Science* (*Educational Review*, Vol. V, pp. 243ff.).
THWING, C. F. *A History of Higher Education in America.*
WHEWELL, W. *History of the Inductive Sciences.*
WHITE, A. D. *Scientific and Industrial Education in the United States* (*Popular Science Monthly*, Vol. V, pp. 170–191).
WILLIAMS, H. S. *History of Science.*
WILLIAMS, H. S. *Story of Nineteenth Century Science.*
YOUMANS, E. L. (Editor). *Culture Demanded by Modern Life.*

CHAPTER XI

PRESENT DAY TENDENCIES IN EDUCATION

At the present day some remarkable movements toward a reconstruction of education are going on.

Recent Attempts at a Reconstruction of Educational Practice.—Because of the remarkable development of science and invention, the nineteenth century has often been referred to as the 'wonderful' century. Such a term affords no better description of material achievement than of the remarkable progress that has taken place in education. The last chapter showed how the growth of the sciences during this period has been reflected in the educational institutions of all countries; and previous chapters have indicated the extent to which, through various movements, education has been broadened and improved in conception and advancement. There has been a continuous gain in the centralization and democratization of schools, in the content of the course of study, in the methods of teaching and the professional training of teachers, and in the liberality with which education has been established and maintained. But momentous as have been these changes and expansion of view, the near future of education will probably witness a much greater development in vision and concrete achievements. At the present time there are constant efforts at a modification and a reconstruction of education in the interest of a better adjustment of the individual to his social environment and of greatly improved conditions in society itself. Educational experimentation and discussion are being conducted along a great variety of lines, and are of a richer and more scientific nature than ever before. It is, of course, impossible to describe all of these movements even in the briefest manner, and it is difficult to select for consideration those most characteristic and promising. Yet some of the present day tendencies that appear most significant must at this point engage our passing attention.

The Growth of Industrial Training.—The movement that is perhaps most emphasized to-day is the introduction of vocational training into the curriculum of education. There is now an especial need for this type of training in industrial lines. Since the industrial revolution and the development of the factory system, the master no longer works by the side of his apprentice and instructs him, and the ambition of the youth can no longer be spurred by the hope that he may himself some day become a master. His experience is no longer broad, but is generally confined to some single process, and only a few of the operatives require anything more than low-grade skill, when productive efficiency becomes the main goal of the system. Nor, as a rule, will the employer undertake any systematic education of his workmen, since the present mobility of labor permits of no guarantee that he will reap the benefit of such efforts, and the modern industrial plant is poorly adapted to supplying the necessary theoretical training for experts. Hence an outside agency, the school, has been called upon to assist in the solution of these new industrial problems.

With the development of the factory system, and the want of high-grade skill, it has become necessary for the school to consider industrial training

Industrial Schools in Germany.—To meet the demand for industrial education, all the principal states of

Europe have maintained training of this sort for at least half a century, and the United States has during the past decade been making rapid strides in the same direction. The especial plans of organization and instruction that have been evolved in each case seem to depend upon the temperament of the people and upon the institutions and industrial conditions of the country or locality concerned. In Germany, where this training has had the longest history and is probably the most effective, the work has been carried on through the *Fortbildungsschulen* ('continuation schools').[1] Institutions of this sort were first established by Würtemberg in 1695, to supplement the meager elementary education, and by the earliest years of the nineteenth century a number of other German states had introduced them. The 'industrial law' of the North German Confederation in 1869 permitted the localities to make attendance at the continuation schools compulsory for all apprentices up to the age of eighteen, and required employers to allow them to attend. And after the Franco-Prussian war, when a desire to enter into industrial competition with the world arose, most of the other states and localities began to follow the example, and this legislation eventually became the basis for an imperial law (1891, 1900). The course in the continuation schools at first consisted largely of review work, but the rapid spread of elementary schools soon enabled them to devote all the time to technical education. Through the establishment of a large number of schools of various sorts, training is afforded not only for the rank and file of workmen in the different trades, but for the higher grades of

Since the Franco-Prussian war the states of Germany have generally made attendance at the 'continuation schools' compulsory for all apprentices until eighteen.

At first the course consisted largely of review work, but, with the increase of elementary schools, all the time was devoted to technical education, and

[1] See p. 288, footnote.

workers, such as foremen, superintendents, and technical office clerks. Similarly, girls are trained in a wide variety of vocations, and in housekeeping and motherhood. Many of these schools, especially in the South German states, have added laboratories and workshops, and the training has proved so valuable that many of the pupils return voluntarily after the period of compulsory attendance.

training is now afforded for higher grades of workers, as well as for the rank and file.

During the last twenty-five years there have also been developed continuation schools for general education, rather than for special industrial training, known as *Gewerbeschulen* ('trade schools') or *Handwerkschulen* ('artisan schools'). These institutions furnish theoretical courses in chemistry, physics, mathematics, book-keeping, drawing, geography, nature study, history, and law. In South Germany there is a tendency to combine theoretical and practical work, and to develop schools adapted to the particular industries of the various localities, but North German States generally confine the courses to theoretical training, and leave the practical side to the care of the employers or associations. The system of industrial education in Munich, organized by Dr. Kerschensteiner, has been especially developed and has attracted much attention. It includes an extra class in the elementary schools with the chief stress upon manual work, to bridge the gap between school life and employment and serve as a preparation for the industrial classes of the continuation schools. The instructors for the industrial schools of Germany are supplied through special training schools, either by giving elementary teachers short industrial courses and making them acquainted with the working of the factory, or by

South Germany tends to combine theoretical and practical work, and North Germany generally confines its courses to theoretical training.

The Munich system, organized by Kerschensteiner, nas an extra class in the elementary schools to serve as a preparation for the industrial classes of the continuation schools.

taking master workmen from the factory, and giving them short courses in methods of teaching.

Switzerland and Austria, like Germany, use apprenticeship, but France has found this feature unsatisfactory, and has undertaken to furnish the entire industrial training through continuation schools.

Industrial Education in France.—In Germany these industrial continuation schools are not intended to be a substitute for apprenticeship, but furnish parallel instruction throughout this period. Switzerland and Austria also use both these features in industrial training, but the one especially emphasizes the apprenticeship and the other the continuation school. Because of unsatisfactory conditions in apprenticeship, France even goes so far as to attempt to eliminate it altogether. More than any other country in Europe, it has made efforts to furnish the entire industrial training through continuation schools articulating with the elementary system. The pupils are admitted at thirteen, and obtain practice in the school workshops for three years. Iron-work is taught to all the boys, but the other courses vary with local needs. Girls learn to make dresses, corsets, millinery, artificial flowers, and other industrial products. A number of these continuation schools have added normal departments, and there is a normal school for industrial training at Paris. There are also throughout the country a number of national schools of arts and trades that are based upon the same principles as these lower industrial schools, and furnish a training for foremen, superintendents, and managers. There are also many evening classes for industrial training under voluntary auspices, but as a whole continuation education has not been nearly as well developed in France as in Germany.

There are also a number of national schools of arts and trades, which furnish training for managers and foremen, and evening industrial classes under voluntary auspices.

Types of English Industrial Training.—In England, despite the rapid industrial development, little attempt was made before the middle of the nineteenth century to improve the vocational skill of workmen. In 1851 grants were made to evening industrial schools and classes, and two years later a Department of Art and Science[1] was established, to encourage instruction in drawing and science and administer the grants. Schools of science were organized in 1872, and shared in the departmental grants. These institutions had at first both day and evening sessions, but after a generation became in many cases regular secondary day schools. There also arose many private organizations, held mainly in the evenings, to teach "such branches of science and the fine arts as benefit commerce and industries." Among these was the City and Guilds of London Institute,[2] which registers, inspects, and examines classes in technology and manual training.

After the middle of the nineteenth century several attempts were made in England to improve vocational skill through industrial education.

At present England has three types of industrial education, each based upon the work of the elementary schools. These embrace the higher elementary schools, which afford a four-year course in practical and theoretical science arranged according to local needs; the day trade schools, furnishing a substitute for apprenticeship, which is now becoming obsolete; and the evening continuation schools for children who have left the elementary schools at fourteen without completing the higher grades. Thus, while industrial education is still in the experimental stage, England has come to recognize that the country cannot successfully enter into world competition without it.

There are at present three types of this training,—higher elementary schools, day trade schools, and evening continuation schools.

Development of Industrial Education in the United States.—The real growth of industrial education did not occur in the United States until late in the nineteenth century. By that time it had become evident that natural ability and adaptability were no longer sufficient,

[1] See pp. 343f. and 345. [2] See p. 343.

but that real skill and technical knowledge were needed. With the immense body of unskilled foreigners and under international competition, American industrial development could be maintained only in the same way as in Europe by training an adequate supply of expert workers.

In the larger cities of the United States, about the middle of the nineteenth century, there arose a number of voluntary evening continuation schools for industrial training, but the public schools were very slow to establish this evening training.

At first this type of education was furnished through philanthropy and private enterprise. Under such auspices there sprang up about the middle of the century a number of evening continuation schools in the larger cities. Among these were the Cooper Union and the Mechanics' Institute in New York, the Franklin Union and the Spring Garden Institute in Philadelphia, the Ohio Mechanics' Institute in Cincinnati, the Virginia Mechanics' Institute in Richmond, and the evening classes of the Young Men's Christian Association of various places. Simple as this beginning was, the public schools were slow to follow the example, and it was not until very recently that evening classes in drawing, mathematics, science, and technical subjects were organized by the public school system.

Day instruction was first offered by the New York Trade School, founded in 1881, and, although for twenty years only two similar institutions were started, during the twentieth century a large number have been organized through

The first vocational institution to be conducted in the daytime was the New York Trade School, founded in 1881 by Richard T. Auchmuty. He wished to have American mechanics trained for the building trades, and believed that apprenticeship could no longer serve the purpose. Because of the economic difficulties in attending, the pupils were at first given a course of only four months. Similar institutions arose slowly. At the end of twenty years there were but two more,—The Williamson Free School of Mechanical Trades near Philadelphia and the Baron de Hirsch Trade School in New York, but since then the development has been more rapid. Since

1910 more than a dozen trade schools have been organized through public and private support and in different parts of the country, and a number of other schools have been opened upon a commercial basis. By 1906 the first public trade school was established. In that year Columbus, Georgia, opened as an integral part of the city system a Secondary Industrial School, in which specific trades were taught. A year later the Milwaukee School of Trades was adopted by the city. These were soon followed by the organization of public trade schools in Philadelphia, Portland (Oregon), Worcester, Indianapolis, and elsewhere. These schools are mostly for youths between sixteen and twenty-five, but 'preparatory trade schools' for younger boys have also been started in New York, Massachusetts, and other states. Such schools offer courses in drawing, elementary science, shop calculations, accounting, business forms, history, and English, and afford a knowledge of shop materials and methods rather than training in a specific trade.

public or private support or upon a commercial basis.

Another recent variety of trade school is the 'part-time' institution, which gives students some theoretical and formal training while they are obtaining their practical experience. These schools somewhat resemble the *Fortbildungsschulen*, but the individualistic spirit of American industry has as yet generally kept employers from releasing their apprentices for instruction during the working period of the day. This part-time alternation of practical and theoretical training is sometimes carried on within a commercial establishment. By such an arrangement the maximum of correlation between the two types of instruction can be accomplished, but the plan has been feasible only in the case of very large corporations.

'Part-time' schools, which afford training during apprenticeship, have recently grown up, and in some instances are conducted within a commercial establishment.

Training for industrial leaders is furnished through endowed or subsidized secondary technical schools, technical high schools, or coöperation between a high school or college and an industrial establishment.

Higher training to equip leaders for the industries with greater skill, technical knowledge, and responsibility has likewise come to be furnished. This has been accomplished through secondary technical schools that are well endowed, supported by men of wealth, or partially subsidized by the state; through the more recent technical high schools established by a number of the larger cities; and through alternating the instruction of a regular high school or college with practical work in an industrial establishment upon some coöperative basis. Hence a great interest and activity in industrial education are now everywhere in evidence, and laws establishing and supervising it have been enacted in a number of the American commonwealths.

The need of schools to prepare for a business career has also come to be generally recognized.

Commercial Education in Germany.—But the modern development of vocational training throughout the leading countries has not been confined to industrial lines. With the extension of the sphere of commerce and the development of its organization that have taken place in the nineteenth century, it has come to be recognized that a thorough preparation is also essential to a business career. Only recently, however, has this training been felt to be a proper function of the schools, since for many years it was opposed by educators as sordid and commercializing, and by business men as unpractical and ineffective. Both classes have now been brought to realize the essential unity of their interests and the need of mutual support, and the rapid growth of commercial education indicates an appreciation of its usefulness and the attempt to respond to a real need. Germany is generally admitted to lead in commercial as in industrial education. The growth of this training has taken place since 1887, but there is now offered under state control a unified and thorough preparation for any line of business. Besides private continuation schools, in which a course of three years in modern languages and elementary commercial studies can be obtained, there have grown up both public secondary schools and university courses in which a thorough general education and theoretical work in commerce, as well as a practical and technical training, are provided. In the higher work of the universities, which is largely a product of the twentieth century, extensive courses, including eight modern languages and a wide range of economics, politics, and law, are offered, and a large amount of specialization is encouraged.

In Germany for this purpose have been evolved private continuation schools, public secondary schools, and university courses.

Commercial Schools in England and France.—Thus Germany has reached a considerable degree of efficiency in commercial education, and has thereby greatly developed her commerce. No other country has advanced so far in this direction. On the other hand, for a nation of commercial supremacy, England has, until lately, been rather indifferent to this type of education, although the leaders in thought and action have awakened and become uneasy about the situation. Examinations upon commercial subjects are now offered by various associations, but there is little coöperation, and the schools still cram their pupils to meet these tests, rather than educate them. There are several varieties of schools, although but relatively few of each kind. Continuation schools have been established and recognized by the Board of Education,[1] a number of private schools and public evening courses have sprung up, a few large cities have started

England has, until recently, been rather indifferent to commercial education; but there have now been established for this purpose a number of continuation schools, private schools, public evening courses, secondary commercial

[1] See p. 306.

schools, and courses in the municipal universities.

secondary commercial schools, and most of the municipal universities [1] have developed courses of wide range and liberal character. But there is as yet a general lack of organization in the various types of institutions. In France there are a few old commercial schools, but the number of pupils is small and the system is not extensive. There are continuation schools under government supervision, private commercial schools, schools established by chambers of commerce, and free evening classes. Likewise, there have been established a number of commercial schools of secondary and even higher grade, like the School of Higher Commercial Studies at Paris. The government control has, however, retarded, rather than aided, the development of these institutions.

In France there are a few old commercial schools, and some secondary and higher instruction, but the work is not extensive.

American Commercial Education.—In the United States we find that commercial education at first developed through the typically American method of the recognition of public need by private enterprise. Early in the nineteenth century, and possibly before that, private schools and classes in book-keeping were established in all the chief cities. These ventures foreshadowed the so-called 'business colleges,' which are under private management and now number about two thousand. They still contain more than one-half the total number of students receiving commercial education of any sort. Penmanship and book-keeping served as their foundation, and are still the main subjects taught. Often commercial arithmetic and commercial law were added, and later stenography and typewriting, but these schools have always been technical and narrow, and their instructors are not infrequently mechanical, deficient in

This type of education began in the United States with private classes and 'business colleges,' which still contain more than half the total number of students.

[1] See p. 310.

education, and swayed by purely pecuniary aims. While usually given the name of 'college,' or even 'university,' the institutions are in reality a species of trade school, and no longer lead in commercial education. In the late eighties many public high schools, normal schools, and universities began to offer commercial instruction, and there began a new era, leading to much development and improvement.

Late in the nineteenth century the public high schools and higher institutions began to offer this work, and while the first courses merely imitated the business colleges, since the twentieth century began, a number of separate high schools of commerce and colleges of commerce, with thorough courses, have arisen.

Until about 1900, however, progress was slow. The high schools at first had the work forced upon them by the taxpayers, who objected when their children had to go to a private school to obtain a business training. The first courses, which lasted only two years, were undertaken as a necessary evil, and were fashioned in imitation of those in the private business colleges, but were often inferior to them. Within the last dozen years, however, some fifteen or twenty cities have opened separate high schools of commerce, and have placed commercial education upon a stable basis. Here the course is like that of any regular high school, except that the studies are commercial, and it covers four or five years of serious study. University schools and colleges of commerce have also sprung up about the same time. The state universities, because of their popular support, have been especially hospitable to this training, but many of the large privately endowed institutions have given considerable attention to it. In fact, a score of years before the real development began, the Wharton School of Finance and Commerce was started at the University of Pennsylvania (1881). Some of these colleges of commerce base their technical work upon a liberal foundation, as in the case of Dartmouth and Harvard; others, like Wharton and the schools in the state universities, coördinate their cultural and practical work; while a few, such as New York University, emphasize the practical element and reduce the liberal to a minimum.

European countries have long since furnished vocational training in agriculture, and during the past generation have organized agricultural instruction of secondary and elementary grade.

Recent Emphasis upon Agricultural Education.—The latest phase of vocational education to be popularized is the agricultural. The European countries have long realized the importance of this training, and during the past generation have everywhere organized agricultural instruction of both secondary and elementary grade. Courses in higher institutions had already been generally established. As early as 1875 France started the *école pratique*, a species of higher primary school with a course of two years, for training the sons of small farmers. These institutions now number about fifty and are most effective. Further, every normal school was in 1879 required to furnish agricultural instruction, and three years later similar legislation was made for the rural elementary schools. For some time the provision was general and indefinite, but in 1896 it was revised and made more specific, and progress has since been very rapid. In Germany secondary work in agriculture is afforded in special institutions at the close of the *Realschule* or after the completion of the sixth year of the *Gymnasium* or *Realgymnasium*.[1] This course offers the natural sciences and agriculture in place of languages and mathematics. Elementary instruction in agriculture has also been furnished in separate schools rather than through the existing elementary schools. England has done but little toward agricultural training in the schools, but several of the British colonies—Canada, Australia,

[1] See pp. 289f.

the West Indies—have introduced it into certain grades.

The United States has of late been especially emphasizing this type of vocational education. The agricultural, or land grant, colleges, started in 1862,[1] increased the knowledge of this subject, stimulated an interest in it, and prepared the way for the extension of agriculture downward into the high school and the grades. This tendency was also promoted by the scientific and nature study movements.[2] Moreover, it was felt that the United States must become a great agricultural nation, and that existing methods of agriculture were exceedingly wasteful. The first agricultural high school was opened at the University of Minnesota in 1888, and was successful from the start. Ten others were organized within a decade, and before long the subject began to be taught at the elementary schools. Since then the movement has been rapid in the secondary and elementary schools. The work is now also presented in county and district agricultural high schools, state and county normal schools, and a variety of private or semi-private institutions. There are now nearly one hundred agricultural high schools in the United States, and the subject is taught as part of the course in several thousand high and elementary school systems. As the movement has developed, both educational and economic results have become far-reaching, and the conceptions of the purpose, needs, methods, and content of education in the American schools have been greatly modified.

The United States started agricultural colleges in 1862, and, through their influence and that of the nature study movement, the subject has been extended until it is now taught in several thousand high and elementary schools.

Moral Training in the Schools of Europe.—But present day tendencies in education have to do with more than

Moral instruction upon a secular basis

[1] See p. 349. [2] See p. 351.

has been greatly developed in the schools of France.

the material side of civilization. There is a rapidly growing sentiment in favor of specific instruction in morals. There are many reasons why this need should be especially felt to-day. One cause has sprung from the impersonal relations that have developed with the growing complexity of business and political life. When men work for impersonal corporations, sell products to people they never see, or intrust their welfare to officials whose names are scarcely known, one strong factor making for honesty and virtue, that of personal relations, is lost, and the temptation to wrongdoing becomes greater. Moreover, it is generally recognized that moral traditions are failing, as a result of the weakening of old religious sanctions, the new conditions in large cities, and other causes.

Such social factors as these are responsible for the attention that has of late been directed to moral training in the schools. Since 1882 specific instruction in morality has been given in the schools of France. This training has been purely secular in its nature, and has excluded religious elements and all appeal to the supernatural. The course has consisted entirely in direct teaching of ethical and civic duties. It has, in consequence, been violently opposed by the clergy, and, since the closing of the Catholic schools in 1904,[1] its efficacy has been seriously doubted, and the whole question is being reopened and considered anew. In English education, on the other hand, the teaching of morality has always been associated with religion. In the 'board' schools this religious instruction has from the first been of a non-sectarian character, but in the 'voluntary' schools the

In English education it has always been given in connection with religion, and since the contest over

[1] See p. 296.

training has occupied more time and has stressed the creed and denominational teaching of some church, usually the Church of England.[1] After the Act of 1902, the contest over religious teaching was brought to a focus, and a self-constituted commission, with Michael E. Sadler as its chairman, undertook to investigate the whole subject of moral instruction. A large and illuminating report on the situation, including the opinions of leading thinkers from many countries, was published in 1908–1909. In Germany and Switzerland the moral and religious instruction in all elementary schools is sectarian, and Catholic and Protestant schools are alike supported, wherever needed, at public expense.

religious teaching was brought to a focus in 1902, the whole subject has been carefully investigated by a commission.

Germany and Switzerland give moral and religious instruction in all elementary schools.

Moral Education in the United States.—During the past decade there has been considerable discussion in the United States concerning moral education. The National Education Association at its annual meeting in 1907 passed the resolution:

> "It is the duty of the teachers to enter at once upon a systematic course of instruction, which shall embrace not only a broader patriotism, but a more extended course of moral instruction, especially in regard to the rights and duties of citizenship, the right of property, and the security and sacredness of human life."

As a result, the committee made a report in 1908–1909 upon various phases of moral training, and recommended special instruction in ethics, not in the form of precepts, but through consideration of existing moral questions, to develop the conscience through reflection. A number of other methods are being investigated. Professor Sharp of the University of Wisconsin is work-

There has recently been much consideration of moral education in the United States; several investigators are experimenting with different methods; and in 1911 the Religious Education Association issued a broad summary of progress in moral education.

[1] See pp. 305f.

ing upon experiments with the high school pupils of the state; Professor Tufts of the University of Chicago has written and lectured upon the possibility of developing public morality by means of a study in the high schools of American industry, business, government, and society; the National Institution for Moral Instruction, through its secretary, Milton Fairchild, has been trying the value of moral lessons illustrated with the lantern; and Felix Adler has organized courses of moral instruction in the Ethical Culture School of New York City, and has striven to introduce direct moral teaching into all schools of the United States. Another medium of great influence is the Religious Education Association, whose convention in 1911 was devoted to moral training, and whose *Journal* gives a broad summary of the progress of moral education in the United States. The report reveals a wide difference of opinion and practice, but an evident tendency to trust other agencies than direct moral instruction. State laws, while often emphasizing the need, do not yet provide for moral instruction in such a way as to have the schools assign a certain amount of time and cover a definite field. Sometimes in a county, city, or school under a single supervising officer a fairly unified system has been put into effect. As a rule, however, legislation has confined itself to instruction in citizenship, the effects of alcohol and narcotics, the humane treatment of animals, and other specific duties.

A characteristic tendency of to-day is the universal attention given to the education of defectives.

The Development of Training for Mental Defectives.— There is another educational movement most characteristic of the present day and more significant of the growth of the humane spirit than even the recent interest in higher moral ideals and conduct. It is found in the modern tendency toward adapting education to all, whatever their peculiarities, defects, or delinquencies. The most striking instance of this is the universal attention now given to the education of mental defectives. The history of the movement is comparatively modern. While institutions for the care of imbeciles were established in Germany, France, England, Scotland, and the United States before the middle of the nineteenth century, it was not until Édouard Seguin (1812–1880) came to America in 1850 that any serious efforts were made to educate them. Seguin began his systematic rational training of idiots at Paris in 1837, but, for political reasons, migrated to the United States and developed his methods here. His general plan was to appeal to the brain through the sense organs by means of a training of the hand, taste and smell, and eye and ear. He used pictures, photographs, cards, patterns, figures, wax, clay, scissors, compasses, and pencils as his chief instruments of education. His achievements were but little short of miraculous, and the stimulus he gave to the training of defectives has been epoch-making, but the exaggerated belief, which sprang up in consequence, that idiocy could be cured, has, of course, not been justified. Feeble-mindedness is largely inherited, and defectives cannot, even in the milder cases, compete successfully in the battle of life, except under most favorable conditions. While there is no point of demarcation at which they can be set off as a class from average or normal persons, and much less can they be discriminated sharply into such grades as 'morons,' feeble-minded, imbeciles, and idiots, they have certain well-known deficiencies in conceptual

This practically began with the 'physiological' methods of Seguin in the United States,

thinking, concentration, and will, and beyond a certain point they seem incapable of development.

which have remained the most effective, although attempts have been made to introduce intellectual elements.

In general, the 'physiological' training of Seguin has remained the most effective means. Since his day there has been a tendency to introduce intellectual elements into the training of the feeble-minded, especially in the case of high-grade defectives, whose education was not undertaken by him, but without much real success. Some institutions have even closely approximated the work of the public schools as far as the third or fourth grade, and have made the manual training quite a subordinate feature. But there is no strong evidence for believing that intellectual studies have at all developed the minds of defectives. The apparent achievements in these lines are mostly the result of parrot repetition, without real assimilation, and do not compensate for the loss of a more useful education or of more kindly disposition in the pupils. The most approved training devotes more than half the time to woodwork, basketry, cooking, knitting, sewing, and other manual and domestic occupations, although the proportions are somewhat governed by the amount of mental deficiency in each case.

In Germany the numerous schools for defectives stress manual education, but give some attention to speech training. They unfortunately allow the pupils to leave at sixteen.

Educational Institutions for Mental Defectives.—All the great nations have now provided schools for the training of defectives. Germany has over one hundred institutions, with some twenty thousand pupils in them, although nine-tenths of them are not supported by the state, but are under church or private auspices. These schools generally stress manual education, but give some attention to intellectual lines, especially to speech training. The most unfortunate feature is that the pupils are allowed to leave the institutions for their homes at sixteen, and in many cases marry and perpetuate mental deficiency. There are but few schools for defectives in France, outside the two near Paris and the juvenile department of the insane hospital at Bicêtre, but these institutions largely follow the physical work of Seguin. In London there is one excellent institution with two thousand pupils, where manual training constitutes almost the entire course. But there are five other schools so located as to serve the various parts of England, in which the training is rather bookish and emphasis is especially laid upon number work.

There are only a few schools for defectives in France, but they largely follow the Seguin training. The large London institution also utilizes manual training, but the five other schools in England attempt a bookish course.

Thanks to the start given by Seguin, America has taken up the education of defectives more fully than any other country. Schools for the feeble-minded now exist in all except a few of the states, and there are some thirty-five or forty private institutions of considerable merit. Not far from twenty thousand defectives are being trained, although this is probably only about one-tenth of the total number of such cases in the country. Several of the commonwealths have laws providing that feeble-minded persons once in an institution must remain there for life, but in other states it is still possible for them to leave at sixteen, as in Germany. The type of education differs greatly according to the institution, ranging from almost purely manual training to a large proportion of the intellectual rudiments, but in all the work is adapted to the various grades in such a way as to raise them a little in the scale of efficiency and to keep them as far as possible from being a burden to themselves and to society.

In America, where the education of defectives is taken up more fully than in any other country, the type of education in the various institutions varies from almost purely manual training to a large proportion of intellectual elements.

Training of Moral Defectives.—Efforts are also being made by progressive nations to afford an education for moral defectives, whose lack appears chiefly in stability

Progressive nations are also training moral defectives, to some extent in the same fashion as mental defectives, and by furnishing exercises and plays, military drill and athletic contests.

and will power. They closely approach the cases of mental deficiency and are often associated with them, and in a large measure they are best trained in a similar fashion. As far, however, as these abnormal persons are the product of unsanitary and immoral surroundings or poor nourishment, much is done by establishing more healthful conditions and furnishing exercises and plays that will develop heart, lung, and nerve power, and stimulate the brain to greater activity. Military drill and athletic contests are often used to develop alertness and prompt obedience to commands, and to supplant selfish spirit with a more wholesome merging in the group interests.

Defectives in a sense organ have also for some time been given a training.

Education of the Deaf and Blind.—Likewise, persons up to the standard mentally, but defective in some sense organ, have for some time been given an education that will minimize the difficulty. There have been two chief methods for teaching the deaf. The manual or 'silent' method of communication was invented by the Abbé Charles Michel de l'Épée (1712–1789) in Paris during the latter part of the eighteenth century, and his school was adopted by the nation in 1791. The other method, the 'oral,' by which the pupil learned to communicate through reading the movements of the lips, was started in Germany early in the eighteenth century, but was not employed to any great extent until the time of Friedrich Moritz Hill (1805–1874). Most of the countries now use the oral method exclusively, or in connection with the older manual system. England abandoned the silent method shortly after the middle of the nineteenth century, although it is still used in Ireland, and both appear in the deaf schools of Scotland and Canada. France followed the sign system exclusively until 1879, when the

The deaf were taught at first by the manual method of l'Épée, but the German oral method is now largely used in most countries.

German method was introduced. Instruction of the deaf by the manual method was begun in the United States at Hartford, Connecticut, in 1817 through Thomas Hopkins Gallaudet (1787–1851), who had studied in France. This system soon spread throughout the union, but, after his visit to Europe in 1843,[1] Horace Mann attempted to have the oral method adopted. While his efforts were not successful, the Clarke School at Northampton, Massachusetts, was established upon that basis, and, after a long controversy, the new system has generally supplanted the manual or has been used in connection with it. Practically every state in the union now has one or more schools for the deaf. Since 1864 higher education has also been furnished by the National Deaf Mute College (now Gallaudet College) at Washington, which is the only institution of its grade in the world.

At Washington a higher education has also been furnished since 1864 by the Gallaudet College.

The first instruction of the blind through raised letters was given by Abbé Valentin Haüy (1746–1822) at Paris. While his schools, owing to a lack of judgment, were failures, the idea spread rapidly. Early in the nineteenth century there were one or more schools in each of the leading countries of Europe, and a generation later institutions of this sort were started in the United States through Samuel Gridley Howe (1801–1876) and others. Since then the number of schools has everywhere multiplied rapidly. Industrial training has in most instances been added to the intellectual, in order to fit every individual to be an independent workman in some line. Even pupils, both deaf and blind, like Laura Bridgeman and Helen Keller, have had their minds reached through the sense of touch.

Instruction of the blind was begun at Paris early in the nineteenth century by Haüy, and the idea spread rapidly through Europe and America.

Industrial training, to secure economic independence, has generally been added to the intellectual.

[1] See p. 173.

A suitable training is likewise being furnished, both by private and public institutions, for extreme individual and racial variations of all sorts.

Training for Extreme Individual Variations.—Similarly, by careful study and wise provision, every possible variation in individuality is now being furnished with the best training possible. Backward, retarded, and nervous pupils are being afforded special instruction even in the public schools. Open air class-rooms and better nourishment are being furnished for anemic and tuberculous children. Cripples and truants are alike given the training best adapted to their peculiar needs. Even the exceptionally brilliant pupil is now in a few school systems allowed the opportunity of improving his genius to the utmost. Negroes and Indians are also provided with the industrial and intellectual education that will in each case be most likely to lead to effective citizenship. Thus the wide differences in economic conditions, future career, and moral, mental, and physical constitution are being carefully considered, and the democratic ideal and the humane spirit are at the present time coming to be most fully realized in education. There is a definite movement toward furnishing opportunities to all according to their ability to utilize them, and toward bringing it to pass that all the schools shall exist for all the people.

Attempts at improved methods have been prominent among modern tendencies in education.

Recent Development of Educational Method.—Nor has the past century witnessed any cessation of the attempts at improved methods of teaching. Various suggestions and systems have been put forward and many have had an important effect upon school procedure. It is impossible, however, to discuss any except two or three of the more influential and prominent, and these can be considered but briefly. The occupational work of Professor Dewey and Colonel Parker's scheme of concentration have especially had a pronounced effect upon methods in the schools of to-day. They have greatly improved upon the motor expression and social participation of even the reconstructed Froebelianism, and have marked the growth of a body of educational theory and practice that places the methods of to-day far in advance of anything previously known. The combination and modification of Ritter, Herbart, and Froebel worked out by Colonel Parker have perhaps received sufficient attention in previous chapters, but we may at this point outline a little more fully the contribution to method made by Professor Dewey.

In the historical study of industries, Dewey found the solution of certain fundamental problems,

The Experimental School of Dewey.—The methods of *John Dewey* (1859–) were developed in an experimental elementary school connected with the University of Chicago from 1896 to 1903. The school did not start with ready-made principles, but sought to solve three fundamental educational problems. It undertook to find out how (1) to bring the school into closer relation with the home and neighborhood life; (2) to introduce subject-matter in history, science, and art that has a positive value and real significance in the child's own life; and (3) to carry on instruction in reading, writing, and figuring with everyday experience and occupation as their background "in such a way that the child shall feel their necessity through their connection with subjects which appeal to him on their own account." The plan for meeting these needs was found largely in the study of industries, on the ground that "the school cannot be a preparation for social life except as it reproduces the typical conditions of social life." The means used in furnishing this industrial activity were evolved mainly along the lines of shopwork, cooking, sewing, and weaving, although many subsidiary industries were also used. These occupations were, of course, intended for a liberalizing, rather than a technical purpose, and considerable time was given to an historical study of them. Dewey declares:[1]

"The industrial history of man is not a materialistic or merely utilitarian affair. It is a matter of intelligence. Its record is the record of how man learned to think, to think to some effect, to transform the conditions of life so that life itself became a different thing. It is an ethical record as well; the account of the conditions which men have patiently wrought out to serve their ends."

and approached the social coöperation and motor expression of Froebel, but did not allow them to become as stereotyped and external.

It can be seen how fully this plan is in accord with the real principles of social coöperation and expression of individual activities underlying the work of Froebel; and "so far as these statements correctly represented Froebel's educational philosophy," Dewey admits that "the school should be regarded as its exponent." But these industrial activities of the Chicago experimental school never became as stereotyped and external as the gifts and even the occupations of the kindergarten have often been. The child was "given, wherever possible, intellectual responsibility for selecting the materials and instruments that are most fit, and given an opportunity to think out his own model and plan of work, led to perceive his own errors, and find how to correct them." Thus the work was never "reduced to a mere routine or custom and its educational value lost." As a result, too, it was the consensus of opinion that "while the children like, or love, to come to school, yet work, and not amusement, has been the spirit and teaching of the school; and that this freedom has been granted under

[1] *Elementary School Record*, p. 200.

such conditions of intelligent and sympathetic oversight as to be a means of upbuilding and strengthening character." Hence, while the Chicago school is now at an end, the experiment in education developed there is still yielding abundant fruitage. It has stimulated similar undertakings elsewhere, and has greatly influenced both the theory and practice of the present day.

The methods of Montessori are similar to Froebel's, but appear to be based upon science, rather than metaphysics.

The Method of Montessori.—The latest development in educational procedure and perhaps the most spectacular is that originating with Montessori at Rome. Because of its novelty and the extravagant claims made for it, it may well be given some detailed consideration. The new methods are not dissimilar to those of Froebel, but they more readily win our confidence from the fact that they appear to be based upon modern science, rather than metaphysics. *Maria Montessori* was the first woman to receive the doctorate in medicine at the University of Rome, and she has since had considerable training in psychiatry, psychology, and scientific pedagogy. She was for a time director of the State Orthophrenic School, and her success in training the feebleminded was most astonishing. She, therefore, naturally desired to try her methods with normal children, and in 1907 accepted the position of educational director of the 'Houses of Childhood' connected with a set of model tenements. The scientific foundation of her practice here is further shown in the conduct of her school. Careful records are kept concerning the heredity, parental occupation, feeding, and infantile sicknesses, and anthropometric measurements are taken at regular intervals. Moreover, an expert inspection is periodically made of the sanitation and economic conditions in the home of each child. It is stated by biologists that many of the scientific statements in Dr. Montessori's *Method of Scientific Pedagogy*[1] are inadequate and incorrect, but if the author is not as strong as she might be in her knowledge of the content of modern science, her system is at least scientific in spirit.

Montessori advocates the freedom of the pupil and 'autoeducation,'

That spirit seems further borne out by the Montessori attitude of allowing the pupil as complete freedom as possible and holding that the chief function of the teacher should be to study the activities of the child. "The transformation of the school," says she, "must be contemporaneous with the preparation of the teacher. For if we make of the teacher an observer, familiar with the experimental methods, then we must make it possible for her to observe and experiment in the school. The fundamental attitude of scientific pedagogy must be, indeed, the *liberty of the pupil.*" In practice, Montessori carries out this fundamental belief more fully than most Froebelians, who also profess it.[2] Instead of holding the children to a fixed and complete order of exercises imposed by the teacher, she maintains that all education worth having is 'autoeducation.' The children should select their own occupations and solve their own difficulties, and should be allowed to develop themselves both mentally and morally. Only when their activities interfere with the general interest or are useless or dangerous, must they be suppressed. While in this latitude toward individual expression Montessori carries out the 'following, not prescriptive' education of Froebel more logically

and carries out this individual expression more logically

[1] *Il Metodo della Pedagogia Scientifica applicato all' educazione nelle Case dei Bambini.*

[2] See pp. 231f.

than that reformer himself, she does not develop participation in group activities to the same extent. Nor is the material used as rich and varied. There is little opportunity afforded for the Froebelian construction and invention, and the development of imagination is ruthlessly nipped in the bud. The interesting plays, songs, and stories of the kindergarten find no parallel in the 'house of childhood.' The conception of 'auto-education' is admirable, but it is difficult to see how genuine activities are to be carried out, except within a very narrow scope, with material so limited as the 'didactic apparatus.'

than Froebel; but she does not develop social participation as fully, and does not use as rich and varied material.

The Montessori Curriculum and Apparatus.—The exercises peculiar to the Montessori schools fall into three main groups. These are connected with (1) activities of practical life, (2) sense training, and (3) formal studies of the elementary curriculum. When the child first enters the school, while he is beginning to find himself, he may take part in the activities of practical life. Besides practice in ordinary courtesy, setting the table, serving a meal, and washing the dishes, the children learn how to button, lace, hook, and clasp various articles of dress by means of a unique apparatus. To the opposite sides of light wooden frames are attached strips of dress material, linen, and leather, which are to be fastened together at the center. Through constant practice with these materials the child learns to dress himself and trains a variety of useful muscular coördinations. Such exercises might well be adopted by the progressive kindergarten or other modern school.

The Montessori apparatus and exercises are connected with:

(1) activities of practical life;

The utility of the sense training is more doubtful. It seems to be clearly based upon the theory of formal disci-

(2) sense training,—

pline and to be intended to train general powers and discriminations. Dr. Montessori maintains that "the aim is not that the child shall know colors, forms, and the different qualities of objects, but that he refine his senses through an exercise of attention, of comparison, of judgment; the exercises are true intellectual exercises." And this underlying theory is clearly revealed by the nature of the apparatus itself. The primal sense of touch is first exercised by passing the finger-tips of the child over various materials and pronouncing their nature as 'rough' or 'smooth'; and then by having him select them by this description. Similarly, other general senses are developed,— the 'thermic,' the 'baric,' the 'stereognostic,' the 'visual,' and the 'chromatic.' Exercises of this sort are of great value, as Montessori found, in training defective children,[1] but the assumption of their usefulness in the education of normal children seems to be largely based upon a false psychology.

tactile, thermic, baric, stereognostic, visual, and chromatic;

and (3) formal studies,—

The feature of the Montessori system, however, that has attracted most attention is its apparent success with the formal studies, especially in the facility and enthusiasm with which the children learn to write and in the beauty of their writing. The inventor of the method, however, declares that this spectacular performance is of little account, save as a single link in the chain of sense development. All the tactile, dimensional, form, and visual training, she holds, leads naturally to the writing coördinations. But Montessori has further invented three exercises by which the approach to the 'spontaneous development of the graphic language' is more directly accomplished. First, the "muscular

writing,

[1] Montessori frankly acknowledges her indebtedness to Seguin.

mechanism to hold and use the instrument in writing" is developed by the child's filling in the outlines of a geometrical form that he has traced upon paper. During this period the child is also engaged in "exercises tending to establish the visual-muscular image of the alphabetical signs" by means of sandpaper letters mounted on cardboard. The teacher shows the child how to follow the contour of a letter with his finger as if writing it and at the same time pronounce the sound (not the name) of the letter distinctly, and then further exercises his memory by saying 'give me *O*' and 'give me *I*,' and by asking 'what is this?' and 'what is that?' Lastly, he is exercised in the composition of words by selecting unmounted cardboard letters from compartments in a set of boxes resembling a compositor's type-cases. "Now the child, it is true, *has never written*, but he has mastered all the acts necessary to writing." This is the secret of the much discussed 'explosion into writing.' The art is learned so unconsciously that the children begin it almost spontaneously and are writing before they realize it. It seems to be the one great achievement of Montessorianism, and if it can be applied to other languages not as phonetic as the Italian, it may be regarded as a permanent contribution to special method.

reading

The Montessori methods in the other formal subjects —reading and arithmetic—are not as striking. Reading is generally acquired after writing through the names of familiar objects written on the blackboard or upon cards. The word is shown the child, and if he interprets the sounds correctly, the teacher has him repeat them more and more rapidly until the word as an entity, and not as a succession of sounds, dawns on his intelligence.

After single words can be read with some facility, progress is made to short phrases and sentences. But there is nothing very novel about this method of securing interest in reading, and, when undertaken with English, where the sounds are so capriciously spelt, it can hardly be effective. Nor do the Montessori methods in arithmetic reveal anything very different in principle from the 'table of units' and other devices of Pestalozzi. The chief feature consists in acquiring the fundamental operations by means of rods of different lengths marked off into sections by coloring them red and blue. After the child has learned to count the sections, the teacher selects a rod at random and asks for the next longer or shorter, or has the child build up all the rods until each result equals the longest. Other exercises are similarly performed until the child has some command of elementary arithmetic.

and arithmetic.

Summary of the Montessori System.—The value of the Montessori system to modern educational theory and methods of teaching is now fairly obvious. It is nominally based upon scientific experiment, and, while its biological statements cannot always be accepted without modification, it is permeated with the scientific spirit that is at present animating modern education. Its emphasis upon individual liberty is most admirable, but the material for exercising this freedom is decidedly limited and social coöperation is somewhat neglected. The exercises in practical activities form a valuable feature and the devices for acquiring writing are possibly a contribution. But it is to be hoped that a new method may yet arise for the lowest classes in our schools, which will combine the best characteristics of both the

While the biological statements of the Montessori system need modification, it is scientific in spirit.

It emphasizes individual liberty, but the material is limited and social coöperation is neglected. Its practical activities and devices for ac-

Froebelian and the Montessorian pedagogy. The existence of either as a mystery, cult, or propaganda must end, and both should be based upon and merged with the wider and more dynamic principles of modern educational practice.

quiring writing, however, are a contribution.

The Statistical Method and Mental Measurements in Education.—One of the most significant of present day movements is the mathematical attitude taken toward the study of education, especially in the United States. In the spirit of the scientific age in which we live, educators are coming to measure variations and changes in intellect, character, and conduct with the same general technique, clearness, and precision that are demanded by the physical and biological sciences. There is a growing tendency in all phases of education to substitute objective, impersonal, and unbiased methods of investigation for the *a priori* judgments of prejudiced and untrained persons or for the unchecked speculations of nebulous theorists. Analytic scrutiny, exact measuring, careful recording, and judging on the basis of observed facts are coming to replace guess work and metaphysics in education. Educational leaders are beginning to seek quantitative knowledge, to describe facts as numerically defined amounts, and to state relations or laws in terms of rigid, unambiguous equations. They are likewise ceasing to exalt the machinery of education and are beginning to examine its product, and, in consequence, they are finding that methods and processes long sanctioned by usage can yet be greatly improved.

There is a very recent tendency in education, especially in the United States, to formulate scientific standards of measurement, and to substitute objective and impersonal methods of investigation for unchecked and prejudiced judgments.

In the methods of educational administration especially, great reforms are taking place along these lines. Individual cards for recording the school history of each

In educational administration, individual

records and definite statistics are making it possible to compare localities, to measure efficiency mathematically, and solve important problems.

pupil are being arranged with ever increasing accuracy, and statistics are being taken after so definite and uniform a plan that the school facts within a given locality are not only made significant and valuable, but may be compared with those of any other section. The degree of efficiency in any system of schools and the relation of any one factor to a resulting condition may be ascertained mathematically and expressed in the terms of a 'coefficient of correlation.' By recording not only those who graduate from a school system each year, but also the number that enter and that are promoted in each grade, the statistics of retardation and its causes and the proportion of those who finish the school can now be calculated with practically absolute certainty. In a similarly accurate way can be determined what is the best age at which to send a child to school, and whether children who have attended the kindergarten complete the grades in less time. A scientific study is likewise made of retardation and elimination, backward pupils, physical defects, fatigue, supernormal children, and other perplexing conditions. Statistical methods are being used not only to throw light upon such isolated and local problems as have been mentioned, but 'educational surveys' are now being instituted in many cities and states, to discover the general educational conditions and the efficiency of the schools. Such investigations have been conducted with great success in Boston, New York, Baltimore, Boise, Montclair, and Orange, and in Wisconsin and Ohio. They are likewise planned for other localities, and are likely to extend to every commonwealth and municipality in the union. If power and means were given it, the United States Bureau of Education would probably be glad to obtain a similarly scientific record of educational facts for the nation.

Similar measurements are being made of individual differences and the part played by sex, age, race family, and environment.

Probably the earliest and most prominent exponent of the new method of intellectual measurements is Professor Edward L. Thorndike of Columbia University. In his *Educational Psychology* he amply illustrates how a quantitative description of individual differences and of the factors that condition them is necessary to throw real light upon educational theory and practice, and how it may completely change school procedure of long standing. He holds that all qualitative differences may be reduced to quantitative, and that the scale for measuring should be not arbitrary and subjective, but objective and impersonal. Such scales for measuring variations in ability and changes that take place through instruction, it is difficult to construct, because of the great complexity of the factors. At present they do not exist to any extent, but Thorndike has shown that they can be formed and has elsewhere specified what their requirements are. An ideal and valid scale of measurement of humanity, as of external nature, should have its points clearly marked, the distances between its points defined, and its zero point absolutely established. Scales that are up to these specifications have already been constructed for handwriting by Thorndike, Ayres, Freeman, and Wilson; for arithmetical abilities by Stone, Courtis, Thorndike, Ayres, and Freeman; for English composition by Hillegas and Thorndike; for spelling by Wallin, Pearson, Whipple, and Suzzallo; and for drawing by Meumann and by Leuba and Hyde.[1] These fields are, of course, more simple than

Scales to measure abilities in various school subjects are also being constructed.

[1] A complete bibliography of the *Standards and Tests for Measuring the Efficiency of Schools* is given in the report of the committee

the teaching of science, history, and literature. There the aims are so intangible that at present it seems impossible to make standards of measure, but this, too, though difficult, must soon be accomplished.

School practices are thus coming to be based upon reason rather than tradition.

Thus advanced educators are coming to make sure that administrative procedure, the studies in the curriculum, and the methods by which they are taught are based upon valid reasons and are not the product of usage and tradition. Scientific methods and accurate scales of measurement seem to have come to stay and to be destined to make rapid progress in the immediate future. Their advantages are evident, but all results coming from these sources, while welcomed, must be frankly challenged and criticized, lest superficial use of these methods or too great an expectation of their achievements throw them into serious disrepute before they are generally established.

The influence of the Darwinian theory of evolution has been greatly felt in modifying the approach to the study of educational problems,

Education and the Theory of Evolution.—But the most characteristic and far-reaching influence in education to-day is that contributed by the Darwinian theory of evolution. This fruitful hypothesis came to be generally accepted during the last quarter of the nineteenth century as the guiding principle of education, and has constantly increased in the illumination it has shed upon the educative process. It has given an entirely new meaning to education, and because of this broadened and deepened conception, it has greatly modified the course of study and revolutionized the method of approaching educational problems. It has wrought very much the same changes in the treatment of intelligence that it did in the biolog-

of which G. D. Strayer was chairman. See *Supplementary Reading*, p. 396.

ical sciences. Consciousness is no longer regarded as a fixed set of entities, but as a developmental process. Instead of classifying and cataloguing mental processes in fixed groups, efforts are made to study their growth from the standpoint both of the race and of the individual. It is held that only through a knowledge of its origin and development can any phase of mentality be properly understood, and that it must be carefully traced from its incipient to its most advanced stages. Studies of mental development in the race, begun by Darwin's *Descent of Man*, which recognized 'sexual' and 'social selection,' as well as 'natural selection,' have been continued by Romanes and Lubbock, and more recently by Lloyd Morgan, G. Stanley Hall, and Thorndike. Equally extensive studies have also been latterly made in the form of writings on genetic psychology, child study, mental development, and adolesence by Preyer, Perez, and Stern, and by Hall, Baldwin, Major, and Shinn. In this way not only observation, but experimentation has been introduced into the study of mental processes, and a large mass of enlightening facts has been accumulated. Likewise, from investigations of this sort have arisen interpretations of certain human psychoses as 'reverberations' or actual 'reversions' to an infra-human ancestry. And there have even been formulated such definite theories as 'recapitulation,' according to which the individual passes through the various stages through which the race has gone in reaching the stage represented by the individual, and as the 'prolongation of infancy' in the human race for the sake of introducing the child to his intellectual and spiritual inheritance.

More revolutionary than this actual increase in

as well as in the revolutionary conception of education itself.

knowledge, however, is the change that has taken place in the conception, imagery, and terminology of education. Educational discussions are now filled with such terms as 'variation,' 'selection,' and 'adaptation,' and such conceptions dominate all educational thinking. Textbooks upon educational psychology, principles of education, and methods of teaching constantly employ the language of evolution. "Education," says Bolton, "is a process of development and of modification or adjustment to environment and to the ideals of perfection conceived by society and the individual."[1] Similar ideas have been expressed by Spencer, Fiske, Butler, Horne, O'Shea, Bagley, Henderson, Ruediger, MacVannel, and a host of others, who have familiarized all progressive teachers with the vocabulary of evolution. Thus education is generally viewed by present day leaders as an evolutionary process, modifying the individual and society, and constantly producing new adjustments. It is regarded as an unfolding of potentialities, and not as a process of addition and accumulation, and the function of the school is held to be the providing of proper stimuli to produce such unfoldment. Probably, therefore, the writers upon education of half a century ago would find themselves listening to a foreign language, if they were to be present at a gathering of recent educational thinkers, for through the reception of Darwinian evolution education has been born again.

Thus accepted practice is being constantly reconstructed.

Enlarging Conceptions of the Function of Education.— Such are a few of the chief tendencies and advances that are being made in education to-day. There is also a great variety of other educational movements, almost

[1] *Principles of Education*, p. 11.

too numerous to be mentioned. In the organization and administration of the public schools there is a decided tendency toward centralization in educational activities, corresponding to the centralization in industrial and political affairs. There are also such matters as the new procedure in school hygiene, arising from the modern attitude toward the prevention of disease; new health regulations, as a result of having so many children housed in the same buildings; medical inspection and open-air schools; new tendencies in school architecture; more extensive training of teachers; a rapid recognition of education as a profession; and the organization of various types of teachers' associations. In connection with higher education there are such new tendencies as university extension, correspondence courses, the correlation of the first two years of college with the secondary school, an increasing number of fields of professional work, university interest in the practical problems of the people, and change in entrance requirements due to the new conceptions of education. Similar tendencies to secure economy, guard health, and cause education to serve democratic ideals are continually arising. Educational theory and practice are in a constant flux, and progress in education is unceasing. Every year accepted practice is being worked over and reconstructed. New activities and functions of education are being sought and developed, and nothing is held so sacred in administration, method, or content as not to be open for reëxamination and forced to justify itself anew. Education has entered upon a most distinctive epoch of experimentation, change, and improvement. While such a situation is not without its perils, and each new proposal should be carefully scrutinized before acceptance, the present tendencies are in the main a sign of progress and life.

SUPPLEMENTARY READING

I. Industrial, Commercial, and Agricultural Education

Bailey, L. H. *On the Training of Persons to Teach Agriculture in the Public Schools* (*United States Bureau of Education, Bulletin,* No. 1, 1908).

Barber, E. M. *A Contribution to the History of Commercial Education.*

Carlton, F. T. *Education and Industrial Evolution.*

Cooley, E. G. *Vocational Education in Europe.*

Davenport, E. *The History of Collegiate Education in Agriculture* (*Address before the Society for the Promotion of Agricultural Science,* 1907).

Ellis, A. C. *The Teaching of Agriculture in the Public Schools.*

Foght, H. W. *The American Rural School.*

Hanus, P. H. *Beginnings in Industrial Education.*

Haskins, C. W. *Business Education and Accounting.*

Hays, W. M. *Education for Country Life* (*United States Department of Agriculture, Office of Experiment Stations, Circular 84*).

Kerschensteiner, G. *Organization und Lehrpläne der obligatorischen Fach- und Fortbildungsschulen.*

Kerschensteiner, G. *Education for Citizenship* (Translated by Pressland).

Person, H. S. *Industrial Education.*

Sadler, M. E. *Continuation Schools in England and Elsewhere.*

True, A. C. *Secondary Education in Agriculture in the United States* (*United States Department of Agriculture, Office of Experiment Stations, Circular 91*).

Ware, F. *Educational Foundations of Trade and Industry.*

Wright, C. D. *The Apprenticeship System in Relation to Industrial Education.*

II. Moral, Civic, and Religious Education

Adler, F. *Moral Instruction of Children.*

Dewey, J. *Moral Principles in Education.*

Hadley, A. T. *Standards of Public Morality.*

Henderson, E. N. *Moral Education* (*Monroe's Cyclopædia of Education*).

Jenks, J. W. *Citizenship and the Schools.*

McAndrew, W., and Others. *Social Education in High Schools* (*Religious Education*, February, 1913, pp. 597–704).

McCunn, J. *The Making of Character.*

Palmer, G. H. *Ethical and Moral Instruction in Schools.*

Religious Education Association. *Education and National Character.*

Roeder, A. *Practical Citizenship.*

Sadler, M. E. *Moral Instruction and Training in Schools.*

Sisson, E. O. *An Educational Emergency* (*The Atlantic Monthly*, July, 1910, pp. 54–63).

Spiller, G. (Editor). *Papers on Moral Education.*

III. Education of Defectives

Armitage, T. *Education and Employment of the Blind.*

Bell, A. G. *Deaf Mute Instruction in Relation to the Work of the Public Schools.*

Farrar, A. *Arnold on the Education of the Deaf.*

Fernald, W. E. *The History of the Treatment of the Feeble-Minded* (*Proceedings of the National Conference of Charities and Corrections*, 1898).

Gallaudet, E. M. *Life of Thomas Hopkins Gallaudet.*

Garber, J. P. *Current Educational Activities.* Chap. II.

Goddard, H. H. *Education of Defectives* (*Monroe's Cyclopædia of Education*).

Illingworth, W. H. *History of the Education of the Blind.*

L'Epée, Abbè de. *La Véritable Manière d'instruire les Sourds et Muets.*

Lincoln, D. F. *The Education of the Feeble-minded in the United*

States (*Report of United States Commissioner of Education*, 1902, Vol. II, pp. 2157–2197).

SEGUIN, E. *Idiocy and Its Treatment by the Physiological Method.*

TREDGOLD, A. F. *Mental Deficiency.*

IV. Modern Educational Method

DEWEY, J., and RUNYON, LAURA L. (Editors). *The Elementary School Record.*

DEWEY, J. *The School and Society.*

FISHER, DOROTHY C. *A Montessori Mother.*

KILPATRICK, W. H. *The Montessori Method Examined.*

MONTESSORI, MARIA. *The Montessori Method* (A translation of *Il Metodo della Pedagogia Scientifica* by Anne E. George).

PARKER, F. W. *Talks on Teaching.*

SMITH, THEODATE L. *The Montessori System in Theory and Practice.*

YOUNG, ELLA F. *Some Types of Modern Educational Theory.*

V. Scientific Measurements in Education

AYRES, L. P. *Measuring Educational Processes through Educational Results* (*The School Review*, May, 1912, pp. 300–310).

AYRES, L. P. *The Binet-Simon Measuring Scale for Intelligence.*

BOBBITT, J. F. *The Supervision of City Schools* (*The Twelfth Year Book of the National Society for the Study of Education*).

GARBER, J. P. *Current Educational Activities.* Pp. 146–152.

STRAYER, G. D. *Measuring Results in Education.*

STRAYER, G. D. (Chairman). *Standards and Tests for Measuring the Efficiency of Schools or Systems of Schools* (Report of the Committee of the National Council of Education in *United States Bureau of Education, Bulletin*, 1913, No. 13).

THORNDIKE, E. L. *Educational Psychology.* Chaps. I and II.

THORNDIKE, E. L. *The Measurement of Educational Products* (*The School Review*, May, 1912, pp. 289–300).

CHAPTER XII

THE EDUCATIONAL OUTLOOK

The destructive attitude of the eighteenth century prepared the way for the social, psychological, and scientific tendencies of modern times.

Progress since the Eighteenth Century.—The discussion of present day tendencies that has just been made, while very brief, serves to show how far we have progressed in educational ideals and practices since the eighteenth century. And even the mere survey of modern movements given in the preceding chapters of this book is sufficient to show how radical and rapid has been our progress since Rousseau undertook so ruthlessly to shatter all educational traditions. His recommendation of isolated education, so palpable in its fallacies, opened the way for the numerous social tendencies in modern education and for great improvement in the aim, organization, and content of education. The development of philanthropic education, which has grown everywhere into universal and national systems of schools, the combination of industrial with intellectual training started by Pestalozzi and Fellenberg, the Herbartian use of history and literature for giving us insight into our duties toward our fellows, Froebel's encouragement of the social instincts by means of stories, songs, play, and constructive work, and many of the modern tendencies looking to social welfare in all directions find some of their roots in the erratic reformer of the eighteenth century who cried aloud for a radical change of front in society. Likewise, by his absolute rejection of books and the standardized knowledge of the past, and his substitution of nature study and observational work, Rousseau opened the way to an increased use of sciences in the modern curriculum and to a more definite crystallization of the scientific movement in education. In partial sequence, we have seen the development of geography, nature study, and elementary science through Basedow, Salzmann, Pestalozzi, Ritter, Guyot, and Parker, the encouragement of scientific and technical institutions and courses in modern education, and the development of the positions of Spencer, Huxley, Youmans, and Eliot. Through Rousseau, too, was indirectly started the study of the child's development and the formulation of his characteristics at different periods, and thus was begun the development of the psychological movement in modern instruction and the remarkable improvements in method. Rousseau, and to a large extent Pestalozzi, made their advances purely through a sympathetic insight into the activities of the child, but with Herbart and Froebel the educational process began to find its justification in an underlying basis of psychology. Then, through the new impulse of evolutionary doctrine, extraordinary developments in genetic psychology, the biological sciences, and sociology yielded a body of educational doctrine and practice that has made possible methods of the most accurate and scientific type.

and, although many of the modern movements were beyond the vision of the reformers,

The Eighteenth Century as the Beginning of Modern Times.—Of course modern education has advanced infinitely beyond anything even implied in Rousseau or any of the reformers of the past century. The educational movements now going on were far in advance of their ken. They may upon occasion have intuitively felt the need of improved conditions in society and more natural practices in education, but such movements as vocational and moral training, the education of defectives, and the use of scientific measurements in education were much beyond the range of their vision. At times they seem to catch a glimpse of the idea of 'natural development,' but they could have had no inkling of the real meaning of evolution and of education as adjustment, which has become fundamental in the view-point and practice of to-day. Yet it is scarcely a strained interpretation to hold that modern education began in the eighteenth century with the effort at eradicating the past and beginning progress anew upon a more natural basis. As indicated in this and previous volumes,[1] educational history may be viewed from the standpoint of the development of individualism, and it has been held that by permitting variations in the social world, just as it has long been recognized in biology, there are evolved and fixed new types that will answer to changed conditions, and growth and progress will ensue without the intervention of conflict and cataclysm.

modern education may be interpreted as beginning with the individualistic recommendations of Rousseau.

From this point of view, the eighteenth century and Rousseau mark the parting of the ways. To follow this interpretation back to the beginning, it may be stated that during the day of primitive man no distinction at all was made between society and the individual, and practically all advancement was impossible, for no one looked beyond the present. With the appearance of the transitional period in the Oriental countries, the indi-

[1] See *History of Education before the Middle Ages*, pp. 295f., and *History of Education during the Transition*, pp. 315ff.

vidual had begun to emerge, but was kept in constant subjection to the social whole, for man was quite enslaved to the past. As the Jewish, Athenian, and Roman civilizations developed, the beginnings of individualism were for the first time revealed, and some regard was had for the future. Then, in the teachings of Christ, there came a larger recognition of the principle of individualism and the brotherhood of man. Owing to a necessity for spreading these enlarged ideals among a barbarous horde of peoples, individualism was repressed, and throughout the Middle Ages the keynote was adherence to authority and preparation for the life to come. The cultural products of Greece and Rome largely disappeared, and all civilization was restricted, fixed, and formal. But the human spirit could not be forever held in bondage, and, after almost a millennium of repression and uniformity, various factors that had accumulated within the Middle Ages produced an intellectual awakening that we know as the 'Renaissance.' Its vitality lasted during the fifteenth century in Italy and to the close of the sixteenth in the Northern countries, but by the dawn of the seventeenth century it had everywhere degenerated into a dry and dead study of the classics. This constituted a formalism almost as dense as that it had superseded, except that linguistic and literary studies had replaced dialectic and theology. A little later than the spread of the Renaissance, though overlapping it somewhat, came the allied movement of the 'Reformation.' This grew in part out of the disposition of the Northern Renaissance to turn to social and moral account the revived intelligence and learning. Yet here also the revival lost its mission, and the tendency to rely upon reason rather than dogma hardened into formalism and a distrust of individualism. Again, in the seventeenth century, apparently as an outgrowth of the same forces, intellectual activity took the form of a search for 'real things.' The movement that culminated in 'sense realism' appeared, but this small and crude beginning of the modern scientific tendency was for some decades yet held within limits. Associated with this realistic tendency, on the religious and political sides also appeared a quickening in such forms as Puritanism and Pietism, which likewise degenerated eventually into fanaticism and hypocrisy. Thus was the way finally opened for the complete break with tradition and authority that occurred in the eighteenth century.

The present tendencies in education make the relation of the individual to the social whole the test of the value of his activities, and attempt to harmonize the individual interests with those of society.

The Harmonization of the Individual and Society.— This destructive tendency, while in France at least most disastrous and costly, was the inevitable result of the unwillingness to reshape society and education in accordance with changing ideals and conditions. Yet out of the attempts at destruction, as we have seen, has grown a nobler structure. For a time individualism triumphed and ground authority under its heel, but when this extremity had been passed, the problem became how to harmonize the individual with society, and to develop personality progressively in keeping with its environment. Thus the nineteenth and twentieth centuries have put forth conscious efforts to justify the eighteenth and to bring out and develop the positions barely hinted at in its negations. It is not alone the individual as such that has been of interest in the modern period, but more and more the individual in relation to the social whole to which he belongs, as only in this way can the value of his activities be estimated. This is revealed in the works of those who followed Rousseau, and, especially in the attempts of leading educational philosophers of the present day to frame a definition of education that shall recognize the importance of affording latitude to the individual without losing sight of the welfare of the social environment in connection with which his efforts are to function. Thus Butler, though recognizing the individual factor, especially stressed the social by declaring education to be "the gradual adjustment of the individual to the spiritual possessions of the race." [1] Then he further declares: "When we hear it sometimes said, 'All education must start from the child,' we must add, 'Yes, and lead into human civilization;' and when it is said on the other hand that 'all education must start from a traditional past,' we must add, 'Yes, and be adapted to the child.'" And the balance between the two factors of the individual and society is even more explicitly preserved in Dewey's statement "that the psychological and social sides are organically related, and that education cannot be regarded as a compromise between the two, or a superimposition of one upon the other." [2] In the same way Bagley has made 'social efficiency' [3] the main aim in educating the individual to-day, and both elements are carefully considered by all modern writers in discussing educational values.

Thus the central problem in education of the twentieth and succeeding centuries is to be a constant reconstruc-

[1] *The Meaning of Education*, p. 15.

[2] *My Pedagogic Creed*, pp. 6f.

[3] *The Educative Process*, pp. 58ff.

tion of the curriculum and methods of teaching so as to harmonize a due regard for the progressive variations of the individual with the welfare of the conservative institutions of society, and a continual effort to hand on the intellectual possessions of the race, but also to stimulate all individuals to add some modification or new element to the product. In this way the succeeding centuries may prove an evolution from the revolutionary eighteenth and may reveal unending possibilities for the development of the individual and society through an education that recognizes both.

INDEX

Printed in the United States
42342LVS00003B/82

9 781410 214980